Praise for Ocean of Sound

'. . . a masterfully innovative and radical work . . . a definite route forward for the pop book.' **Melody Maker**

'. . . as styles of music multiply and divide at an accelerating pace, [*Ocean of Sound*] challenges the way we hear, and more importantly, how we interpret what we hear around us.' **The Daily Telegraph**

'*Ocean of Sound* shatters consensual reality with a cumulative force that's both frightening and compelling. Buy it, read it and let it remix your head.' **i-D**

'. . . an encyclopaedic work, uncommonly knowledgeable and wide in its scope . . . a rare and subversive read.' **DJ Magazine**

'. . . a scintillating and illuminating read.' **Mojo**

'Its parallels aren't music books at all, but rather Italo Calvino's *Invisible Cities*, Michel Leiris's *Afrique Phantôme*, William Gibson's *Neuromancer* . . . David Toop is our Calvino and our Leiris, our Gibson. *Ocean of Sound* is as alien as the 20th century, as utterly Now as the 21st. An essential mix.' **The Wire**

'An extraordinary and revelatory book, *Ocean of Sound* reads like an alternative history of 20th century music, tracking the passage of organised sound into strange and new environments of vapour and abstraction.' **Tony Herrington**

'At the end of the millennium, we can see two trends in music, one proactive, the other reactive . . . Toop's *Ocean of Sound* brilliantly elaborates both these processes, like sonic fact for our sci-fi present, a Martian Chronicle from this Planet Earth.' **The Face**

'This Encyclopaedia of Heavenly Music is an heroic endeavour brought off with elegance and charm. The play of ideas is downright musical and, vitally, the author writes like a mad enthusiast rather than a snob.' **NME**

'Always the rigorous pluralist, [Toop] sees no reason *not* to expect wisdoms from rival cultures, tribal or club, nor emptiness or stupidity either. His sense of the absurd, of potential darkness and madness, is a bullshit detector never turned off.' **New Statesman & Society**

Also by David Toop and published by Serpent's Tail

Exotica: Fabricated Soundscapes in a Real World
Rap Attack #3

David Toop is a musician, author and music curator. His first book, *Rap Attack*, is now in its third edition. Since the publication of *Ocean of Sound* in 1995 he has recorded five solo albums, including *Screen Ceremonies*, *Pink Noir* and *Spirit World* and published *Exotica: Fabricated Soundscapes in a Real World*. He lives in London with his daughter, Juliette.

ocean of sound

aether talk, ambient sound and imaginary worlds

david toop

Library of Congress Catalog Card Number: 00-108741

A catalogue record for this book is available from the
British Library on request

First published in 1995 by Serpent's Tail
an imprint of Profile Books Ltd
Profile Books,
3 Holford Yard,
Bevin Way,
WC1X 9HD
www.serpentstail.com

First published in this 5-star edition in 2001

Set in 10pt Garamond by Avon Dataset, Warwickshire
Printed and bound by CPI Group (UK) Ltd, Croydon, CR0 4YY

10 9 8 7

contents

for Leslie John Toop (1913–95)
and for
Kimberley (1959–95)
... in a green sunny place ...

acknowledgements

The raw material for this book has been gathered over twenty-five years of study and music making. Picking out key individuals who have contributed to my knowledge and experience over such a lengthy period seems arbitrary, yet some names stand out in terms of the subjects I discuss: Madeau Stewart, now retired from BBC Radio Three, who responded to some eccentric ideas with encouragement rather than dismissal; Brian Eno, who did the same and continues to do so; Paul Burwell and Max Eastley, who continue to inspire me after all these years of musical collaboration and friendship; Paul Schütze, John Wall and Tony Herrington, who kept tabs on my general condition throughout the writing of the book and then read the manuscript; Jon Hassell, Sheila Hayman, Tom Recchion and Paul Sanders for the aether talk; musicians and artists such as John Zorn, John Oswald, Steve Beresford, Marie Yates, John Latham, Hugh Davies, Evan Parker, Annabel Nicolson and Derek Bailey, with whom I feel privileged to have shared conversation and collaboration; Mike Barnett, David Thompson, Jon Tye, Kevin Martin, Tony Thorpe and all the other recording conduits; all the interviewees; all my friends, neighbours and family for support during difficult times, including Musa Kalamulah, Pamela Marre, Liz Stringer, Veena and Nick Ellsworth, Justine Picardie, Neill McColl, Scott and Nick Hall, Sue Steward, Cathy and Andrew Brenner, Nancy Brenner, Sheryl Garrett, Kate Flett, Nick and Julie Logan and so many others.

Sections of the book have appeared in different form in a number of publications, particularly *The Face*, *The Wire* and *Mixmag*. Some of the editors have already been thanked above for support which has extended far beyond the professional. I would also like to thank Mark Sinker, formerly at *The Wire*, and Richard Morrison at *The Times*, both of whom said "yes" to projects which have found their way into this text. In Japan, Nobuhisa Shimoda deserves an especially warm greeting for his assistance and enthusiasm. The earthquake which destroyed large sections of Kobe happened after I had written about musical activities in the city; this section should be read with the knowledge that life changed dramatically in those few moments. Gratitude goes to my editor, Laurence O'Toole, who negotiated the territory between bluntness and sensitivity with elegance and so helped to make a better book. A number of people who were vital to different aspects of the book died during the time I was writing it. With great sadness: Stuart Marshall, John Stevens, Kimberley Leston and my father. The deepest thanks go to my daughter Juliette who, in innocence, earths me and helps me to look far ahead.

prologue: fragments and mantras

What follows is a collection of diverse views, thoughts, experiences. They trace an expansiveness, an opening out of music during the past one hundred years, examining some of the ways in which music has reflected the world back to itself and to its listeners.

This is not a book about categories of music – ambient, electronic, environmental or any of those other separations which lay claim to the creation of order and sense but actually serve business interests. What I have followed, starting with Debussy in 1889, is an erosion of categories, a peeling open of systems to make space for stimuli, new ideas, new influences, from a rapidly changing environment. Then, as now, this environment included sounds of the world – previously unheard musics and ambient sounds of all kinds, urban noise and bioacoustic signals – as well as experiments in presentation rituals, technological innovations, unfamiliar tuning systems and structuring principles, improvisation and chance.

The sound object, represented most dramatically by the romantic symphonies of the nineteenth century, has been fractured and remade into a shifting, open lattice on which new ideas can hang, or through which they can pass and interweave. This is one metaphor. Landscape is another – a conjured place through which the music moves and in which the listener can wander.

Musicians have always reflected their environments in ways which are incorporated into the music's structure and purpose. The unverifiable origins of music are located by most musicologists either in bioacoustic and meteorological sounds or language. After a subtle examination of origin theories, Anthony Storr makes the following conclusion in his

Music and the Mind: "It will never be possible to establish the origins of human music with any certainty; however, it seems probable that music developed from the prosodic exchanges between mother and infant which foster the bond between them." So sounds which we would describe as ambient, functional or mysteriously alien have laid the foundations of musical creativity.

But the day when Claude Debussy heard Javanese music performed at the Paris Exposition of 1889 seems particularly symbolic. From that point – in my view the beginning of the musical twentieth century – accelerating communications and cultural confrontations became a focal point of musical expression. An ethereal culture, absorbed in perfume, light, silence and ambient sound, developed in response to the intangibility of twentieth century communications. Sound was used to find meaning in changing circumstances, rather than imposed as a familiar model on a barely recognisable world. Inevitably, some of this music has remained in fragments; some has been moulded from fragments into mantras and other solid structures.

Much of the music I discuss could be characterised as drifting or simply existing in stasis rather than developing in any dramatic fashion. Structure emerges slowly, minimally or apparently not at all, encouraging states of reverie and receptivity in the listener that suggest (on the good side of boredom) a very positive rootlessness. At the same time, a search for meaningful rituals recurs again and again, surely a response to the contemporary sense that life can drift towards death without direction or purpose. So this is a book about journeys, some actual, some imaginary, some caught in the ambiguity between the two. Although the narrative jumps, loses itself and digresses, my central image was signals transmitted across the aether. This applies as much to the Javanese musicians and Debussy in the colonial era of the nineteenth century as it applies to music in the digital age at the turn of the millennium. This past hundred years of expansiveness in music, a predominantly fluid, non-verbal, non-linear medium, has been preparing us for the electronic ocean of the next century. As the world has moved towards becoming an information ocean, so music has become immersive. Listeners float in that ocean; musicians have become virtual travellers, creators of sonic theatre, transmitters of all the signals received across the aether.

August 1995

1 memory

*sound and evocation; Muzak, ambience and
aethereal culture; Brian Eno and perfume; Bali,
Java, Debussy*

Sitting quietly in never-never land, I am listening to
summer fleas jump off my small female cat on to the polished
wood floor. Outside, starlings are squabbling in the fig tree
and from behind me I can hear swifts wheeling over rooftops.
An ambulance siren, full panic mode, passes from behind the
left centre of my head to starboard front. Next door, the neighbours are screaming – "... fuck you ... I didn't ... get out
that door ..." – but I tune that out. The ambient hum of night
air and low frequency motor vehicle drone merges with insect
hum called back from the 1970s, a country garden somewhere, high summer in the afternoon. The snow has settled. I
can smell woodsmoke. Looking for fires I open the front door,
peer out into the shining dark and hear stillness. Not country
stillness but urban shutdown. So tranquil.

Truthfully, I am lying in intensive care. Wired, plugged and
electronically connected, I have glided from coma into a sonic
simulation of past, and passed, life. As befits an altered state,
the memories have been superimposed, stripped of context,
conflated from seasons, times, eras, moments, even fictions,
into a concentrated essence of my existence in the soundworld.

These sounds reconnect me to a world from which I had
disengaged. Sound places us in the real universe. Looking
ahead, I can see a plane enlivened by visually represented

objects. I can touch within a limited radius. I can smell a body, a glass of beer, burning dust. But sound comes from everywhere, unbidden. My brain seeks it out, sorts it, makes me feel the immensity of the universe even when I have no wish to look or absorb.

There are ear plugs, but then I just hear the sound of my own shell.

Not long born, still unable to control most of my own body, I stared at colour shapes and gripped objects as they came near. Far away, a dog barked. Then there were two worlds.

Now I am very old, too old. A stone-deaf baby. Who am I? These people sitting around my bed; who are they? One of them holds my hand. I press the button. Sound pictures wash them away. I am listening to a song in a school classroom: "Oh soldier, soldier . . ." Somebody is carrying a radio and an old pop song is playing: "See the pyramids . . ." I can hear the metal phase echoes of footsteps moving along an alleyway, wind in drainpipes, a tied-up dog howling. Enfolded in the stillness of Christmas Eve, church bells, police sirens and domestic rows. Sea sucked back over stones through the narrow rock corridor at Clodgy Point, Cornwall. A cave down on the beach; inside, I sound the echo with a bone trumpet, water dripping in a steady tattoo. Fences rattling in the wind on Dartmoor. Walking after midnight down the long tunnel of an underground station. A man walks alongside me, bright eyed with chemical joy. Australian vowels. "Hear that? Sirens. The sound of London." He looks down at my feet as we stride quickly in parallel. "Squeaky boots."

A bee trapped in a chimney flue, its buzzing amplified to room dimensions. The fizzing drone of a street light. A hotel room in Italy and close by a man and a woman are screaming their way to orgasm. Somebody shouts in the distance, drunk. Toads belch in the deep night and a motorbike whines by. I have a daughter; she is singing "Daisy, Daisy . . ." Sounds that have remained mysteries for decades: walking by a railway terminal on a Saturday morning and stopped dead by the eerie lament of a train whistle choir. All those horns and whistles blowing at once. The air buckles. Did somebody die? Paradise is so dull. I listen for a moment to the woomph of mortar fire in thick jungle, vultures tearing strips from a corpse, car alarms, fire alarms, smoke detectors, house alarms and cement mixers.

And then the comfort note of air conditioning, the slow glide of electronic curtains. My exit, probably. But I still hear the sound of fleas jumping off my small female cat on to the polished wood floor.

soundbites

At a conference in Cairns, Australia, a scientist member of the American Rock Art Research Association claimed that prehistoric cave-painting sites were chosen by the artists for their reverberant acoustic character. Steven Waller speculated that each painting site reveals a correspondence between the animals depicted on the walls and the nature of any sound activating the echoes in that space. In caves such as Lascaux, where large animals were painted, the echoes are overwhelmingly loud, whereas in sites where felines adorn the walls, the decibel level of the reverberations is very low.

New Scientist, 28 November 1992

Seals straying from the North Sea into Lincolnshire's River Glen feast on freshwater fish stocks customarily assumed to be the natural prey of local roach anglers. To drive the seal family back into the North Sea, the National Rivers Authority have been playing recordings of killer-whale songs under the surface of the Glen. "We are playing the music using hydrophones," said a spokeswoman for the NRA.

The Times, 31 October 1994

"The best thing that ever happened to background music was foreground music," reported *Billboard* in a special sixtieth anniversary advertising supplement devoted to Muzak®. "If you go into a store and you think you're hearing Muzak, it probably isn't Muzak," said Bruce Funkhouser, Muzak programming and licencing VP. "There are still a couple of companies out there doing that old-style 1,001-strings, ruin-your-favorite-song kind of thing, but we dropped all that in '87." Since that momentous year, Muzak has switched 11 of its 12 music channels to so-called foreground music (the original hit record by the original artist). The 12th is called the Environmental Music channel. This features instrumental re-recordings of those hits. "A far cry from the 'oceans of beautiful music' of the past," *Billboard* continued, "the new channels are hip, current and extensively researched."

Billboard, 29 October 1994

pre-echoes

In his dazzling novel of Southern Californian subculture, *The Crying of Lot 49* (first published in 1966), Thomas Pynchon predicted the replacement of human musicians by digital processing. Listening to muzak in a pizzeria, a character hears one violinist playing sharp. "They could dispense with live musicians", he suggests. "Put together all the right overtones at all the right power levels so it'd come out like a violin."

Pynchon also foresaw a world in which people would get drunk in electronic music clubs, Stockhausen records playing on the jukebox. "We're the only bar in the area, you know, has a strictly electronic music policy", brags the barman of an LA outskirts bar called The Scope. "Come on around Saturdays, starting midnight we have your Sinewave Session, that's a live get-together, fellas come in just to jam from all over the state . . . We got a whole back room full of your audio oscillators, gunshot machines, contact mikes, everything man."

In *Vermilion Sands* (published in 1971), J.G. Ballard celebrated leisure, artifice, ennui and ambient drift in his portrayal of a desert resort. Among the lotus-eating pleasures of Vermilion Sands are choro-florists selling singing plants and sonic sculptures growing on the reefs. The latter are incorporated into commercially available singing statues. The narrator, a sound sculptor, cheats one of his customers by augmenting a statue's interactive sensory mechanisms with a tape. Then he finds that the statue has assumed the divinatory properties of a mirror or quartz globe for the rich buyer. "I went out one dusk to the sand reefs where the sonic sculptures grow", the sculptor says, emptied by the realisations that followed the sale of his fake. "As I approached, they were creaking in the wind whenever the thermal gradients cut through them. I walked up the long slopes, listening to them mewl and whine, searching for one that would serve as the sonic core for a new statue."

With startling awareness of the evolutionary links between player pianos and simulacra (of which more later), Philip K. Dick's *We Can Build You* (published in 1972) begins in Oregon, at the headquarters of an imaginary musical-instrument manufacturer which is falling behind in the technological race. Its competitors, Hammerstein and Waldteufel, make keyboard instruments which exploit brain-mapping research and directly stimulate the hypothalamus. The book's narrator, locked in argument with his partner in the firm, is a sceptic. "Like most people", he says, "I've dabbled at the keys of a Hammerstein Mood Organ, and I enjoy it. But there's nothing creative about it. True, you can hit on new configurations of brain stimulation, and hence produce entirely new emotions in your head which would never otherwise show up there. You might – theoretically – even hit on the combination that will put you in the state of nirvana. Both the Hammerstein and Waldteufel corporations have a big prize for that. But that's not music. That's escape. Who wants it?"

More than twenty years later, at the close of the twentieth century, a deafening answer roars back: "We want it."

And at the end of the nineteenth century, a Parisian writer, clerk and dabbler in magic named Joris-Karl Huysmans explored *fin de siècle* ideas of vicarious (or virtual?) living and neurotic aestheticism through a character called Des Esseintes. *À Rebours* (*Against Nature*, published in 1884) follows Des Esseintes through his quintessentially Decadent immersion in scent and colour, cruelty and eroticism, Orientalism, increasingly refined diets and strange pleasures. In one scene, he recreates a passage from Gustave Flaubert's

The Temptation of Saint Anthony by setting up a tableau of two miniatures – a sphinx and a chimera – in the darkened bedroom. Lying back in reverie, he listens as a female ventriloquist intones a rehearsed dialogue, "like voices from another world", between the two carvings. "I seek new perfumes, larger blossoms, pleasures still untasted", she chants, and Des Esseintes imagines that Flaubert's words are addressed directly to him, amplifying his "craving to escape from the horrible realities of life". The scene ends, by implication, with sex, but the pleasure is not shared by the ventriloquist.

After reading Charles Dickens, Des Esseintes decides to travel to England. Preparing to take the boat, he prevaricates endlessly, ricocheting between culinary and literary flavours in taverns, deciding finally that reality is a disappointment when compared with art. His journey progresses no further than Paris. "After all", he reflects, "what was the good of moving, when a fellow could travel so magnificently sitting in a chair?" So the couch potato, the sofa surfer, the virtual nomad, was born.

Although Des Esseintes absorbs more than he creates, he plays games with his environment. But the intended subtlety of the games is overwhelmed by a heaviness of execution. Epitomising the triumph of materialism over aether, a tortoise is gilded and encrusted with unusual gem stones in order to set off a mobile counterpoint to the iridescent colours of an Oriental carpet. Understandably, the overloaded animal roots itself to a secluded spot. Des Esseintes blends musical correspondences with tiny drops of liqueur from a dispensing device he calls his mouth organ, fantasising whole ensembles from the synaesthetic linkage of dry curaçao with clarinets, anisette with flutes and gin with cornets. From long practice, he could recreate complex musical compositions on his tongue.

Another of his active skills, or obsessions, is the manipulation of scents. "After all, he argued, it was no more abnormal to have an art that consisted of picking out odorous fluids than it was to have other arts based on a selection of sound waves . . ." So, in mounting excitement, he paints an epic canvas in his dressing room with a bewildering sequence of exotic teas, delicate perfume sprays, sprinkled scents and rubbed pellets of odiferous substances. The final effect of this orchestration is drastic. As he airs the room, other smells crowd back in like a haunting of Medieval spirits. Overwrought and oppressed by his own art, Des Esseintes finally faints across his windowsill.

Against Nature mixed observations, often satirical, of the artistic and social atmosphere of the period with Huysmans's own adventures in imaginal esoterica. On the one hand, there were performances such as the total-art spectacle of Paul-Napoléon Roinard's *Cantique des Cantiques*, staged by Paul Fort at the Théâtre Moderne in 1891, in front of an audience which included Debussy and the occult-poet Joseph Péladan. The poetry was augmented by music, colour projections and perfume sprayed rather ineffectually from the theatre boxes and balcony. Fights broke out and shots were fired near the ticket office. On the other hand, Huysmans was influenced by French occultists such as the Abbé Boullan. At one point, he found himself caught up in a magical war. Despite defending himself with miraculous hosts, he claimed that at bedtime he was being beaten on the head by "fluidic blows".

Some of these esoteric pursuits mirror the desire for "pleasures still untasted" characteristic of our own time. "There is talk of 'the sophisticated life' ", wrote Italian design historian Claudia Donà in a 1988 essay entitled "Invisible Design", "of the 'renaissance of subtlety', of 'soft' and 'hard' design, of 'fluid' objects whose new, 'suggestive' pleasures, associated with smells or sounds or lights, are supplanting the old values of aesthetic form or utility. There is talk of the object of the future as something evanescent, light, psychic; of immaterial objects akin to images or holograms. On the eve of the twenty-first century, we are seeing an era focused on the heightening of sensation – a development provoked by a more destructured use of language, but which will usher in a new harmonics."

suggestive pleasures

Functionalism and the ineffable meet in air. Unconscious material is coaxed into the light with the same cunning employed by the shaman Ame-no-Uzume-no-Mikoto (the Heavenly Alarming Female) when she danced, lewdly and loudly as eighth-century Japanese myth relates, in order to trick the sun goddess out of her sulk in a cave and bathe the world in light once more.

Brian Eno, better known for his successful record production of bands such as U2 than his art installations, created a work in Hamburg called "The Future Will Be Like Perfume". Exhibited in February 1993, the title was a clear indicator of the ethereality of so much contemporary experience. Also, he released *Neroli (Thinking Music Part IV)*, an austere album even by Eno standards. This piece, originally recorded for installations in 1988 and lasting to within a few minutes of one hour, was named after the orange-blossom scent and related to its relaxing, uplifting, thought-clarifying properties. "I never intended to release that piece originally", he explains, "and I made it as a study. I found I very often put it on when I was writing or sitting reading. I never really thought of it as music, in particular. I thought it made a nice space to think in." Paradoxically, Eno himself failed to recognise the musical substance of *Neroli* until the piece was released on compact disc. A contradiction arises.

The previous year Brian had delivered a lecture and slide installation at Sadler's Wells Theatre, London, entitled "Perfume, Defence & David Bowie's Wedding". "A coriander king", the *Guardian* called him in its post-mortem of the event. Among the observations made and descriptions given during the Perfume section of this lecture were the following: "**Orris butter,** a complex derivative of the roots of Iris, is vaguely floral in small amounts, but almost obscenely fleshy (like the smell beneath a breast or between buttocks) in quantity, or **Civet,** from the anal gland of the civet cat, is intensely disagreeable as soon as it is recognizable, but amazingly sexy in subliminal doses."

Anal scents: what was their relation to a cultural shift?

In 1975, Brian had begun to talk in press interviews about the prospect of insinuating music into chosen environments as a sort of perfume or tint. Writing for a short-lived paper called *Street Life* in November of that year, he touched briefly upon changing listening behaviour: "I believe that we are moving towards a position of *using* music and recorded sound with the variety of options that we presently use colour – we might simply use it to 'tint' the environment, we might use it 'diagramatically', we might use it to modify our moods in almost subliminal ways. I predict that the concept of 'muzak', once it sheds its connotations of aural garbage, might enjoy a new (and very fruitful) lease of life." By 1978, he had shaped these ideas into a manifesto. "An ambience is defined as an atmosphere", he wrote for the sleevenotes of *Music For Airports*, "or a surrounding influence: a tint. My intention is to produce original pieces ostensibly (but not exclusively) for particular times and situations with a view to building up a small but versatile catalogue of environmental music suited to a wide variety of moods and atmospheres." But the idea was to highlight "acoustic and atmospheric idiosyncracies", rather than muffle them with Muzak®. "Ambient Music is intended to induce calm and a space to think", he concluded. "Ambient Music must be able to accommodate many levels of listening attention without enforcing one in particular: it must be as ignorable as it is interesting."

This last statement, in particular, was anathema to those who believe that art should focus our emotions, our higher intelligence, by occupying the centre of attention, lifting us above the mundane environment which burdens our souls. Yet what Eno was doing, as often happens when somebody grasps the flavour of the moment, was predicting a movement already in existence. The measurable, graspable narrative of self-contained, highly composed, emotionally engaging sound objects had been shattered by missiles flung from every point of the artistic and technological compass. His words were important for projecting this trend towards open works into the realms of design (even social design) and popular music. Once art became design or, better still, pop design, designer pop (or any other permutation), then a radical idea could turn into a media event.

In a sense Thomas Pynchon, J.G. Ballard and Philip K. Dick predicted Brian Eno: Pynchon with his image of electronic sound as ambient entertainment; Ballard with his scenes of Vermilion Sands' cloud sculptors and sonic statue salesmen; Dick with his musical reverie technology. And, as with any science-fiction author, at the heart of his speculations are a collection of present-day realities. Background music is everywhere, most of it carefully selected to reflect the fine tribal and class divisions of leisure pursuits: a hi-tech restaurant playing jazz recorded within a time-slice of 1955–1965; a wood and posters bar playing so-called "roots" and "world" music; a pub playing 1970s' pop; an Indian restaurant playing Bollywood film songs; a slightly more expensive Indian restaurant playing Enya, Sade, Kenny G, maybe even The Orb; a family theme-park café playing standard tunes in pre-1987, 1001-strings Muzak style, and so on. Cable television flickers on the edge of vision; loops of New Age music endlessly repeat their soothing arpeggios in sealife parks to accompany the glides and backrolls of stingrays; the sub-bass and bass drum of high-volume jungle tracks booming from a car bulldozers the air in a mobile fifty-yard radius; music floats around in the aether of the WorldWide Web, waiting to be downloaded, hoping to talk to somebody.

The general lack of deep engagement with all this stimulus is disarming, alarming or enthralling. It depends on your mood, your point of view, your vested interest in products and solid values, or invisible, intangible, emergent, shifting communications. "We are, in short", Brian continued in his Perfume lecture, "increasingly un-centred, un-moored, living day to day, engaged in an ongoing attempt to cobble together a credible, or at least workable, set of values, ready to shed it and work out another when the situation demands. I find my-self enjoying this more, watching us all becoming dilettante perfume blenders, poking inquisitive fingers through a great library of ingredients and seeing which combinations make some sense for us – gathering *experience* – the possibility of making better guesses – without demanding certainty."

What this book seeks to explore is the path by which sound (and music, in particular) has come to express this alternately disorientating and inspiring openness through which all that is solid melts into aether. People talking of killer-whale com-munication sounds as music, or searching for long-absent animal echoes in prehistoric cave-painting sites; recordings on which sheer noise, minimalism or non-narrative drift is sold and used as a kind of pop music; clubs where the periph-eral status of the music, its extreme eclecticism, or its cut-up diffusion, is regarded as an environmental enhancement; music chopped out and laminated on to thick layered slices of seemingly incompatible sound events; music constructed from private telephone conversations stolen out of the air (and "private" lives) by means of a hand-held scanner; music ex-ploring the language of physical sensation; music in which a blankness prevails, ambient dread or bliss, calm and near-silence, extreme minimalism, or a spacious landscape, a tropic or frozen atmosphere in which the listener can insert her or himself, occupy the foreground, wander the imaginary space for hours at a time.

In a 1989 essay entitled "Why Minimalism Now?", Claire Polin paralleled the emergence of the minimalist musical genre, particularly La Monte Young, Terry Riley, Philip Glass and Steve Reich, with minimal American painting of the late 1950s and early 1960s exemplified by Mark Rothko's huge slabs of muted colour and Ad Reinhardt's black canvases. She

quotes Reinhardt's outline of the new aesthetic: " . . . no texture, no drawing, no light, no space, no movement, no object,
no subject, no symbol, no form . . . no pleasure, no pain." She
goes on to say: "Followers, like Olitsky, produced works of
unnameable luminous mixed colours that appeared to float in
infinite space, or in a spaceless infinity, recalling Pascal's
words: 'the silence of infinite space fills me with terror'. One
feels a weariness of the human spirit, a desire to escape into
an enfolding quietude from the pressures of a frenetic, discordant world, a world which, according to Carl André,
'contains too many objects, and now requires some blankness, some tabula rasa'."

The trance of blankness can invade us in supermarket
aisles, waiting in queues, stuck in traffic, driving fast on a
motorway, watching television, working a dull job, talking on
the telephone, eating in restaurants, even making love. Jack
Gladney, narrator of Don DeLillo's *White Noise*, hears "an eerie static" emanating from plastic food wrap in his freezer.
The sound makes him think of dormant life, moving on the
edges of awareness. He searches for certainties, despite fear-
ing them, in a sea of shifting, irrelevant information. In the
evenings he watches from the overpass as a drama of spectacular, toxically provoked sunsets unfolds. "May the days be
aimless", he tells himself. "Let the seasons drift."

Blankness – at best a stillness which suggests, rightly or
wrongly, political passivity; at worst, a numbness which confirms it – may be one aspect of losing the anchor, circling
around an empty centre or whatever the condition is. But
openness, another symptom of the condition, may be more
significant. Musicians have always stolen, borrowed, ex-
changed or imposed influences, but for the past one hundred
years music has become voracious in its openness – vampiric
in one respect, colonial in its rabid exploitation, restless, un-
centred, but also asking to be informed and enriched by new
input and the transfer of gifts.

overtones

"[H]yper-artificiality, through which design is enabled to approach more nearly to the natural, is a condition at once super-technological and poetic, a condition of whose potential we are still too little aware. Endowed with quasi-divine powers – speed, omnisience, ubiquity – we have become Telematic Nomads, whose attributes approximate ever more closely to those of the ancient gods of mythology."

Claudia Donà, "Invisible Design"

Ubud, Bali. A mist of fat raindrops. I shelter under a wooden platform in the tropical darkness, listening to a rubbery lattice of frog voices warping in the rice fields. Some distance away, the lighting for a gamelan performance glows in a magic arc. Wind flurries throw slivers of gong overtones and buried drum beats across the water, whipping them in then out of earshot. Rain and humidity, insects and frogs, darkness and quietude.

I had seen Balinese and Javanese gamelan performances before: in a tent at the first Womad Festival in Somerset and, rather more formally, in two London concert halls. In 1977 I previewed a Sadler's Wells Theatre season of Gong Kebyar from Sebatu, central Bali, for *Time Out* magazine. My Venezuelan friend, Nestor, accompanied me. We stopped for a drink after the show, as always, and the delay awarded us the privilege of seeing a group of Balinese musicians and dancers gathered outside a hole-in-the-wall Chinese takeaway on the Clerkenwell Road. Not a delicate rice offering in sight.

During his Balinese sojourn shortly before the Pacific war, the Canadian–American composer Colin McPhee experienced ambivalent feelings on hearing the newly developing gamelan music called *kebyar*. "Forever changing", he wrote in his beautiful little book *A House In Bali*, "brilliant and sombre by turn, the moody music seemed to express a new spiritual restlessness, an impatience and lack of direction, for it was as unpredictable as the intermittent play of sunlight from a clouded sky."

In his time, McPhee was a pioneer among musicians who had fallen, or were to fall, under the spell of Indonesian music. Varying degrees of gamelan influence can be detected in the work of John Cage, Harry Partch, Lou Harrison, Philip Corner, Olivier Messaien, Steve Reich, Gavin Bryars, Terry Riley, Peter Sculthorpe, Wendy Carlos, Don Cherry, Jon Hassell and, in very recent times, Australian composer Paul Schütze and London sampling band Loop Guru. A sound akin to Javanese and Balinese gamelan filtered through dense layers of contemporary sources suffuses feature-film scores such as Ryuichi Sakamoto's *Merry Christmas Mr Lawrence*, Maurice Jarre's *The Year of Living Dangerously* and Yamashiro Shoji's *Akira*. This last, a *Carmina Burana* for the electronic, post-linear, folk-digital age, hypnotically counterpoints a relentless dark rush of Manga apocalypse imagery with hyperactive percussion, electronics and "Balinese Tantra" (whatever that may be), courtesy of Ida Bagus Sugata.

The CD cover hypes the score as "music for the 21st century". Perhaps this is not as trivial as it sounds. Music in the future will almost certainly hybridise hybrids to such an extent that the idea of a traceable source will become an anachronism. On a 1993 Japanese recording of Detty Kurnia, the daughter of a Sundanese (west Java) gamelan player, the entwinement of Javanese pop, traditional and neo-traditional styles, modern Asian pop and Hong Kong atmospherics, Japanese studio technology and quasi hip-hop drum programming can becalm the listener in an uncharted ocean. The experience is entrancing and disturbing, like trying to follow a map that changes its boundaries before your eyes.

Colin McPhee was not the first aficionado of Southeast Asian music. Centuries before him were the seafaring explorers, traders and colonial administrators from Holland, Portugal and England, some of whom were affected positively by the music. Piloting *The Golden Hind* around the world in 1580, Sir Francis Drake dropped anchor off the coast of south Java, where he heard "country-musick, which though it were of a very strange kind, yet the sound was pleasant and delightfull". Thomas Stamford Raffles, lieutenant-governer of Java in 1811, returned from Southeast Asia with two collections of gamelan instruments. In 1817 he wrote: "It is the harmony and pleasing sound of all the instruments united, which gives the music of Java its peculiar character among Asiatics." To Raffles, some of what he heard bore "a strong resemblance to the oldest music of Scotland". Clearly, he sensed possibilities in this music that in some respects extended the European traditions in which he grew up. "The airs", he wrote, "however simple and monotonous they may appear of themselves, when played on the *gámbang káyu*, or accompanied by the other instruments, never tire on the ear, and it is not unusual for the gamelan to play for many days and nights in succession". This passing comment illuminates a particular quality of Javanese gamelan and helps to explain, perhaps, why the music of such a small Southeast Asian archipelago has so strongly influenced music in the twentieth century. In 1937, Leonard Huinzinga expressed the nature of this quality more poetically. "This music does not create a song for our ears", he wrote. "It is a 'state', such as moonlight poured over the fields."

Aside from the *sound* of the music – a fractal vibration of harmonics which contains immeasurable variety – the transmission of the music introduced to European culture the idea of performance as a kind of ambience. Colin McPhee vividly described all-night events in Bali: he would fall asleep as fatigue overshadowed the spirited cacophony of a barong dance, finally waking at dawn in time to watch the concluding movement. The long rhythmic cycles and leisurely development within performances of Indonesian music allowed listeners to vary their concentration; intense focus, even a literal entrancement, could be alternated with peripheral listening, eating, drinking or, ultimately, sleep. The ambient music of Brian Eno has some origins in these ideas, since he was influenced by the music and ideas of the American minimalists. In their turn, they were influenced by the musical events of India, Bali, Java, Morocco and many other parts of the world, events which might run all night and allow for a less sharply focused style of listening.

A Balinese gamelan orchestra from Peliatan performed in Paris in 1931. "Early in 1940", wrote Klaus Wachsmann in a Royal Anthropological Institute lecture entitled "Spencer to Hood: a changing view of non-European music", "the [Amsterdam Tropen] Museum had made use of Indonesian shore personnel, in the employ of an Indonesian shipping line, to play gamelan music, and their concerts drew thousands of visitors." Then other gamelan ensembles toured Europe and America after World War II. From the 1950s onwards, gamelan ensembles flourished in museums and the musicology departments of American and European universities to such an extent that a new genre of non-Indonesian gamelan music emerged and the purchase of historic gamelans, particularly by American institutions, was described in 1971 by R.M. Wasisto Surjodiningrat, author of *Gamelan Dance and Wayang in Jogjakarta*, as a competition. "We have to be proud that the appreciation of the outside world for our gamelan music is increasing", he wrote. "On the other hand we are afraid that this will lead to the loss of our most cherished heritage for the prize of a mere couple of thousand dollars."

The first of the virtual explorers witnessed a gamelan performance in a similar spirit, in exactly the city and within a few years of the moment in which Huysmans's Des Esseintes was discovering the advantages of armchair travel.

Claude Debussy's father had plans for his son to become a sailor but Claude, at the age of eight, was described by his sister as spending "whole days sitting on a chair thinking, no one knew of what". This dedication to a life in the imagination was underlined by a letter to another French composer, André Messager, in which Debussy wrote: "I have endless memories which are worth more than reality." In 1888 Debussy visited Bayreuth to hear Richard Wagner's *Parsifal* and *The*

Mastersingers; the following year he went again, this time to
hear *Tristan and Isolde*. Still under the spell of Wagner's German romanticism, he visited the Paris Exposition Universelle,
a colonial exhibition held in 1889 to commemorate the cente-
nary of the French Revolution. He heard performances of
music and dance-dramas from Japan, Cambodia, Vietnam and
Java. A drawing by René Lacker shows us the Javanese group.
Five musicians sit crosslegged in front of a fence-like structure
made from bamboo. One plays a suling flute, one plays the
bowed *rebab*, in the centre is a man poised with his mallet to
strike a small, flat-key metallophone (perhaps a *saron* or
slentem, the instruments which play the melodic theme of the
music); at one end of the semi-circle a *kendang* drummer
plays barehanded, and at the other sits a rather dazed-looking
player of a *bonang*, a tuned metallophone of upturned bronze
kettles which elaborates on the central melody in muted
tones.

None of the instruments looks particularly ornate and the
group is small, though Lacker may have been sketching in
haste. The musicians seem to be in a state of semi-concentra-
tion, yet all of them show signs, some furtive, some direct, of
watching their watchers. According to one of Debussy's biog-
raphers, Edward Lockspeiser, the musicians accompanied
bedaya dancers, a performance which somebody compared
with Wagner's flower maidens in *Parsifal*. Never mind the
inappropriate comparison; if this is accurate, then Debussy
was fortunate. The *bedaya* (also *bedhaya*, or *bedoyo*) dances
– Bedaya Semang and Bedaya Ketawang – are sacred, ancient
and very beautiful court dances from Jogjakarta and Surakata.
Bedaya Semang, the story of a sultan who goes to live with an
unearthly queen in her palace at the bottom of the sea, is said
to have been created at the end of the eighteenth century;
Ketawang, regarded as a sacred heirloom, may date as far back
as the reign of Sultan Agung in the first half of the seventeenth
century and, according to Wasisto Surjodiningrat, was danced
exclusively within Jogjakarta palace walls until 1918. Per-

formed by nine female dancers who are prone to collapse
from the strain of their costume preparations, Bedaya Ketawang has a similar theme to Bedaya Semang: Sultan Agung
sees a performance in the underwater palace of the goddess
of the South Sea and converts his inspiration into a terrestrial
dance.

There are other, less sacred *bedaya* dances, and perhaps
the importation of one of these to nineteenth-century Paris is
more likely. But all *bedaya* music and dances are performed
with the slow, eerie grace of a loris and, to my knowledge, all
are based around watery themes. In the mid-eighteenth century, the first sultan of Jogjakarta built a water castle of
artificial lakes, tropical gardens and ornate architecture called
Taman Sari. Surely this background detail was unknown in
1889, yet how significant it turned out to be for Debussy, who
composed liquid works such as *La mer, Reflets dans l'eau,
Jardins sous la pluie* and *Poissons d'or* only a few years after
his experience at the exposition.

Psychologically, these Javanese myths, along with the
music itself, suggest an emergence of dreams and unconscious
desire into the tangible world of consensus reality, the feminine other dredged up into a domain of masculine logic and
action. The compulsive, almost occult attraction of liquidity,
the floating world, the ungraspable emergence of reflections,
sunlight on ripples, waveforms, the abyssal darkness down (or
up) there, was characteristic of *fin de siècle* Europe, just as it
is now on a global scale. Debussy found himself in sympathy
with the French symbolist writers – Mallarmé, Valéry,
Rimbaud, Huysmans, Verlaine and Victor Segalan – as well as
being influenced by the Egyptian craze that followed Napoleon's Egyptian expedition, the Japanese woodcuts of Hokusai
and, briefly, the Pre-Raphaelites and Russian exoticists –
Mussorgsky, Borodin, who was inspired by reading an account of Japanese tortures, and Rimsky-Korsakov the fantasist
who inflated folktales into epics.

Debussy was open to a world of sound beyond rules and

convention. As a successful but rebellious composition student in 1883, he shocked members of another class at the Conservatoire by playing a pianistic impression, full of strange and unresolved chords, of buses travelling along the Faubourg Poissonière. Harmony and counterpoint existed to be ignored according to whim and intuition. His reaction to the music he heard at the exposition was interesting, being couched in terms which appear respectful, curious, even slightly over-awed (although he did write about "charming little peoples who learned music as simply as one learns to breathe"). He was affected profoundly by the simplicity and emotional power of a Vietnamese (or Annamite, as it was known then) dance-drama. His famous comparison of Javanese with Palestrina's counterpoint came twenty-four years later, when he wrote about the exposition experience to his friend, the poet and author Pierre Louys. Along with *Aphrodite*, a "classic" of Orientalist soft pornography crammed with masturbation, sexual violence, erotogenic philtres, lesbian flute players, paedophilia and fake antiquity, Louys wrote *Chanson de Bilitis*, a pseudo-Greek literary hoax which was set to music by Debussy and performed at the Paris Exposition Universelle of 1900. Louys also held intellectual salons, and Debussy held forth on one of these occasions with a prophetic idea: "I would like to see, and I will succeed myself in producing, music which is entirely free from 'motifs', or rather consisting of one continuous 'motif' which nothing interrupts and which never turns back on itself."

Louys and Debussy seemed to share similar dreams of a pagan cosmos of half-human flautists fucking in forest glades. Debussy's reverie was realised in his gorgeous *Prélude à l'après-midi d'un faune* and *Syrinx*, a flute solo composed in 1913 which depicted Pan justifiably lamenting the transformation of his nymph lover into an aeolian reed flute. In *Aphrodite*, Louys describes a garden temple of pleasure, populated by 1400 exotic prostitutes from all over Asia, Africa and primitive Europe. Women from the most remote regions are portrayed as "tiny, slow-moving creatures whose language no one knew and who looked like yellow monkeys . . . all their lives these girls remained as shy as stray animals". Others live like "a flock of sheep" or "only coupled in animal posture". The scene suggests a zoo, a sexual menagerie, perhaps an exposition.

The Paris expositions were enormously influential. Not only did they introduce many forms of unknown culture and crafts to Europe, they were also a showcase for contemporary work created closer to home. At the 1889 exposition, Rimsky-Korsakov conducted a number of Russian works; to celebrate the exposition of 1900 a number of composers, Erik Satie among them, were allotted a few pages for posterity in huge, leatherbound albums of officially recognised art. A physician named Félix-Louis Regnault, a pioneer of ethnographic documentary, made a film of a Wolof woman making pots at the Exposition Ethnographique de l'Afrique Occidentale in 1895, the same year that the Lumières publicly demonstrated *cinématographe* films of steam trains and crying babies for the first time. Commercial cinema was born, the armchair traveller was up and lounging, the virtual traveller was seeded and already visible as a tiny dot on the far horizon.

In *A Theory of Expositions*, Umberto Eco describes collection and assemblage throughout history as a representation of "apocalyptic insecurity and hope for the future". "It was only with the expositions of the nineteenth century", he continues, "that the marvels of the year 2000 began to be announced. And it is only with Disneyland and Disney World that concern with the space age is combined with nostalgia for a fairytale past." These expositions were models of the shopping mall, as well as being the precursors of themed entertainments, trade shows, post-Woodstock I rock festivals and the kind of fast-foods-of-the-world "grazing" restaurant clusters that can be found in Miami malls. In Paris, world cultures were laid out in a kind of forged map as choice fruits of empire, living proof of conquest and self-aggrandisement in the face of imminent decline.

Edward Said performed a comprehensive demolition job on the West's obsessive appropriation of the East in *Orientalism*. "Every European traveller or resident in the Orient has had to protect himself from its unsettling influences", he wrote. Sex was particularly unsettling for the nineteenth-century Europeans, he added. "But there were other sorts of threats than sex. All of them wore away the European discreteness and rationality of time, space and personal identity." All of that sounds like a welcome effect. Debussy's admiration for the "unsettling influences" of Vietnamese drama or Javanese percussion and counterpoint, despite being locked in colonial realities, was a catalyst for his break from the powerful influence of Wagner and, by extension, Wagner's sinister enthusiasm for the master-race theories of Houston Stewart Chamberlain and Arthur de Gobineau.

Strolling through the 1889 exposition, Debussy, the stay-at-home, drifted into unknown sound zones, discovering answers to impulses which had already percolated through his European skin. At the mid point of the twentieth century his legacy may have been more prevalent in overblown feature-film scores than in the cerebral experimental music of that time, but near the end of the millennium his open, intuitive, impressionistic soundworld seems once more inspirational.

Increasing numbers of musicians are creating works which grasp at the transparency of water, seek to track the journeys of telematic nomads, bottle moods and atmospheres, rub out chaos and noise pollution with quiet, concentrate on sonic microcosms, absorb quotations and digital snapshots of sound into themselves, avoid form in favour of impression, concoct synthetic wilderness in urban laboratories, explore a restricted sound range or single technological process over long durations, seek to effect physiological change rather than pursue intellectual rigour, or depict impossible, imaginary environments of beauty or terror. Music that aspires to the condition of perfume, music that searches for new relationships between maker and listener, maker and machine, sound and context. Music that leads the listener into a shifting zone which Peter Lamborne Wilson has described as the "sacred drift", a mode of imaginal travel "in which the landscape will once again be invested with meaning, or rather with a liberatory aesthetics".

Various forms of this music have been called, with varying levels of appropriateness, ambient, environmental, deep listening, ambient techno, ambient dub, electronica, electronic listening music, isolationist, post-industrial ambient, space music, beautiful music, sound art, sound design, electronic music without beats, brainwave music, picture music, ambient jungle, steady state music, holy minimalism, Fourth World, New Age, chill out, or, the useless one to cap them all, new music. But no genre category adds up to much more than media shorthand or a marketing ploy. Open music might be a more useful catch-all name for what I am talking about, except for the fact that a proportion of this music, sometimes a high proportion, is vacuum sealed, zipped up in a droning Om-zone of discarnate reverie resistant to intervention and crackling quietly at the back of the freezer.

Besides Claude Debussy and the *bedaya* musicians of Java, where did so-called ambient music and all its bedfellows come from? What follows in this book is more a personal nomadic drift than a detached chronological history. This drift will trace a web of sources. In my biased opinion, compromised by first-hand involvement, these are the sources that have led to a musical environment which is, despite my reservations, a hydra of creative potentials for now and the next century. There are other sources, but those are other books.

2 if you find earth boring ...

travels in the outer imagination with Sun Ra

Everybody in the hotel lounge is sleeping; everybody except me. Over there in the armchair is Marshall Allen, saxophonist, flautist, oboist and performer on the self-invented morrow (as in to-), and sitting here in front of me, serene in repose, orange-died beard, dressed in a long robe decorated with star shapes and dots of distant galaxies, is Sun Ra. A quiet young man, hair matted into dreadlocks, gently touches him on the shoulder. His eyes open. "I am listening", he says. Space vibrations have been keeping Sun Ra awake for the past month. "The frequency moves so fast", he complains.

Ra had been listening to space vibrations and painting his musical pictures of infinity for at least thirty-five years. Sun Ra was probably seventy-six when I met him. That same year, he suffered a stroke; refusing to allow the fire of vision inside him to be quenched, he played concerts while sitting in a wheelchair. Finally, he passed on to other galaxies in 1993. His life had never been easy, either in terms of financial reward, critical support or the rigours of maintaining a large touring Arkestra, complete with otherworldly costumes and personnel, for decades after the big bands were supposed to have died.

His first UK performance with the Intergalactic Research Arkestra, held in the Queen Elizabeth Hall in 1970, was one of the most spectacular concerts ever held in this country. Not spectacular so much in terms of effects, which were low on budget but high on strange atmosphere; spectacular in terms of presenting a complete world view, so occult, so *other*, to all of us in the audience that the only possible responses were outright dismissal or complete intuitive empathy with a man who had chosen to discard all the possibilities of a normal life, even a normal jazz life, in favour of an unremitting alien identity. Fire eaters, a golden-robed dancer carrying a sun symbol, tornadoes of percussion, eerie cello glissandi, ferocious blasts and tendrils of electronic sound from Sun Ra on Farfisa organ and Moog synthesiser, futuristic lyrics of the advertising age sung by June Tyson – "If you find earth boring, just the same old same thing, come on sign up for Outer Spaceways Incorporated" – saxophone riffs repeated over and over by Pat Patrick and Danny Thompson as they moved down the seating aisles towards the stage while John Gilmore shredded and blistered a ribbon of multiphonics from his tenor, film images of Africa and outer space . . . As depictions of archaic futures, shamanistic theatre, images of divined worlds, these devices of cumulative sensory overload were regarded at the time as distractions from the music. But those who concentrated solely on the music ignored Ra's role as a political messenger.

As with everything else in his life, the formation of his first band in Chicago was an event surrounded by deliberate mystification. A photograph exists, dated circa 1956, which shows a group called Sun Ra and His Men, smiling for the camera, all dressed conventionally in dark suits and striped ties. Marshall Allen had arrived in Chicago in 1952, 1953, he can't remember precisely when. He and a drummer went looking for Sun Ra's band. "When they played jobs", Marshall tells me, "they always had somethin' different, something original on, somethin', a hat . . .". He joined the band and started looking original himself. "It didn't bother me. I had to get used to that. It was the *music*, see, that music that I couldn't just, ahh, flow with. But I said, I spent all this time lookin'. This *must* be it. It was good for me. Gave me some discipline." He chuckles, as if to say that discipline was not his strong point at that juncture.

Already, the song titles reflected Ra's philosophy: "Tapestry From An Asteroid", "Lullaby For Realville", "Kingdom of Not". "I've done it all along", Ra says, "but secretly. I used to compose some songs every day for the Creator. Just for the Creator, not for the public. I did that for years, then some got away. It got out of hand, it got to the people and people started listening. That was it." Bang, a fist on the table. "I had no preconceived notion, just playing sounds. It was fantastic. We was playing in the Grand Terrace, got the bandstand, got steps on the side for the chorus girls to come out. They didn't much approve of what I was doing."

He continues with a strange story about being kidnapped in Berlin many years later. "I was gone for about an hour and the band looked for me everywhere. We went through the Berlin Wall. Then they asked me questions about space, what kind of fuel on the ships? Then they came back to the hotel, they televised me, and again, asked me about space travel. Then I told them that there would come a day when you wouldn't have to use gasoline. You'd simply take a cassette and put it in your car, let it run. You'd have to have the proper type of music. Like you take two sticks, put 'em together, make fire. You take some notes and rub 'em together – dum, dum, dum, dum – fire, cosmic fire."

Ra's science-fiction sound paintings of alternative destiny could be linked historically with the percussive blocks of sounds composed into dark, mythic shapes by Edgard Varèse, or the jazz composing/arranging of Tadd Dameron and Duke Ellington, particularly Dameron on *Fontainebleau* and Ellington's wonderful "jungle" band of the late 1920s. Sun Ra acknowledges the beauty of pieces such as "Prelude To A Kiss" and "Day Dream" but claims that Ellington's musicians were not right for him. Revealingly, the judgement is based on social difficulties within Ellington's orchestra, rather than the musicians' undoubted playing abilities. Sun Ra valued his responsibilities as a guru, a benign cult leader, more than he valued musical virtuosity.

The earliest of Ra's recordings are marked by a strong sense of his first steps towards an artistic rebirth, a shamanistic transformation of himself as the central force in a bizarre and virtually self-contained universe. For this reason, he resisted all temptations to reveal his early life in any detail. By spurning the undermining, sacrilegious effects of biographical archaeology and its fugitive fame, he could better maintain the sacred integrity of his magical universe. Was he born on Saturn or in Birmingham, Alabama? critics would ask. Perhaps Alabama was a stranger place than Saturn in 1914. As we talk he slips out tantalising morsels: "Comic books was telling about all kinds of inventions that they'd done today. I used to read them all the time. I go by the Bible in a lot of things. It says God takes foolish things to dumbfound the world. So I consider comic books as foolish things so I read all the comic books. Sure enough, they wrote about the first atomic bomb in a comic book, TV wristwatch, all these things in the comic books were happening."

We walk slowly from the restaurant to the hotel, Sun Ra telling me about an important meeting in Turkey. He and the Arkestra had performed in Moscow, invited to celebrate the space flight of Yuri Gagarin. Following a concert in Turkey, a group of teenagers handed him a typed manuscript. "I've been talking about space all along", he said as we dodged puddles. "Compositions talking about space, following, you might say, intuition. Talking about things that are totally impossible but still holding to it that its true. It's just like being a scientist. People think, 'Impossible, couldn't happen'. Now I'm talking even more impossible things." Walking with the assistance of a stick, he pulls some papers out of a plastic carrier bag, dropping some on the wet pavement. Mindful of the fact that these may save the planet, we scrabble to save them from the wind. "I found this proof in Turkey. It's more fantastic than science fiction." My assessment may be biased, since I can only judge the contents from Sun Ra's fragmentary description of the contents, but from what he passes on to me, the general drift of this channelled wisdom is classic science fiction: superior alien beings wish to raise the consciousness of humans because the mess we are making is threatening the balance of the cosmos, so they transmit secret knowledge to a place where the vibrations are right.

America, particularly America, is dotted with eccentrics, psychedelic visionaries, conspiracy theorists and isolated crackpots who ordain themselves as spiritual leaders of mail-order churches, pouring out philosophy on energy streams of lunacy channelled direct from passing UFOs, predicting the end of the world, a return of the Golden Age. How was Sun Ra different? Partly because of his humorous self-awareness. Ra claimed in one of his drily catchy songs that the end of the world had already been and gone, so he knew how to play with the rules of the apocalypse business. In other respects, he matched the profile – a folk prophet who collaged self-taught knowledge into a crazy patchwork of profound wisdom, hokum and glossolalia. The music embraced similar contradictions – one moment on Saturn, the next moment back down on earth in a Chicago burlesque club. This irrational divergence was baffling to European intellectual mystic composers such as Karlheinz Stockhausen. "It was so highly powered", Stockhausen enthused to *Melody Maker* in 1971 after seeing Sun Ra perform. "I tell you, this first 20 minutes was first-class avant-garde experimental music that you can't put in any box. It was incredibly asymmetric! . . . But after this piece came some saloon wishy-washy music. I didn't like it at all. Sort of cheap, movie music."

One day Sun Ra may be contextualised in a mystico-political undercurrent of black American thought alongside Marcus Garvey and the turbaned founder of the Moorish Science Temple, prophet Noble Ali Drew. In *As Serious As Your Life*, Valerie Wilmer noted that Ra led a Chicago-based nationalist organisation, distributing pamphlets about the future importance of electronic technology, and there are rumours of his influence on the ideas of Elijah Muhammad, the founder of the Nation of Islam. Wilmer also passes on a story told by saxophonist Red Holloway, who remembered Sun Ra planning to go to New York to buy some books but then, like Des Esseintes, deciding that physical travel was unnecessary. "He said he just sent his body . . .", Holloway told Wilmer, "his – oh, I've forgotten the words that he used – astral projection? Yeah, that's it. And he said he got the information he wanted." When others laughed, Holloway would challenge them: "Well, can you prove that he's wrong?"

Mocked, belittled, patronised or written out of the jazz tradition, patient in his role as an unwelcome prophet, Sun Ra believed in the moment of revelation, the thunderbolt conversion. "I've seen incidents where people could", he yawns, then bangs the coffee table hard enough to blot out the next word, " . . . in one second, just one chord. I met a fellow in Chicago named Sharkey. He was gonna take an audition. He was sitting in a booth with his head on the table. I didn't know then he was so high. I tell you, none of the other instruments could wake him up. But as soon as I hit the chord he sat up and say, 'Who's there?' and got up, just from that."

The part of his message that could never be understood by Stockhausen came from Ra's experience as a black man in America. "Because of segregation", he once wrote, "I have only a vague knowledge of the white world and that knowledge is superficial. Because I know more about black than I do white, I know my needs and naturalness. I know my intuition is to be what it is natural to be – that is the law of nature everywhere." With sound, light, words, colour and costume, Ra concocted a moving, glittering hallucination of ancient Egypt, deep space, the kingdoms of Africa – Nubia, Ashanti, Hausa, Yoruba, Mandinka, Songhai, Sudan, Mali, Malinke, Xhosa – a history of the future with which he battled for the souls of his people against the legacy of slavery, segregation, drugs, alcohol, apathy and the corrupting powers of capitalism.

An extraordinary film made in 1974 gives us the clearest insight into Sun Ra's perception of his purpose as well as mirroring many of the mythopoeic elements of his life. *Space Is the Place*, unique as a cosmic blaxploitation Biblical sci-fi fantasy, begins in a Chicago club, in 1943. Ra is playing piano for the floor show. A man named The Overseer demands his dismissal. Ra plays strange chords which almost destroy the club. The scene switches to the desert, where Ra and The Overseer engage in a magical battle. Ra and his Arkestra then land on earth in a spaceship and sign a promotional deal. Ra is kidnapped, rescued, plays a concert and then leaves earth before it is shattered by a huge explosion. One scene in which Ra visits a youth community centre, is particularly revealing. "How we know you not some old hippie or something?" one woman demands. "How do you know I'm real?" Ra asks in reply. "I'm not real. I'm just like you. You don't exist in this society. If you did, your people wouldn't be seeking equal rights. You're not real. If you were, you'd have some status among the nations of the world. I come to you as the myth, because that's what black people are. I came from a dream that the black man dreamed long ago."

The periodic rediscovery of Sun Ra's music seems to coincide with each new phase of environmental awareness or spiritual hunger. His depiction of black cultural history, captured as in a dream and projected into the space age, has an appeal to anybody who yearns for a life more dignified and magical than the one they are living. Ra was not discouraged by the peaks and dips of public enthusiasm. "This planet has always rejected innovators", he says. Commercial record companies occasionally funded a recording but the majority of his album releases – estimated to be in the hundreds – appeared under his own imprint. Labels such as Thoth and El Saturn, sometimes recorded in Solar Fidelity or Galacto-Fidelity, captured every phase of Sun Ra's development. But records cannot convey the unique blend of low-budget spectacle, gravity and sly humour contained within a Sun Ra performance. Seated at the grand piano in his hotel lounge, dressed in robes and a hat which can best be described as inspired extraterrestrial Oxfam chic, he drifts into a jet-lagged reverie and improvises a solo piece which encompasses impressionistic tone clusters, rhapsodic runs, hints of Harlem stride piano, all built around a melancholy jazz ballad. The image is at once absurd and affecting. No other musician has created a myth of such dogged thoroughness.

Little is known of Sun Ra's background. He was born in Birmingham, Alabama, where he received a scholarship to help his music studies. "I never wanted to be a leader", he says. "Even in high school they elected me a valedictorian. I turned it down. I didn't want that because I saw what was happening to leaders. I thought leaders were an endangered species." He moved to Chicago and played in Fletcher Henderson's band, contributing his advanced harmonies and feel for sound. Eventually, the need to lead his own band became too strong to ignore. During the 1960s, he recorded unparalleled music: albums such as *Art Forms From Dimensions Tomorrow*, *Cosmic Tones For Mental Therapy*, two volumes of *The Heliocentric Worlds of Sun Ra*, *Atlantis*, *Strange Strings* and *The Magic City*. Every record was an apocrypha, a vibrant cosmic map of unknown regions, lush solarised rainforests, cold domains of infinite darkness, astral storms, paradisical pleasure zones, scenes of ritual procession, solemn ceremony and wild celebration. Space was the place. Noise and silence clashed in the void; the instruments of darkness squalling, rumbling, throbbing – split-note oboe and piccolo, rolling tympani, spiral cymbals bells dragon drums thunder drums warped in echo, trembling heterodyning of massed flutes, electronic celestial footsteps of angels dancing on bass marimbas, humming-bird cello, the howler-monkey belching roar of baritone saxophones and bass clarinets, outer space explored in the extruded plastic, labour-saving, swept-fin cockpits of the Clavioline, Rocksichord, Farfisa organ, Fender Rhodes electric piano, Hohner Clavinet and Moog synthesiser. Music to play for 5-D readings of mid-twentieth-century sci-fi comics and magazines such as *Fantastic Adventures*, *From Unknown Worlds*, *Wonders of the Spaceways* and *Tales of Tomorrow*.

spell

" 'The god comes in peace', say they who are in the full moon; they have given to me appearings in glory with Ra. Ascending to the sky, to the place where Ra is."
  Middle Kingdom Egyptian coffin text.

eye of Ra/hymn to the setting sun

"Reality is too harsh," Ra says. "Imagination makes everything nice. Use your imagination and get out of the most drab places by simply holding on to the imagination and making it real." I ask him, do you feel optimistic?

"Mystic?"

"Optimistic."

"Oh, mystic, you got opti." He laughs. "That could mean something else. Opti-mystic. Another word to deal with. Opti of course, you got op, that could be eye. Optimistic, that's very nice. That way, we got something else. You can take a word and move it out into other planes."

"It could turn around into mystic vision."

"Right, that is very beautiful. It's just like taking notes, taking them and making something beautiful." He reads sections from the Turkish/cosmic council manuscript, passages about the coding of consciousness, the failings of our leaders, the difficulties of Planet Earth. "Things are moving fast," he murmurs, sounding uncharacteristically bewildered, perhaps conscious that death is not so far away. "I don't know whether the sun's going round faster but the days are going by so fast."

Sun Ra's dream

"I had a vision that I saw some materials that defy description. I saw some jewellery that's like nothing you've got on this planet. It was like a big supermarket that was the supermarket of the Omniverse. Everything in the Omniverse was in this market. I didn't see any walls. It was so big there were no walls.

"I stopped at one counter where they had some socks. These socks were like they were alive. They were glittering like diamonds. I wondered how that could be. It wasn't like sequins. This was like they were *alive*. I wanted to know how much they cost. They said it was ninety dollars for one pair of socks. I said, 'Well, I've never seen anything like this before. I'd better go and see about the *pants*.' I went over to the pants and they were one hundred and eighty dollars. Finally they said, 'Since you're from another place, our tax here for everything is eighty dollars.'

"I was still standing there trying to figure out whether I wanted the pants or the socks. Then I came back here. I wondered if I had paid for them, they'd have been in the bed with me?"

3   scanning: aether talk

ambient in the 1990s; Scanner, John Cage, acid house, disco; AMM; Telepathic Fish, Biosphere, Mixmaster Morris, Land of Oz, The Orb, The KLF

59-73, 59-73 ". . . and ejaculation and all those sort of things . . . right, mixture . . " sub-aqua dial tone triad, low bass, hiss and crackle, Erik Satie's *Vexations* running underneath as unresolved counterpoint, a ride cymbal briefly, subliminal chatter, "oh yeah, oh yeah", a thump like the underwater pressure from the air guns of an oil rig, a faster rhythm, the whisper voice of professional sex, "I put two fingers inside . . . mmm, nice . . . gently and up and down . . . very nice . . .", "I will not be treated like a child", "you should know that", "yeah, well I can sum it up now . . . would you respond by talking or by writing? . . . also you might find it easier to write . . .", a repetitive keyboard line that could have been lifted from a Terry Riley piece, sibilant voices distorted into electronic sandpaper, radio voices, echoes, ritualistic banging, laughter, the impression of a forest canopy arcing above us, but not trees, rather signals, transmissions, radiophonic fizz, verbal voyages across time zones and round the curvature of the earth, a telephone rings, 'and he gets upset with me . . . this coat has got so beautiful" . . . "1,2,3,4,5,6,7,8," . . . crackle moving across the stereo field, "leave it with ya, tata boy" . . . more radio voices, muted speech, modulated by fading signals, the nostalgic sound of cold war espionage, a fierce burst of crackle across the flat lands, the iron grey seas, "You've upset people too much, for the wrong reasons, that's the problem", pop song, warble, faint high tones, string glissandi, more *Vexations*? then crackle, a deep, lazy voice: "naah, I just had a nice easy day today". . .

Scanner, "Mass Observation" (twenty-four-minute ambient remix by Robin Rimbaud, Robert Hampson, Jim

O'Rourke) verbalised.

field recordings

Robin Rimbaud snakes out a cheap television aerial across my sofa and tunes in his hand-held scanner to the invisible, private world. Private no longer. Somewhere nearby, a man is talking on the telephone to a woman, telling her he is about to buy a large loaf of bread in a local baker's. Children are singing in a weird heterophonic chorus behind the foreground conversation. The exchange is mundane but then he says "I always wear black to match the colour of my car", and banal talk is revealed as a Trojan horse carrying other levels of communication: status, style and sexual promise.

As well as organising a London club called The Electronic Lounge, Robin makes records based around material snooped, via the scanner, from telephone conversations. Sounds, atmospheres and sometimes beats are added but the core material is people talking in the mistaken knowledge that nobody else is listening. Hearing these records is a compulsive experience. The voyeuristic urge proves to be very strong.

But in addition to exposing the dynamics of interaction, scanners can also track unconscious desires as they irrupt into the glue of ordinary dialogue. Uninhibited by physical proximity, blank to the environment, focused on a disembodied voice, the imagination relaxes and allows its less housetrained *habitués* to scuttle into the light. Hearing these strange conversations plucked out of the air makes me think of an H.P. Lovecraft short story called "From Beyond", in which he wrote about an electrical machine which made visible "the creatures that form what men call the pure air and the blue sky" and that "come out of places where aesthetic standards are – *very different*". The story concludes with the narrator shooting the machine.

"I've always been interested in field recordings", says Robin. "When I was younger, when I was thirteen or fourteen, I used to hang microphones out of the window of my family's house and used to record what was outside in the street. I've got hours of tape – I don't know what you would call it. A good way of putting it with the scanner stuff is *mapping the city*. I don't want to sound like I sit in my little palace, picking up all the classes, but it's like mapping the movements of people during different periods of the day. It's fairly predictable. In the early morning, very quiet, lots of people ringing in saying 'I'll be late for work', or 'goodbye love', all this affection stuff; you very quickly move into the work rota and you're mapping out the system and the way people interact. You get to a lunch period when things lull and people start ringing up their friends, then it's back to work again. Around six to seven it's people ringing home. Then in the evening, that's where the riot happens. That's when it gets really exciting because all hell gets let loose. The phone rates go down and people have the most surreal conversations.

"I've always been interested in the spaces in these conversations. From a very early age I've never liked the telephone. I talk a lot on the telephone because it's the only way you can communicate with many people but I just don't like it. You can't have a natural pause because you just get ages of static. The etiquette's all gone, the organisation. Who's going to talk next? It amazed me with mobile phones, which are much more expensive than standard phones – you get these enormous gaps happening. They're the points that really interest me. What's happening in there. What I've often done is sampled these little parts of the background as well. A big part of the work I've done has been sampling a soundtrack in the background, be it people moving around the room, a radio on or whatever, looping it, manipulating it, using it as a texture. But that's the point where it really opens up. Interaction between individuals really happens at that point, or doesn't happen.

"It still shocks me that people have phone sex. With pornography, there is no interaction. They're listening to a tape recording most times. You're listening to somebody listening.

If you're talking to somebody on the phone, you usually say goodbye. The pornographic ones are disturbing because the phone goes dead. You know that's it. They've finished up, they've got their Kleenex and it's done.

"A big aspect for me is that it's so random. You never know quite what you're going to pick up. When I do a live gig and I do an improvisational set, I never know whether all I'm going to get is static. That's just as valid. If there's nothing there, there's nothing there."

This recalls the notorious first performance of John Cage's four-minute piece for twelve radios – "Imaginary Landscape No. 4" – premiered at Columbia University, New York, in 1951. Two players shared control of tone, volume and tuning for each radio. The performance began after midnight when the air waves were relatively quiet and composer Henry Cowell decided that this had spoiled the piece. Cage disagreed. His biographer, Davill Revill, quotes one of the operators, poet Harold Norse: "The effect was similar to an automobile ride at night on an American highway in which neon signs and patches of noise from radios and automobiles flash into the distance."

"I remember going to a lecture by John Cage a long time ago", says Robin. "I found it really liberating when he was talking about listening to music at home and there was building work going on next door. Somebody said to him, 'Was it disruptive?' and he just had to accept the fact that this was part of the sound. Once you embrace that, then everything's OK."

orientation

What is ambient music? Calm, therapeutic sounds for chilling out or music which taps into the disturbing, chaotic undertow of the environment? There are two separate, quite different moments in the past twenty years which tend to define interpretations. The first moment is Brian Eno's but, before I come to that, this is the second one. The story, or my version of it, goes as follows: Between 1986 and 1989, a number of import 12" singles appeared in the UK, almost all of them from either house-music clubs in Chicago, techno musicians of Detroit or garage-house producers from New York; most of them reduced the elements of dance music to a bare minimum in order to explore the new textures and rhythms of machine music. Phuture's "Acid Tracks" and "Slam", Larry "Mr Fingers", Heard's "Washing Machine", "Beyond the Clouds" and "Can You Feel It", Model 500's "No UFOs" and "Night Drive (Thru-Babylon)", Reese and Santonio's "The Sound", Virgo's "Do You Know Who You Are", Tyree's "Acid Over", Armando's "Land of Confusion", Lil' Louis's "French Kiss", Rythim Is Rythim's "Strings of Life" and "Nude Photo", Metro's "Angel of Mercy", Truth's "Open Our Eyes" and many others contributed to an emergent movement in Britain, now enshrined in popular mythology as rave. The full scope of that story lies outside this book but its development is relevant since without the Ecstasy-fuelled liberation, accompanying media circus and subsequent repressive legislation that accompanied so-called acid house and rave, the polar opposite – chill-out rooms and quiet clubs for ambient listening – might have remained the pipe dreams of a few solitary explorers.

Two of the key records that helped to shake British youth into a new phase of hedonism, self-belief and communal dissent were "Acid Tracks" (1987), produced by Marshall Jefferson, and "Washing Machine" (1986), made entirely by Larry Heard. Both had their origins in the black, predominantly, though not exclusively, gay warehouse clubs of Chicago. Accounts of how these two minimalist machine instrumentals came into being share a similar feeling, if only because both records were a consequence of home experiments which subverted the intended purpose of one or two pieces of music technology. This is how Marshall Jefferson described the moment to me, when I interviewed him in 1988: "Oh shoot, man. 'Acid Tracks' wasn't pre-programmed, man. 'Acid Tracks' was an accident, man. When you get an acid machine you don't pre-programme anything. You just hit some notes on a machine, man. DJ Pierre, he was over and he was just messing with this thing and he came up with that pattern, man. You know, dah-dah-dah-gwon-gwon-gyown-ga-gyown. So we were listening to it, getting drunk man. 'Hey, this is kinda hot, man. This is a great mood, man. Let's put it out. What the fuck?' You know? We played it at the Music Box, man, and everybody was flipping.

"When I did Sleezy D, 'I've Lost Control', man that's got screaming in it. Really, I was trying to get a mood something like the old Black Sabbath records or Led Zeppelin. So that's how it got the name Acid Tracks, because it's supposed to put you in a mood, you know? For one thing, the tune is eleven minutes long of the same thing. Slight changes, but not that noticeable. Like when you listen to a real long solo in the old days it's the same bass line going and everybody's doing some-thing different over it. That's supposed to capture a mood. Now what everybody thought acid house was after that was a drum machine and that acid machine, the Roland TB-303, which was not the truth. Acid house was meant to be the cap-turing of moods. You don't have to use the same machine all the time. You can use different instruments. I hate that ma-chine with a passion now. Everybody's using it wrong. The way they're doing it now it's not capturing any moods. It's disrupting thought patterns, man. That just hurts when you listen to it all night. It stabs your brain, man. You hear doh-doh-doh-doh-doh-dit and I hate it, you know, when it goes dit-dit-dit-dit-dit-wheoghwowowweogh. Oh man! It's like scratching a chalk board with your fingernails, man! Man, I *hate* that."

The basic components of "Acid Tracks" epitomise the prin-ciple of less means more: a Roland TB-303 Bassline playing patterns which sweep up and down through frequency and filtering as they run; the thudding, dry bass drum, hi-hat, clap and toms playing straight disco beats from a Roland 909 drum machine; the cowbell and whistle from a Roland 727 and some unidentifiable synthesiser swooshes in the background. Simple, but ferociously effective, particularly if drugs are involved. This was music without narrative; music as function; music as a technical process. Jefferson may have come to regret what he, DJ Pierre, Spanky and Herbert J put together that drunken evening in Chicago but, for disrupting thought patterns, "Acid Tracks" was powerfully psycho-active, black science fiction.

Larry Heard's "Washing Machine" was even more direct: a repeating, rolling melodic line with unusual intervals, spongy like a rubber ball in texture, bald of recognisable emotion except for occasional moments of musical tension and a slight suggestion of exuberance. Little touches of reverb introduce fleeting suggestions of physical space around the sounds, there are short silences or a bar of hi-hat cymbal. The drum programming is more eccentric than "Acid Tracks", perhaps a reflection of Larry Heard's career as a drummer in Chicago bands playing anything from R&B and jazz fusion to rock. "We did a lot of abstract rock", he told me when I interviewed him in 1989. "Yes, Rush and Genesis. I was a drummer so I was really crazy about Neil Peart. It was good for me to practise off of stuff like that."

Both Jefferson's enthusiasm for Black Sabbath and Heard's idolisation of progressive rock drummer Peart were bemusing at the time. According to stereotypical divisions of taste by skin colour and culture, black musicians were supposed to be listening to soul. An accumulation of personal histories has forced an adjustment of that picture: many techno and house-music innovators were inspired by a mixture of rock, jazz fusion, industrial music and the techno pop of YMO, Kraftwerk, Depeche Mode and Gary Numan.

The new technology of MIDI (Musical Instrument Digital Interface)-linked, programmable, polyphonic synthesisers and drum machines offered an escape route from a dying live-music scene, a chance to experiment in isolation, free from peer pressure to conform, and a means of composing and recording without using expensive studios. Larry began by borrowing an analogue Roland Juno 6 from a friend who had left town for the weekend. "I had always been interested in music", he told me. "I had four brothers and they all played guitar. I was, like, kinda left out. So when I did finally pick up an instrument I wanted it to be different to what they were doing. I started playing drums but I had always tinkered around with keyboards 'cos I was fascinated by the sounds of the synthesisers."

While his friend was away, Larry wrote two tunes. One, called "Mysteries Of Love", was a moody, inspirational track. The other was an instrumental, "Washing Machine". "It was just random sounds running over a beat", said Larry. "I've always been weird in my musical tastes. I always wanna hear something different from the things you hear on the radio all the time, just wanna hear someone venture out, take a chance when they're making music. It sounded weird to me. In the end my little brothers liked it. They thought it was kinda cool." They also thought it sounded like a washing machine, so that became the name. Never happy to be tied down to one style, Heard was capable of writing anything from strange compositions for drum machine, gorgeous mid-tempo ballads, tracks that sounded like Pink Floyd, backdrops for beatnik poetry or electronic jazz-fusion instrumentals which depicted lush environments of the imagination. With the dance frenzy at its height at the end of the 1980s, the potential context for such a broad sweep of quietly non-formulaic music seemed unpromising. Where did Heard envisage people listening to his records? "In clubs, of course, but maybe real late-night things. Some of the stuff, without the drum beats, I feel could be soundtrack-type stuff. Just for listening, everyday listening."

As we shall see later in this book, when Brian Eno applied the term "ambient music" to his activities he switched the emphasis away from making music, focusing instead on the act of listening. Inevitably the spotlight returns to the creator, if only for expedient reasons of maintaining a career, keeping up magazine circulations or boosting record-company profits. But many forces were chipping away at the hierarchical, separated roles of producers and consumers. Before Eno's theoretical dismantling of this relationship, early disco DJs had also eroded fixed definitions of performance, performer and audience.

The aim of dancing your ass off, sacred or profane, was inspired by disco's flow motion, the seamless mix that transformed three-minute pop songs (Phil Spector's little symphonies for the kids) into long-form epics. Like an all-night performance of Balinese gamelan or a Central African cult ceremony, the music moved through dusk until dawn. This nocturnal rhythm was bisected with sexual rhythms and the rhythms of crosstown, crosscountry, transworld movement. The futuristic vision of hypnotic living and machine sex was imported from Europe: from Germany came Kraftwerk with "Autobahn" and "Trans-Europe Express"; from France came Jean-Marc Cerrone with "Supernature" and from the South Tyrol, crucially placed in the centre of German, Italian and Swiss culture, came Giorgio Morodor with Donna Summer's "Love To Love You Baby" and "I Feel Love". Even The Bee Gees' "Jive Talking" was inspired by the rhythm of car wheels bumping over a railway track.

Speaking to Giorgio Moroder in 1992, I asked him why he and his co-producer, Pete Bellotte, had decided to extend "Love To Love You Baby" into seventeen minutes of orgasm theatre. He laid the blame on the coffin of the late Neil Bogart, once the notorious president of Casablanca Records. "He liked the song so much he wanted to have a long version of it", claimed Moroder, "and that's when I did the seventeen-minute one. The official story is that he was playing it at a party and people wanted to hear it over and over. I think the real one was more like the bad story. He was doing some other thing than dancing." So a revolution in music was catalysed by a record executive's desire for his own personal sexual soundtrack.

Actually, the story was more complicated. According to Vince Aletti, writing in *Rolling Stone* in 1973, some of the earliest records played in New York's underground of "juice bars, after-hours clubs, private lofts open on weekends to members only, floating groups of partygoers who take over the ballrooms of old hotels from midnight to dawn" were unusual imports from France and Spain, hybrids of rock, jazz and Afro funk.

African, Latin and jazz influences were dissolving the boundaries of rock. In the latter half of the 1960s, reciprocal motion agitated and enlivened music. Miles Davis, Sly Stone, Santana, War, The Temptations, Cream, The Velvet Underground, La Monte Young, Jimi Hendrix, Pharoah Sanders, The Grateful Dead and Terry Riley all indulged in marathon trance grooves, rippling with strange currents, often stretching beyond the limits of endurance into boredom, but hunting ecstatic release through repetition.

Zen

One of John Cage's many famous stories concerned a music class he gave in Oriental music. He played a record of a Buddhist service that began with a microtonal chant and then continued with the repetitious beat of a percussion instrument. After fifteen minutes, one woman in the class stood up, screamed, and then shouted, "Take it off. I can't bear it any longer." Cage took the record off. Then another class member – a man – got irate. "Why'd you take it off?" he demanded. "I was just getting interested."

John Cage, "*Silence*"

Bob Dylan may have regarded Smokey Robinson as a great poet, but the effect of Dylan on Motown was more obvious. Whatever it was that Bob Dylan, The Beatles and The Rolling Stones had done by copying, then transforming black music, a lot of black artists wanted the freedom to follow. Motown producer Norman Whitfield's response to acid rock – at least to Sly and The Family Stone's rainbow coalition version – was to produce psychedelic soul for The Temptations and Undisputed Truth. In Philadelphia, another producer/songwriter – Thom Bell – was moving in the opposite direction, enveloping a romantic vocal group called The Delfonics in a jacuzzi of French horns, flugelhorns, flutes, strings, harps, tinkerbell glockenspiels and even Indian sitars. As individual developments, both directions were destined to run themselves into the ground. Copied *ad nauseam*, Whitfield's funk-rock workouts degenerated into a monotonous grind, while Bell's crisp, quasi-classical arranging was caricatured by lesser talents and eventually melted to slush. Fused, however, they metamorphosed into a creature that conjured improbable oppositional visions of carnality and sentimentality, motion and stasis, delicacy and brutality, earth and aether.

If nineteenth-century composers such as Mahler, Scriabin, Mussorgsky, Prokofiev and Richard Strauss had collaborated as equals with musicians from the European colonies of Brazil, Cuba, Haiti, Nigeria, Ghana, Cameroon, Congo and Indonesia, what a sound they would have made. Or what a sound they would not have made, more likely, since whereas synthetic hybrids often match our imaginings to perfection, human attempts at impossible collaborations often fall short of the speculative reach of machines. Although disco reached many high points in its romanticisation of escape, its enduring legacy is less idealistic, yet still utopian. Disco mixing, the merging of records by a DJ, denied the musician as performer, denied the integrity of any individual performance, denied the problems of mixing musical styles or cultural difference, denied the conclusion of a work. Communication, the human problem, could take place in the machine: first, record decks and tape editing, then samplers, then hard-disk drives. Gradually, the DJ became the artist. Gradually, the song, the composition, was decomposed. After its first formative years, during which the global soundbanks were plundered for empathetic records, disco began to work on the principle of decomposing songs into modular and interchangeable fragments, sliced and repatched into an order which departed from the rules of Tin Pan Alley. This new order was designed to suit the nocturnal rhythms of a participatory, ecstatic audience, rather than any model of consensual, concise, classic proportions demanded by pop listeners.

Songs became liquid. They became vehicles for improvisation, or source materials, field recordings almost, that could be reconfigured or remixed to suit the future. In a humiliating way, musicians became technicians, alongside recording engineers, tape ops, editors and all the other technocratic laboratory assistants cleaning their glasses in the back room. At the front end of the medium was the DJ, ruling the disco, playing music and people as one fluid substance. Disco embraced the science of possession: motion codified into a biofeedback system of sonic driving leading to a form of trance, a meeting held in the virtual space of the spirit world. The discotheque (the literal meaning of which is record library), evolving over two decades into the club, became an indicator of atomised lives within the city. The club, as a generic concept, had come to synthesise historical strands as diverse as the Cabaret Voltaire, organised in 1915 by Dadaists Hugo Ball and Emmy Hennings in Zurich, or, less than fifteen years later, the exotic, sexually charged "jungle" floorshows of Harlem's Cotton Club. A gathering point and one of the most significant stages for the theatre of the new urban speed tribes, the club is also a dark refuge where new worlds can be tempted into the light. The DJ (often mistakenly elevated to shaman): librarian, *bricoleur*, scryer.

chilled out . . .

Chill: African-American slang for murder (1940); the coldness of the dead; cool enough to be close to the dead, detached from the consensus morality of the living, as in Iceberg Slim, or Texas blues guitarist Albert "the Ice Man" Collins, recordist of "Frosty", "The Freeze", "Sno-Cone" – the artist as coldblooded slayer. Cool, the coolest. At an extreme, emotionally frozen. Africa to America. In *Flash of the Spirit*, Robert Farris Thompson relates the concept of cool to the West African, Yoruban "mystic coolness" (*itutu*). "To the degree that we live generously and discreetly", he wrote, "exhibiting grace under pressure, our appearance and our acts gradually assume virtual royal power. And as we become noble, fully realising the spark of creative goodness God endowed us with – the shining *ororo* bird of thought and aspiration – we find the confidence to cope with all kinds of situations. This is *àshe*. This is character. This is mystic coolness. All one." By the early 1980s, New York dance records were full of references to chilling out. Bobby Orlando recorded a bass-heavy underground disco track – "Chill Out" – and old-school hip-hop was a forum for juvenile storytellers who had taken a chill pill, or were chilly the most. Chilling out was hip-hop vernacular for relaxation.

polaroids

1967, The Roundhouse, Chalk Farm, London. Waiting at the head of the queue, late in the evening, then almost first into the building – an emptied, circular shell once used for turning steam engines. The interior has the dark, soaring atmosphere of a ruined abbey, an abandoned factory of shadowed, grim corners and filthy alcoves. Lights are being rigged from the roof of a small hut in the centre of the floor. On stage, men are aimlessly busy, or busily aimless. One, wearing a short raincoat, blows soft flurries through a tenor saxophone; one, a man with sharp cheekbones and a goatee beard, assembles a drum kit, plays crisp rolls on the snare, then disassembles the kit and packs cymbals, stands and drums back in their cases; two men crouch on the floor, wrestling with wires, plugs, sockets, devices, a guitar. Loud bursts of noises are emitted, none of them having any perceivable relationship to other sounds. Standing at the edge of the stage, looking around me, I can see that nobody else in the audience realises that this is a performance. I have to break through a conception of performance to find this realisation myself. Later that night, Geno Washington and the Ramjam Band play musically poor but rabble-rousing versions of "Knock On Wood" and other soul favourites, followed by the new (and first) supergroup of Eric Clapton, Jack Bruce and Ginger Baker: Cream. Shortly after this key event, when mod turned psychedelic, brushing against improvisation and the ideas of John Cage as it revolved, I learned that these seemingly aimless characters on stage were called AMM. They had names. The saxophonist was Lou Gare, the drummer was Eddie Prevost, the two crouching men were Cornelius Cardew and Keith Rowe. Geno Washington vanished into lost memories many years ago; although Eric Clapton is now a global celebrity and both Jack Bruce and Ginger Baker are still musically active, Cream is barely known by a new generation of metal fans. One member of AMM is now dead, one has left the group, but a track by the latest AMM incarnation was included on Virgin Records' *Ambient 4: Isolationism* album in 1994.

1994, The Roundhouse, Chalk Farm, London. Chantal Passemonde, co-organiser of Telepathic Fish ambient parties, recalls a different event (same venue but another era): "It was cold, that's the best description. It was traveller people like Andy Blockhead, rather than club people, who had this idea that they wanted to do not a Rainbow Gathering, but a Rainbow Gathering sort of thing, if you know what I mean, in the Roundhouse on New Year's Day. What with the Criminal Justice Bill coming up and all that, and they felt it was really a powerful space to do it in. I knew Andy Blockhead, just from free festivals and partying. They'd been to Fish things and they said would we like to come and do it with them? In the end it turned out to be totally brilliant but the first seven hours were complete hell. I was playing with Paul and we played, we DJd, for eight hours. At the end I had an asthma attack.

"One of the guys knew one of the Roundhouse owners and asked for permission and he said yes. Then the day before, he said no, then yes, then no, then they wanted a lot of money.

Eventually we were saying we were going to squat it. Fuck them, we realised we could get access into it. In the end he was all right about it. All we saw was a fat Mercedes. We had the owner's permission provided it stayed ambient, because of the potential trouble they thought they'd get if it was a full-on rave, which they'd had when Spiral Tribe had done stuff there. So that's how the ambient thing came into it. The whole point was for people to gather after where they'd been on New Year's Eve. We were there all night and then it started at six in the morning. By about seven or eight o'clock that night they'd got in a big heater which made a big difference and then everything started going insanely psychedelic and bizarre. Two bands played – really traveller bands. Pan was one – an insane sort of progressive, psychedelic rock thing. There was loads of shamanic drumming, you know the insanity that occurs. Then Mixmaster Morris played and it went right through the night into Sunday.

"It looked amazing. Do you know Nick Mindscape, the guy who does Megatripolis visuals? He had these unbelievably huge screens that hung round one half of the circle, like right down, almost to the floor, and they were projected on. Then on the other side, there were these three vertical drops that were hung so that they were in free form, and they just moved, like billowed in the wind. There were projections on that. That was when it was dark. Matt Black was there and he was doing stuff. Everyone was really colourful, wearing jumpers and stuff. And during the day it was really lovely because all the light comes through the roof. I remember at one point we were playing the first track on B12's *Electro Soma* album, it's all very ethereal, and people were blowing bubbles. The whole place was full of bubbles. It did look like a really bizarre, post-apocalyptic, insane thing. People got so cold they were lighting fires. It was like something out of *Mad Max*. The building is just a shell but it's so powerful. Everyone was gathered in the inner circle of pillars and there was fire juggling. I wasn't on any drugs but it was weird. You just felt that there was some magic – you know that feeling you get when something is really special and it's miserable as well?"

... to chill out

Amsterdam is cold, this Friday night, October 1993. Inside the Melkweg, two men in pyjamas are pretending to sleep standing upright. A woman in black high heels watches television and three men wearing dark suits stand on a table at one end of the room. A couple encased in multi-hued, poly-vinyl Julian Clary-type outfits camp around in a gloom lit by luminous globes wrapped in sheets and bubble lights produced by a bank of projectors. Garden gnomes sit on green toadstools, their pointy ears attuned to a background drone of Indian tambouras and what may be the sound of herding songs recorded in some chilly northern climate.

Bored with this throwback to early 1970s' audience participation performance art, I wander into the other rooms to hear live performances of programmed music. The following night, part two of Amsterdam's first Ambient Weekend, I peruse some of the evolving curiosities of the ambient clubbing phenomenon from the balcony of the Melkweg. Following a live didgeridoo duet (the revenge of the native Australian?) delivered just to one side of DJ decks ringed with flowers, Chris and Cosey are performing.

Veterans of Throbbing Gristle's early 1980s' grey industrial electronica, they loom behind their keyboards like a couple of monochrome mannequins. They are static, the music is static, the place is packed and DJ Per, who has organised the event with his brother, is very happy. He is also very amused by the irony of the situation he sees below him. Having finally cast out its dopers' mattress, along with a 20 year reputation as the hippie centre of Europe, the Melkweg is occupied, once more, by supine catatonics skunked out on soft furnishings.

One of the frequent criticisms aimed at new ambient and electronic music is that the music lacks stars, focal points, magazine-cover fodder, dynamic performers. By definition, a computer-driven, pre-programmed performance is pre-determined. Only a few operators can transcend the knowledge that they, along with the audience, are passive witnesses to the computer's blind need to work through a programme from start to cut off. The only error, or danger, is that the machine may crash.

Saturday night at the Melkweg and all this is true of Biosphere's set. Have Macintosh Power Book will travel, yet with visuals and a keen sense of how to pace the music, he conjures real excitement, mystery and tension from digital information. Geir Jenssen, the man behind Biosphere, began his career with a Norwegian band called Bel Canto, a Nordic answer to Australia's post-punk, Medievalist ambience band, Dead Can Dance. After abandoning that ship, he recorded a promising Belgian New Beat/acid album – *The North Pole By Submarine* – as Bleep in 1989, some of it sampled from radio transmissions, and then released his first Biosphere album, *Microgravity*, on Renaat and Sabine Vandepapeliere's Belgian-based Apollo label in 1992.

As Biosphere performs, a time-transported punk, armed with spiked mohican and Exploited T-shirt, sits in the lotus position in front of the stage and meditates, while Saturday night party people scan the prospects, bug eyed, looking to pull. A hippie lying on his back on the mattress in the centre of the dancefloor flicks a used-up but still glowing spliff into the air, oblivious to the inflammable people around him. A tough audience to please.

From the PA, two children's voices loop round and round, a sample taken from a feature film to form the basis of a Biosphere track called "Phantasm": *We had a dream last night . . . we had the same dream*. A nagging two-note ostinato and these two creepy voices build tangible tension in the room. Photographs of earth shot from a space shuttle, acquired from NASA or from Tromsø's local science station, fill the screen behind Geir, and when the bass drum finally kicks in, this tough crowd goes wild.

Drinking beer with Geir in the Melkweg café earlier in the evening, I asked him if his home environment in Tromsø in Norway exerts an influence on the atmospheres in his music. On first impressions an intense, rather melancholy soul, Geir looks like the kind of character who could have played well in Hollywood horror movies of the 1930s. This is deceptive. Actually, he is a wistful man who makes amusing company. Tromsø, he explains, has no sun for two or three months of every year. Winter lasts for seven or eight months. "I feel at my most creative when the sun is gone", he admits. "When it's a Christmas feeling and it's dark all the time, you can see the Northern Lights. You see the houses with all the lamps inside. It's very cosy."

This picture strikes us as being rather funny, bearing in mind the fact that techno avoids references to community (other than the techno "community"), security or domesticity, so we talk about signals transmitted across great distances, of technology and isolation and the dramatic image of invisible connections across a void. "I think it's great to sit in the darkness with computers", he muses. "I like this combination of desolate areas and hi-tech equipment. In my home town, if a fishing boat is going under, it can send a signal up to a satellite and they can see it on the computer where the boat is. It happened last week. Five people were saved because of that. They can also see if boats are spilling oil illegally."

We think about that prospect for a second. "Green space", laughs Geir. "You can sit wherever you want on the planet because you can bring the technology. You can sit on the North Pole and pick up sounds from radios and satellites. I have this idea. If possible, I would like to be the first one making music in the space shuttle – composing music and weightless. Don't tell anybody this idea or Jean-Michel Jarre will steal it." Before Geir goes on stage to press the first button, he wants to lay one more ambient cliché to rest: "I hate it if people use my music as a background. When I was listening to Jon Hassell and Brian Eno, I was inspired to know more about the Himalayas or astronomy, Egypt and archaeology. I want people to get inspired to read astronomy or to get another view of the universe. To be curious."

Mountains, stars, satellites, space travel; weightlessness and computers, an escape from the body. The urge to transcend the body is a dominant theme in any conversation about the technological future. Virtual-reality fantasies and the spectacle of the wired world express an alienated yearning to leave the biological prison and transmute into a cyborg state. In the *fin de siècle* mind, immateriality, spirituality and electronics are synonymous. The body has become dangerous. "I also think reality is an interesting subject because I think we are all immersed all day every day in reality", said future designer Douglas Trumbull to future designer Syd Mead (the visual illusionists who created a dystopian archaic-future look for *Blade Runner*) in that bible for cyborgian transcendentalists, *Mondo 2000*. "What we seek is super reality, or *hyper* reality or altered states of some kind. I think the attractions in this area that are going to be the most successful will be the most extreme states or out of body experiences."

In their view, psychedelic shamanism has become a metaphorical holy grail, not only in the quest for new identities in a fragmented world, but in the search for the ultimate commercial, theme park, drug machine. As glamorous compulsions of advertising surfaces spread in a sweet sticky flood over the subterranean desires and revelations of altered states, so the future designers rave about human brain interfaces and the direct implantation of visions into the human mind.

the milky way

On the hunt for a psychedelic skinhead acid pixie bare-knuckle backstreet fighter to cast in your new computer game you could do worse than ink a contract with Mixmaster Morris. Acting, as always, the pugnacious silver surfer of ambient, Morris, The Irresistible Force, DJ, recording artist and tireless advocate of ambient music, elbows the air, screws up a physiognomy that is already mashed potatoes and narrows his eyes to Stanley blade slits.

"Who's got some roach material?" he demands, avoiding eyelock with any of the humans in this cold dressing room backstage at Amsterdam's Melkweg. Morris is not a person to whom questions are addressed. He just rolls out soundbites for the interrogator to gather up in a shopping bag and reassemble at leisure. A typical example: "We've had sixty, seventy years of making records. That's stage one. Now we sample them."

We last met in Soho Ambient during the summer of ambient that was still in progress in 1993 as autumn turned to winter. Soho Ambient was, at that point, a hole-in-the-wall trading post. Lurking at the rear of a hippie emporium hidden by the greengrocery of Berwick Street market, this modest enterprise with its limited stock of CDs and vinyl was symptomatic of the peculiar rise of ambient.

The very first time we met, Morris and I talked at length in the front room of his Camberwell flat. "My dream", he confessed during that sunny afternoon, "was to get a roomful of people to take psychedelic drugs and to operate samplers and sequencers in front of them. That seemed like an impossible goal six or seven years ago. Now it seems rather trivial." In between playing computer games, Morris's other guest of the day talked to me about making brain machines.

Back in Amsterdam, Morris and I exchange notes on our respective bafflement. Ever since the Land of Oz chill-out nights in 1989, plus rare early sightings of electronic fluffiness from Fingers Inc. and Virgo in Chicago or The Orb and The KLF in London, the oxymoron of ambient house – dance music for sitting still – had become accepted into common usage. Ambient had turned into one of those polysemous glue words which stick wherever they land. Morris, always on the move, saw ambient rise in Frankfurt, Hamburg, Berlin, San Francisco, finally to survey an international movement in the making. Aside from Holland, Belgium and the inevitable Goa, he had found embryonic scenes in Japan, Austria, Finland, even St Petersburg and Chicago. "I'm happy there's an ambient movement and not just an Orb movement", he says. At the very least, there is a new category in the record shops. "I'm much more interested in a revolution than a category", he continues. "It's definitely a window of opportunity. I can see us taking on artists that nobody in history would have taken on – the really crazy ones. There's a lot of crazy ones following me about – giving me tapes of really crazy music and ringing me at three o' clock in the morning, saying, have you listened to that tape yet that you got in the post this morning? It does drive me crazy but some of these people are the next generation. Even if I never made any more music I would be happy to have been a conduit just to let all that stuff through."

Ambient had been one symptom of a shift in music production in the UK. Not a revolution like the hippie movement or punk, which had songs about revolution, but a sudden reorganisation of all the pieces into new formations. As with psychedelia and punk, the big cash might or might not fall from the skies after the main event had blown itself out. But for the moment, there was a perceptible openness, a sensation of feeling another cultural movement flex its muscles.

Something like three in the morning at the Melkweg, Friday night, and Dave Wheels and Bobby Bird of Higher Intelligence Agency are giving a compelling demonstration of one way in which music making is changing. In Chris Heath's *Pet Shop Boys versus America* book, Neil Tennant comes up with a phrase: "It's machines playing live." That will do nicely. HIA are in there, on the floor with the dancers like a reggae sound system. The machines are playing live and the atmosphere is white hot. Nobody is pretending to replace machine processes with crotch pumping and choreography. There's some knob twiddling, effects processing and track muting, along with a lot of concentration, but the purism of the thing, the idea that this music happens in real time as the machines respond to messages stored on data disks, is imperceptible except as an intangible energy – a clarity of sound and purpose. "Live electronics can enhance the mood of where it's being performed", Dave Wheels explains, "with the energies of the people performing it being picked up by the people they're working with and going back out to the people they're getting it off." I think I follow that. "You build it up like that", he says. "That's the aim."

Despite persistent associations of New Age values, most of the new ambient is fiercely urban and now age. Some clubs double as marketplaces for ineffectual and overpriced "smart" drugs, Tarot readers, luminous jewellery, masseurs, digeridoos and "tribal" drumming, but in general these elements seem to denote spiritual hunger, activism stemming from disillusionment, an alternative economy or simple social discontent, rather than a withdrawal into the élite white light of New Age evolutionism.

21 September. I talked to Future Sound of London at their studio in north-west London. We discussed a track called "Dead Skin Cells" from their *Lifeforms* album: the huge enlargements from microscopic photographs of dust mites, the possibility that emergent bodies lay in dusty piles of shed skin. "What we term ambient has been misconstrued", Gary, the talkative half of FSOL, tells me as the taciturn half, Brian, paces the room, "because it's like – put on a space suit – I am weird because I come from outer space. I'm not interested in that. I think *this* . . ." (raises eyebrows to indicate planet earth) ". . . is a weird place. What our music, I think, represents is a weird perspective of this space now. It's like a re-evaluation of yourself in your space, rather than escapism."

David Morley's first track for Renaat Vandepapeliere's rapidly expanding Apollo label was a crackling, blue-label, lucky-if-you-own-one slab of vinyl called "Evolution". David, blond, British born and self-confessedly plagued by nervousness, mixed baby gurgles so high on one side of that particular record that Renaat objected. "It was meant to be a bit stressful", he admits. "That's another thing about ambient at the minute. It's always considered soft, mushy, smooth, which I like as well, but I think it can also be tense. The word – ambient – just means anything around you that affects you in some way." So people began to talk about dark ambient, and then isolationism, as a contrast to the beatific German electronic music typified by Ralf Hildenbeutel and Oliver Lieb on Sven Väth's Recycle Or Die label.

networks

For Higher Intelligence Agency, it was all about getting something going in Birmingham. They started their club, Oscillate, in May 1992. "The first Oscillates were above a pub," says Dave Wheels, "the only place we could find cheap enough to put it on. You know, everyone was unemployed, on benefit. The first one, I seem to recall, two people turned up. Nobody was interested. Twenty people were there. It was so unpredictable." Then they moved the club to a Friday. Ultramarine played there. Mixmaster Morris played an ambient set (nearly getting himself electrocuted by Jonny Easterby's sound sculptures in the process) and then Orbital, one of the few techno acts to make a successful jump from studio technocracy to outdoor rock festivals, played a one off to test the computer-age resolve of post-industrial Birmingham. The club was jammed. By this time, HIA had connected to Mike Barnett's Birmingham-based Beyond label. "That's another strange story", says Bobby. Resigned to being lone pioneers of their own hybrid genre, they suddenly heard about a label being launched in their own city, specifically to cater for ambient dub. His face still registers astonishment at the absurdity of it all. "We couldn't believe it."

And in London, there was Spacetime and Telepathic Fish. Held in a warehouse in Cable Street, London's East End, in 1990–91, the Spacetime parties were organised by techno/ ambient musician Jonah Sharp and holographic clothing designer Richard Sharpe, both of them now living in San Francisco where Jonah runs his Reflective Records label.

"They were really experimental", says Jonah. "We used to have Morris playing all night. The whole idea behind the music was that people would come and talk. It allowed him to try a lot of things out. I used to play live at them. It was people sitting in the corner, tinkling on keyboards. The whole holographic thing is synonymous with what I've done. Richard is an inventor – he invented this fabric and he's totally into visual art. We used to decorate the entire room with holographic foil. There was a fountain in the middle and we had a massive dish with terrapins and a bowl of punch. The entrance was a bottle of wine. Two hundred people maximum and it was a lot of fun. Good conversations, which was an important thing. Instead of losing yourself in your own little space, there was a lot of interaction. I think a lot of people met at those parties. That was what made me aware of the possibilities of the chill-out space. That environment within a big rave was just starting to happen at that time. I think Alex Patterson was playing at Land of Oz but I didn't know about that. For me, the ambient room or chill-out room was a platform for live music. I was never interested in DJing at all. The DJ was someone who filled in if the keyboard blew up. Morris used to always play live. He had a computer and a little drum machine." After five of these events, The Shamen's Mr C took over the DJ decks. "He completely ripped it up", Jonah laughs. "Spacetime got thrown out the building. The landlord turfed us all out. There were people on the roof. It was mad."

Telepathic Fish grew from similar origins as a small squat party to a growing public event with its own fanzine, *Mind Food*. "It's like being in someone's living room", Hex/Coldcut 'Macpunk' Matt Black said to me in October 1993 as we watched somebody step around the inert bodies, the dogs on strings and the double baby buggies, carrying a tray of drinks and eats. On that occasion, held in Brixton's Cooltan Arts Centre, Telepathic Fish ran from noon until 10 p.m. on a Sunday. You could buy Indian tea and cheese rolls (the latter constructed in situ with a Swiss army knife) from a low table

set up in one corner of the main room. This looked for all the
world like a 1960s' arts lab: bubble lights, computer graphics,
inflatables, sleepers, drone music, squat aesthetics.

My first and foolish action was to sit on a mattress which
has been out in the rain for a month. For half an hour, only
professional interest keeps me from screaming out of there in
a shower of sparks but then I relax. No, it's fine. This is ambient in the 1990s – the 1960s'/70s'/80s'retro future rolled into
a package too open, loose and scruffy to be anything other
than a manifestation of real commitment and enthusiasm. Telepathic Fish was started by a group of art students and
computer freaks – Mario Tracey-Ageura, Kevin Foakes and
David Vallade – who lived together in a house in Dulwich.
Later, Chantal Passemonde moved into the house, shortly after the parties had begun. Kevin was a hip-hop fan, David
liked heavy metal and Chantal listened to the ambient end of
indie music: Spacemen 3 and 4AD label bands such as This
Mortal Coil. There were no shared musical visions; simply an
idea that the environment for listening to music could be
different.

"It all happened one day when Kevin went to get some
dope off this real bizarre Rastafarian in Brixton", says Chantal.
"He had this whole theory about feeding the five thousand. It
was all very unclear, but it was about taking the fish and making it a part of you. It becomes part of your mind and spirit,
and somehow that linked up with telepathy. How, I still don't
know. They were all tripping at the time so we never managed
to get the complete story. What they did was this bizarre ritual
of swallowing a goldfish."

For the first party, held in the Dulwich house, six hundred
people turned up through word of mouth and Mixmaster Morris DJd. Then they planned a May Day teaparty. The fliers were
teabags. Mixmaster Morris wanted a German ambient DJ, Dr
Atmo, to play at the party, along with Richard "Aphex Twin"
James, a recent addition to Morris's wide circle of friends and
fellow psychic nomads. "We realised that the whole party was

going to be too big for the place we were going to have it,"
explains Chantal, "which basically was a garden, so we rushed
around. Morris knew some people and we found this squat in
Brixton, which was run by these completely insane people.
Just real squattie types, right over the edge. It was from Sunday tea on May bank holiday and people just turned up in
dribs and drabs all through the night. We got Vegetable Vision
in to do the lights. We ran around and got mattresses from on
the street round Brixton and we had some of my friends doing the tea. We made lots of jelly and there was plenty of acid
about. That went on for about fourteen, fifteen hours, with
people lying around. That was the first proper Telepathic Fish,
May 1st, '93. Then, there was no such thing. There probably
was on a small scale, lots of people chilling out in their bedrooms – the post-clubbing experience when everyone comes
round and you play tunes, but we'd never been to anything
like that. We just did what we would like. We'd all missed Land
of Oz, we'd missed everything. It felt like something big was
about to happen. You could feel that people wanted it but they
didn't quite know what it was."

Of the clubs and parties that Telepathic Fish and Jonah
Sharp missed, Land of Oz generated the widest ripples. The
convergence of influences found at this short-lived event typified a refreshing dissolution of tribal boundaries and
behaviour. Land of Oz was a Monday night house-music club
organised at a central London club – Heaven – by DJ Paul
Oakenfold in 1989. A chill-out room was added in the upstairs
VIP room. You could chill, but you had to be a somebody on
the club scene. Since there were no ground rules for this type
of event, misunderstandings could take on a life of their own.
Steve Hillage, for example, was invited to Land of Oz because
he was a friend of the man who designed the sound system.
Better known as a hippie guitarist from Gong and a successful rock producer, Hillage was discovering that the acid-house
upsurge was capable of recharging more than one vintage of
battery. Wandering around the chill-out room upstairs, he was

pleased to hear a track from his own *Rainbow Dome Musick*. This was something he had recorded ten years earlier, a sort of meditational underscore for the rainbow dome constructed as a central feature of the 1979 Festival for Mind–Body–Spirit. Held in the vast hall of Olympia, London, these spiritual hypermarkets were early warnings that the Californian New Age movement was taking hold in the UK. His collaborator on these two long pieces – "Garden of Paradise" and "Four Ever Rainbow" – was Miquette Giraudy, a French keyboard player who had acted in Barbet Schroeder's 1972 film *La Vallée*, a confused story set in Papua New Guinea but given some commercial impetus by Pink Floyd's *Obscured By Clouds'* soundtrack.

Chiming Tibetan bells and slow electric piano arpeggios were musical components that had been outlawed by every youth movement since punk. Hillage was agreeably surprised, then, to find his work back in favour, particularly adjacent to the white heat of house music. He introduced himself to the DJ, Alex Patterson, who had no idea who Hillage was. At that time, Patterson was working in an A&R capacity at EG Records, the King's Road company that specialised in ambient music in its first incarnation, releasing records by Brian Eno, Robert Fripp, Michael Nyman, Michael Brook, Harold Budd, Jon Hassell and, indeed, myself. Patterson knew nobody from this generation. Brian Eno once gave him a nod when they passed on the King's Road but that was it. Instead, he was plugging into the British and German dance scenes, listening to nascent techno from the UK underground, trying to sign the publishing for A Guy Called Gerald in Manchester, travelling to Chicago in an attempt to negotiate a publishing deal with Larry Heard and, in the process, hearing Heard's drumless remixes.

Patterson had met The KLF – Bill Drummond and Jimi Cauty – and had already started a collaboration with Cauty under the name of The Orb, releasing a single called "The Kiss" in July 1989. "Cross-over potential: nil" predicted the press release. True enough for that single, but slightly wide of the mark by the time The Orb became one of the most successful bands in the UK. Credited to Two Fat Belgians – perhaps a dig at the Belgian New Beat craze (dismally slow, sample-heavy dance records that were failing to export Belgian culture with any success) – "The Kiss" was one of a number of samplemanic, scratch 'n' sniff, blip culture records released at the time: Drummond and Cauty's Justified Ancients of Mu Mu, Coldcut, New York and Miami hip-hop, Bomb the Bass and M/A/R/R/S. The same approach could be applied to club DJing: throwing any possible source into the mix and gluing together the disparity with beats. But what if the beats were taken out, the volume pulled down, the tempo varied or slowed down to stasis, the diversity taken to extremes? This is what Patterson and Cauty started at the now legendary sessions at Land of Oz.

"Legendary?" muses Patterson, sitting in the chill-out room of The Orb's studio, tracksuited and smoking one spliff after another. "It was just like a bar, a VIP bar upstairs. We were just given the room every Monday for about six months. I'd met Nancy Noise, who introduced me to Paul Oakenfold. We were talking about it with Jimi Cauty. I think he liked the idea of me and Jimi. We spent the Sundays looping one sample from, like, 808 State or 'Sueño Latino', or something that was, like, very obvious – the Hovis advert." At this point, the idea of ambient was not entirely an underground concept. "Sueño Latino" was an Italian house-music single, produced in Bologna by the DFC team: Riki Persi, Claudino Collino and Andrea Gemolotto. The basic tune was taken from a strange electronic disco-minimalist album, *E2–E4*, recorded in the early 1980s by Manuel Göttsching and released by Klaus Schulze. *E2–E4* already had a dancefloor pedigree; it had been a part of the eclectic mix of records played at Manhattan's Paradise Garage club. The simple addition of heavier drums and bass, plus loon sounds (a bird commonly spotted hiding in digital samplers) and a multi-orgasmic monologue spoken by Carolina

Damas in Italian, was novel enough to send "Sueño Latino" into the UK charts. Even at this early stage, the elements feeding into the ambient side of dance music were surprisingly varied. Göttsching, for example, was the guitarist for a German rock band named Ash Ra Tempel, co-founded in 1970 with Schulze. By 1977, Ash Ra Tempel had slimmed down to Ash Ra. Albums such as *New Age of Earth* epitomised the difference between UK and European rock; pictured on the back of the album cover, Göttsching was still dressed like a 1969 hippie – long hair, flowing scarf, Gibson guitar. The music titles – "Ocean of Tenderness" in particular – were alien to the post-punk spirit of Britain and East Coast USA. These were signals that had been consigned to the dustbin of history. But the style rule in Britain is to adopt the opposite of whatever has become entrenched, institutionalised or boring.

So Patterson and Cauty fused the mellow side of house with slow music, ethereal music, hippie music (despite the denial), bioacoustic music and spliff music, feeding them through all available montage techniques. Nothing was sacred. Ear witnesses have reported The Eagles, Strauss waltzes, Brian Eno, BBC birdsong albums, 10cc's "I'm Not In Love". "We'd build melodies up", Patterson explains, "and then take an eight-track, or it was a twelve-track, into Heaven, just linking it up to three decks, loads of CD players, loads of cassettes and this loop, which would then become an eight hour version of 'Sueño Latino', 'cause there's a loop of it in there. We used to keep it very, very quiet. We never used to play any drums in there. It'd be just like, you know, BBC sound effects, really."

What was the original reaction? "We used to get six or seven or eight or nine kids who always used to come and sit at the front and just sit there all night and listen to what we did. There was a hard-core of about nine, maybe ten people listening. There wasn't that many people stayed there all night. And then it gradually got bigger. It depended. If it was a bank holiday then it got packed, people just completely off their heads escaping all the loud noises from everywhere else.

But you needed a VIP pass to get in there, which made it weirdly special. If you could get in and listen to it in the first place you were lucky. All the DJs, they liked it because they could sit down and talk work, rather than being in a room crammed full of loud music and sweaty people, trying to get a conversation going behind the DJ booth. *NME* started to pick up on it – ambient house, music for the 1990s – but there was no ambient bands around. They tried to claim there was loads of clubs all over Britain that were on the same network. There was probably three or four clubs, one of them being Mardi Gras in Liverpool.

"The simple reason why it was popular, or became, as you say, legendary in a sense, was because nobody had even thought about doing that in a club since the late sixties, early seventies. And that was playing hippie music, which we weren't at all. I spent four or five hours playing really early dub reggae. You don't have to dance to it, you just nod your head to it. It's still ambient to me. Some of the effects on those records – a four-track, in a hut in Orange Street, Kingston, and they'd make sounds like that. It puts us to shame when you think of how much we've got to play with.

"Land of Oz – it only lasted six months. It's the diversity that created it. We used to play the German version of Kraftwerk, War – *Galaxy*, *The World Is A Ghetto* – 'Four Cornered Room' especially off that album. Ummm . . . *For All Mankind* videos. We had white screens so we could put visuals up as well. We had home movies of ducks in the park. We'd go for everything. It was all laying on top of each other – what The Orb later became with four thousand people standing watching. This was a little room with a hundred people in there at the most."

That last point is important to an understanding of why ambient music is more a way of listening, an umbrella term for attitude, rather than a single identifiable style. As Patterson has suggested, the DJ came to the forefront of music. As a semi-anonymous *bricoleur*, a cut-up artisan, the DJ could montage any form of music to create a mood, an environment. Records began to appear which reflected this cavalier approach. What had been a process became identifiable product. As Jimi Cauty told *Face* magazine editor Sheryl Garratt at the time: "People keep ringing me to ask if I want to DJ at their New Age night, but I've only got four records!" The KLF released a drumless mix of "Madriga Eterna"; still calling themselves The Orb, Patterson and Cauty released "A Huge Ever Growing Pulsating Brain That Rules From the Centre of the Ultraworld" in December 1989. Ambient house for the E generation they called it – a neat marketing phrase which happened to be exactly right for a brief time.

The Orb single was sampladelic, rather than drumless: church bells, babies crying, celestial choirs, relentless arpeggiated synth sequences in the style of Tangerine Dream, a heavy breakbeat and, at the centre of the Ultraworld, the late Minnie Riperton singing her touching but nevertheless rather sickly ballad: "Loving You". This was not the first time Minnie had been electronically, unwittingly transplanted. After her death from cancer, her unfinished vocals were built up through overdubbing and editing into a posthumous album, a reiteration of music's status as a shifting conglomerate of manipulable bits, rather than a finished entity. The dead are no more immune to this process than the living.

More links were being made here, particularly the connection between ambient music's calming intentions and the nice-and-easy-does-it mood of easy listening. In 1990, The KLF released two albums which could be described as ambient. *Space* was an electronic tour of planetary influences, not quite Gustav Holst's *The Planets* performed on sequenced synthesisers, but close enough in the vastness of its cosmic rumblings and heavenly choirs to infer such Rick Wakeman-style prog-rock concepts. *Chill Out,* on the other hand, manipulated more bits and pieces with a subtlety and focus that has not been evident in their activities either before or since. Two significant landmarks of pop muzak were sampled into the soundscape: Acker Bilk's "Stranger on the Shore" and Fleetwood Mac's "Albatross" along with Elvis Presley's "In the Ghetto" and snatches of KLF singles. A sticker on the front cover instructed "file under Ambient". Critics received a manifesto with their copy, a list of eighteen "facts?" which included the following:

3. Ambient house is not New Age music.

11. Ambient house does not come to you: you have to go to it.

15. Ambient house is just a Monday night clique in the VIP bar at Heaven.

16. Ambient house is the first major music movement of the Nineties.

All of which were partially true. Whatever The KLF (or K Foundation) have done in the name of confronting musical, artistic or business conventions and conceits, whether burning money, ridiculing art prizes, sampling The Beatles, recording with Tammy Wynette or making hit singles, the music has been treated as a side effect. Their early singles captured the flow of movement associated with outdoor raves – orbital travel around the M25, searching for a field somewhere, dancing at "3am Eternal", life held in a perfect moment of time.

Chill Out is movement in the imagination, oscillating in a strange dream space between radio reception and virtual travel. Listening with detachment, I feel simultaneously as if I am moving across vast spaces, yet immobilised in one spot in the Gobi desert, watching the world go by, tuned in to organic and synthetic rhythms normally inaudible to the human ear without radio receivers, hydrophones, parabolic sound reflectors, satellite listening stations. Trains passing, a flock of sheep herded nearby, Mongolian throat singers floating in the air above me, motorbikes and cars roaring across the soundfield, a pedal steel guitar lament falling like dusk, a black preacher's hoarse "Get ready, get ready . . . East Coast, come back fat as a rat", night insects buzzing, dolphins, waves on the seashore, "Stranger on the Shore" . . . "A Melody From a Past Life Keeps Pulling Me Back", "Dream Time In Lake Jackson", "The Lights of Baton Rouge Pass By", like Harold Norse in 1951, standing on a stage in New York City after midnight, tuning a radio for John Cage and experiencing "an automobile ride at night on an American highway in which neon signs and patches of noise from radios and automobiles flash into the distance".

4 burial rites

noise and silence, myth and reality; electrical war and the Futurists; Edgard Varèse and Charlie Parker

In the second volume of his *Introduction to a Science of Mythology, From Honey To Ashes*, Claude Lévi-Strauss associates noise-making instruments with death, decomposition, social disorder and cosmic disruption. The instruments of darkness, he calls them. He documents a ceremony of the Bororo Indians of central Brazil. When a chief dies, his funeral and the investiture of the new chief are marked by a rite at which individuals personifying the *parabára* spirits (Parabára being the inventor of the bamboo rattling cane used in the ceremony) walk around the grave of the dead man, carrying split bamboos. When the leader of the ritual announces his arrival, the bamboos are rattled. Then they place their noisemakers on the grave and leave.

Revealing and deciphering the language of myth, Lévi-Strauss analyses many strange stories told by the Indians of Brazil's Amazonas rainforest: jaguars murder howling babies by farting in their faces; an Indian drums on the distended, gas-filled belly of a dead monkey, making it fart in order to combat the banging, crackling noises of demons; a split hollow tree trunk is thrown on the ground – the noise is a trick designed to draw an old woman out of her house after she has killed and eaten Indians while transformed into the guise of a jaguar; bullroarers (whirled instruments made from narrow, flat, often fish-shaped pieces of wood) are played in imitation

of a stinking, mud-covered river monster's bellow – a man discovers that he will become a shaman during a dream in which
the aquatic spirit (*aigé*) holds him yet he feels no objections
to the filth or stink of rot which clings to its skin; in a world
of permanant daylight, a well-sealed palm nut chirps with the
sound of crickets and night toads – when the seal is broken on
the nut, living things and inanimate objects are transformed,
darkness falls and two balls of thread have to be changed into
nocturnal and dawn birds to demarcate night from day.

Buried in anthropological esoterica, there are descriptions
of obscure, ritual sound makers which could match the hallucinatory design of the myth instruments. In the early 1930s, a
man named Geoffrey Christian witnessed a demonstration of
an instrument used on the Upper Purari river, Papua New
Guinea, during full-moon dances. For the ten to sixteen days
of this ceremony, the men ate very little but drank huge
amounts of water through long bamboo pipes. Five or six of
them would then sit in a circle and balance large, polished
hardwood disks on their toes or knees. "Each man lifts his
diaphragm", wrote Christian, "and the edge of the disk is
thrust deeply into the pit of the stomach; all then depress their
diaphragms on to the upper surface of the circumference of
the disk and open their mouths. An old man then takes a stone-
headed hammer and gently hits the centre of the disk. The
sound appears to reverberate from the distended lungs, and
issues forth from the mouths of the seated men; the effect is a
deep booming sound, similar to the sound of the big skin-
headed drums of other parts."

Other documentations of inventive, impossible ritual instruments used for rites of passage, cosmic transitions and the
music of non-humans (spirits, ancestors, animal familiars) include the following selection: One of the simplest of all,
called a Lion's Roar – once found in Ethiopia – by shouting
into a tapering hole dug out of the earth; rock gong complexes
found in sites as far apart as Uganda and Wales – ringing rocks
scarred by the so-called "chatter marks" of non-random but

repetitious striking; African voice disguisers, used at night to simulate the speech of ancestral spirits, made from tubes sealed with membranes of distorting materials such as spiders' egg cysts or bats' wings; a circumcision mask named Mask That Eats Water (recorded in 1965 among the Dan people of Côte d'Ivoire), built from a pit dug in the earth, covered with bark through which were passed vegetable fibres which were made to groan by hand friction; anthropomorphic wooden trumpets, carved as larger-than-lifesize human forms, held by the arms and blown through a mouthpiece set in the back of each, used in funeral rites with dwindling frequency in the mid 1960s by the Ba-Bembé people of Congo; a shaman's clay ocarina, unearthed in Hungary, moulded to the shape of a human head with symbolic trepanation (skull perforation) marked on the top; giant slit gongs of Cameroon – both zoomorphic slit gongs used for funerary purposes by male secret societies in the Bamileke chiefdoms, and monumental slit gongs of the Bamum court, some twice as high as a tall man, used for signalling war or crisis and left to rot in the open air after the death of a king.

One particularly imposing example was photographed in 1912. A crouching simian, like ET with genitals, squats on top of the wooden gong. On a more elaborate instrument, a human figure sits above crocodiles and other carvings, a knife in one hand, human head in the other. The explorer who saw it recorded the fact that dried leaves were wreathed around it. Two weeks later, he came back to find the leaves gone and the figure richly encrusted with blood. Intrigued, he asked questions. Human blood or animal?

purity and danger

In *The Pursuit of the Millennium*, Norman Cohn related the story of a millennial messiah named Hans Böhm. A shepherd who played drum and pipes for dancing in taverns and markets during his time off from the sheep, the Drummer of Niklashausen (as he became known) started a minor social revolution in his south German village. Böhm began in 1476 with a straightforward Virgin Mary vision – stop dancing, throw away the golden necklaces and pointy shoes, start the pilgrimages. This escalated swiftly, supported by increasingly large numbers of followers, to that hardy perennial of possibilities: no priests, no class divisions, no taxes, no rents, the fruits of nature ripe and available to all. But as Cohn observed, "the bishops during the first half of the century were wildly extravagant and could pay their debts only by levying ever heavier taxes". With his followers reaching a fever pitch of devotion, the Drummer had to go. An ecclesiastical court found him guilty of heresy and sorcery. His life ended in flames; tied to a stake, singing hymns to the Virgin, but his prophesies began with another symbolic consumption by fire: in front of the parish church he had burned his drum.

Away from the naked bodies, biodiversity and communal magic of the tropical rainforest, deep in the doomed megalopolis, the urban present, noise persistently draws on the metaphorical resource of dark powers. *Fin de millénium* visions puncture the skin. In recent times, terms such as grunge, black metal, grindcore, jungle, the darkside or dark ambient, have been tagged on to musics which are fierce, distorted, morbid, malevolent or menacing. Musics for the dance of death, in other words, rather than the music of the spheres. Heaven and hell; in some cases both, in opposition or in balance. I am listening to two jungle tracks as I write this: "The Burial" by Leviticus, and "Meditation" by DJ Crystl. Both play moods of euphoria off an undercurrent of disquiet, balancing oceanic dreams with the clattering, libidinous rush of body processes and urban movement.

Less willingly, I listen to the apocalyptic industrial grind of Skinny Puppy's "Dog Shit" – hoarse screams of "jaw hell piss fuck head rest pure acid hell filthy world mutation laughing hound" – or Nine Inch Nails' Trent Reznor shouting into the void on "Broken": "Dress up this rotten carcass just to make it look alive". In 1990 I walked from my house in north London to Konk Studios, where Trent and his producer, Flood, were remixing an album track. Trent talked, fragmented but intelligent, about balancing imbalances, contrasting contradictory signals, working against stereotypical correspondences – "I think there's something cool about electronic music that's aggressive . . . There's something seductive about aggression . . . maybe not sing about traditional industrial death lyrics . . . For me, I think the key is anger-fuelled, something other than fast or loud" – never reaching a conclusion about the symbology of noise and silence, death and speed, purity and corruption.

extinguished fires

Fifty years into the first millennium, the Roman emperor Nero attempted to improve his singing technique by lying under sheets of lead and administering enemas into his own back passage. For pleasure, he and his male "wife" enjoyed dressing in animal skins and attacking the genitals of men and women tied to stakes. He also anticipated the crowd manipulation techniques of fascism and rock music, using five thousand noise makers to influence the mood of the people during public meetings, categorising the catalytic sounds into *bombi* – like bees buzzing, *imbrices* – like rain or hail on a roof, and *testae* – like pots crashing. In his survey of the political economy of music, *Noise*, Jacques Attali quotes Adolf Hitler writing for the *Manual of German Radio* in 1938: "Without the loudspeaker, we would never have conquered Germany." We are much more interested in the digital global transmission of combined text, sound and moving image now, but sounds that traversed long distances or spoke with abnormal volume once possessed a special mystique. These properties of sound – ascribed to pagan forces – survived a Christianising influence in Europe, with bells being rung to subdue storms at sea; during a plague in 1625 a doctor wrote the following prescription: "Lett the bells in cities and townes be rung often, and great ordinance discharged thereby the aire is purified."

At the conclusion of the first volume of his mythological epic – *The Raw and the Cooked* – Lévi-Strauss investigated a European custom called charivari, a din made with cooking pots and pans, wash basins and other domestic utensils with noise potential. The point of the racket was to express communal disapproval of marriages made between two people of disparate ages, women having affairs with married men and other social "crimes". The charivari would descend on women who beat their husbands, though not, apparently, in reverse circumstances. None of this lies any further back in history than Debussy's experience at the Paris exposition or Erik Satie's *Musique d'ameublement* (more later of Satie's furniture music). Thomas Hardy's *The Mayor of Casterbridge* was first serialised in 1893. In one section of the novel Hardy sketches in a charivari, known in his part of the world as a skimmington ride. "What do they mean by a skimmity-ride?" asks a man in an inn. "Oh, sir," said the landlady swinging her long ear-rings with deprecating modesty; " 'tis a old foolish thing they do in these parts, when a man's wife is – well, not too particularly his own." Hardy goes on to list the odd, archaic instruments used for a skimmington: "the din of cleavers, tongs, tambourines, kits, crouds, humstrums, serpents, rams'-horns, and other historical forms of music". Challenged by a magistrate, one of the riders claims he might have heard the wind in the trees making a "peculiar poetical-like murmur", all the while concealing a pair of kitchen tongs and a cow's horn under his waistcoat.

In a diminutive version of the Futurist idea that machines in factories would be tuned into "intoxicating orchestras", one of Karlheinz Stockhausen's great unrealised visions for utopia was a prediction that domestic appliances – food mixers, washing machines, perhaps even coffee grinders – would one day be sound-designed to make pleasing combinations of tones as they whirred, spun and masticated. Perhaps he underestimated the dark covert history of the kitchen. *The Raw and*

the Cooked links the practice of charivari or skimmington riding with another noisy occasion – the eclipse of the sun – an
event which has been known to precipitate loud crashing and
banging of kitchenware, drums or gongs all over the world.
"The function of noise", writes Lévi-Strauss, "is to draw attention to an anomaly in the unfolding of a syntagmatic
sequence." He notes situations in which the contrast between
silence and noise became dramatically significant: "Among
the Warramunga of Australia, when a sick man was on his
deathbed, noise was prescribed before his death, and silence
afterward. Correspondingly, the great Bororo rite of the visit
of the souls (which is a kind of symbolic and temporary res-
urrection of the ancestors) begins at night in darkness and in
total silence and after all fires have been extinguished. The
souls are frightened of noise; but their arrival is greeted by a
tremendous outburst of noise. The same thing happens when
an animal that has been killed during a hunt is brought into
the village, and when the shaman invokes the spirits so that
they may take possession of him."

Tipu's tiger

Of all the noise instruments in history, one of the least
equivocal in its intent is Tipu's Tiger. Captured in India by the
British army after the defeat and death by bullet and bayonet
of Tipu Sultan in 1799, this large and amazing object is now
housed in the Victoria and Albert Museum, London. The most
succinct and evocative description was written by an em-
ployee of the East India Company: "This piece of Mechanism
represents a Royal Tyger in the act of devouring a prostrate
European. There are some barrels in imitation of an Organ,
within the body of the Tyger, and a row of Keys of natural
Notes. The sounds produced by the Organ are intended to re-
semble the Cries of a person in distress intermixed with the
roar of a Tyger. The machinery is so contrived that while the
Organ is playing, the hand of the European is often lifted up,
to express his helpless and deplorable condition."

John Keats saw Tipu's Tiger in the East India Company's offices and later referred to it in a satire he wrote on the Prince Regent: " that little buzzing noise, Whate'er your palmistry may make of it, Comes from a play-thing of the Emperor's choice, From a Man-Tiger-Organ, prettiest of his toys." And when the tiger was first exhibited in the newly opened Victoria and Albert Museum, the public cranked the handle to make it roar with such sadistic, joyful frequency that students in the adjacent library were driven half-mad by the distraction.

In a technical analysis of the instrument, Henry Willis speculated that "the intended method of use for the keyboard organ was to run the knuckles up and down the scale to produce the effects of a screaming man being killed by a tiger". Because the design and materials suggest a European rather than an Indian maker, Willis suggested that the tiger and its victim were constructed by either a malicious Frenchman or a renegade Englishman. But whoever made this wonderfully macabre sculpture, Tipu certainly enjoyed it. He was obsessed with tigers, for one thing; for another, as a Muslim whose wealth and land had been plundered by the colonialists, he hated the British. Reportedly, he used to circumcise them when he took prisoners. His walls were decorated with scenes depicting soldiers being dismembered, crushed by elephants, eaten by tigers and other fates too obscene for the British major who saw them to form a verbal description.

"Better to die like a soldier than to live a miserable dependent on the infidels on the list of their pensioned *rajas* and *nabobs*", Tipu said at his last military conference. Delicious irony: through the preservation of imperial spoils, albeit mute and frozen in the act of mauling within a glass case, the objectification of Tipu's hatred endures.

electrical war

Throughout this century of rapid technological change, the drive of modernism has been harnessed to the dances and songs of machines. In Italy, Filippo Marinetti, the author in 1909 of the first Manifesto of Futurism, visualised speed, electricity, violence and war as empowering elements. (In 1929 he portrayed Benito Mussolini as a man of "square crushing jaws" and "scornful jutting lips".) "I listened to the lyric initiative of electricity flowing through the sheaths of the quadruple turret guns", Marinetti wrote in 1914, clearly quivering with similar ecstasies after witnessing minor skirmishes from the trenches. For the Futurists *and* their opponents, art was war. During a performance of Bralilla Pratella's orchestral work, supposedly depicting urban industrial noise, the musicians were pelted with coal. As they retired hurt, Marinetti shouted "Rotten syphilitic" and "Son of a priest" at the perpetrators.

Marinetti was almost certainly influenced by Alfred Jarry, the Parisian "author with pistols" and the founder of pataphysics, the science of imaginary solutions. Following Jarry's example, Marinetti and the other Italian Futurists stepped up the assault on bourgeois values through the new medium of performance: words as declaimed, intoned sounds partially freed from syntax; music as noise; body gestures; sonic impressions of battle; the sounds of a boxing match; tirades, insults, practical jokes and fist fights.

Multimedia, the most overworked term of the late twentieth century, began here (or hereabouts). Valentine de Saint-Pont danced her *Poem of Atmosphere* in Paris, masked and Orientalist, splayed in mock-Egyptian flat relief, colour and mathematical equations projected on to every surface around her, music by Satie and Debussy providing the soundtrack to her celebration of sexual freedom. And in Russia, Futurist performance was enacted on a grand scale: a spectacular symphony of "proletarian music" was played by factory sirens, steam whistles, foghorns, artillery, machine guns and aircraft on 7 November 1922, all of these conducted from the rooftops of Baku.

One of the specific aims of Futurist music was the eradication of inflated romanticism, particularly that of Wagner.

"How shall we avoid *Parsifal* and its cloudbursts, puddles and bogs of mystical tears?" implored Marinetti. For him, the answer lay with electrical war and a world in which he predicted with fair accuracy that "[t]he energy of distant winds, the rebellions of the sea, transformed by man's genius into many millions of Kilowatts, will penetrate every muscle, artery and nerve of the peninsula, needing no wires, controlled from keyboards with a fertilising abundance that throbs beneath the fingers of the engineers". The days of the symphony were numbered. "Now we have had enough of them", wrote Luigi Russolo, "and we delight much more in combining in our thoughts the noises of trams, of automobile engines, of carriages and brawling crowds, than in hearing again the 'Eroica' or the 'Pastorale'."

Irrepressibly pugnacious, Marinetti had slipped his own incontinent ideas into Pratella's sober sounding *Technical Manifesto of Futurism*. Russolo, a man blessed with high cheekbones and eyes so intense they seemed to bore through the camera lens and directly into the film, had been inspired by a Pratella performance – "Perhaps", as musician and researcher Hugh Davies has suggested, "just as some musicians (including myself) have some of their best ideas in the concert hall when listening to music that bores them, Russolo felt that if this was typical Futurist music, he could do better."

So Luigi Russolo, a painter of marked Symbolist leanings, began writing a series of polemical essays which have come to be grouped under the general heading *The Art of Noises*. In company with a painter named Ugo Piatti, he started work also on the *intonarumori*. Based on the scraped string principle of the hurdy-gurdy but also combining aspects of the slide guitar and Indian *khamak* string drum (extremely unlikely that either of these would have been known to Russolo), the *intonarumori* sound as if they might have been terrifying on disc if Russolo had been able to wait until the 1950s to record them. He divided them into categories, all variations on the basic idea, and the names recall the instruments of darkness: the Howler, the Hummer, the Crackler, the Burster, the Whistler and the Gurgler. Despite some remarkable research (particularly by Davies) and even reconstructions of Russolo's instruments, the unavoidable truth remains that the one recording made of the instruments is ruined by the compositional meanderings of his brother, Antonio. Even without Antonio's inconsequential salon music, the recording technology of 1924 was not really up to the task of capturing these growling monsters.

In a live setting, however, the noise must have been disturbing. "No more!" the audience shouted during a performance at the London Coliseum. A critic compared their sounds with the "rigging of a channel steamer" and Davies quotes one witness, interviewed in 1982 at the age of ninety, whose recall of this 1914 concert was sufficiently fresh to describe the music as "funny burps" and "like battleships pooping off". Not very loud, though, he thought.

This combination of war sounds with the noise of human wind neatly links the instruments of darkness of Brazil's rainforest with their twentieth-century equivalent. Like Marinetti, Russolo wrote about battle sounds with enthusiasm. He was more the academic or technician, however, as he analysed and classified the whistles of varying shell calibers, the enharmonic Doppler effect of falling pitch as the shells flew from cannon barrel to final explosion, the *tok-tok-tok-tok* of machine guns, the *tek-poom* of Austrian rifles, the *tek-tak-trak* of rifle bolts, the *tseeoo* of bullets and the physics of acoustics. "Modern war cannot be expressed lyrically without the noise instrumentation of Futurist *free words*", he wrote. These free words had been devised by Marinetti during a battle; he ranted and raved with uncomfortably infectious verve about the hygiene of war, not a tenable theory at the best of times, but easier to carry off after a few colonial encounters in Libya and Bulgaria than after the horror of World War I trench carnage and the subsequent killing grounds of the twentieth century. But, like a film critic taking notes at a snuff

movie, Russolo chills the blood more thoroughly than
Marinetti, just for the dispassionate poetry, ultimately the ped-
antry, of his observations. Some of his images are affecting –
soldiers wrapping their hob-nail boots in trench sacks for a
silent attack – but his prime concern is a hunger for dramatic,
enharmonic sounds, particularly glissandi which sweep
across a sound field, echoes, and violent explosions.

Hugh Davies regrets the fact that none of the composers
who enthused over Russolo's noise instruments chose to incorporate them in their work. If Stravinsky had included
growlers and hummers in *Le Sacre du Printemps*, for example, (my idea, not Davies's), then Russolo's inventions might
not have slipped into the terminal obscurity of being too
avant-garde for the avant-garde. I make the suggestion, knowing it was impossible. Stravinsky worked on *Le Sacre du
Printemps* from 1910, when he had a dream in which a pagan
rite was enacted: a circle of wise elders watched a young girl
dance herself to death (more sex, death, paganism and anthropology). Stravinsky was invited to Marinetti's house to hear
the noise makers, having expressed some interest in incorpo-
rating them in a ballet. "A Crackler crackled and sent up a
thousand sparks like a gloomy torrent. Stravinsky leapt from
the divan like an exploding bedspring, with a whistle of over-
joyed excitement", wrote Francesco Canguilo, a Futurist poet
and sculptor. But this was in 1914, a year after the notorious
first performance of *Le Sacre du Printemps*, the concert
which set a twentieth-century standard for violent audience
reactions to modern music. Perhaps Stravinsky was thrilled to
hear something that might cause an even bigger riot than his
own work.

I disagree (very mildly) with Davies, because these grinding, humming, growling pagan noises clamoured in the air
without any help from the Futurists. From the industrial revolution onwards, functional machines had let them loose.
Those who composed for the orchestra – particularly
Stravinsky in his formative years and Varèse throughout his

life – could hear the sounds of an increasingly noisy sound-scape as music in their minds' ears, and strained to reproduce them. In fact, the English Vorticist Wyndham Lewis delivered a patriotic and rather snooty dismissal of Futurism during a taxi ride with Marinetti. Machine society was invented by the English, he said, so why should London show any enthusiasm for machine art at such a late stage. Marinetti was apoplectic.

Russolo took a brave step, but only one. Noise, sound, musical rules, the growing clamour of mechanised life, the lines drawn between them were blurring, vanishing into thin air. The solid objects of European composition – the score, the orchestra, the composer, pitch relationships, tuning and harmony, the boundary between music and not-music – were about to be dismembered.

Varèse's dream

He was in a telephone booth in New York, talking to his wife Louise, who was in Paris. As they spoke his body became lighter, eventually losing all substance and disinte-grating, one limb at a time. In this non-corporeal form, he flew to Paris where he was reintegrated, the physical self that was Varèse reborn as spirit.

new worlds on earth

A photograph: Varèse's basement studio in New York City. A bricked-in fireplace, paintings by Miró, a grand piano littered with gourds, a woodblock, beaters, an African shaker, rattles. Metal frames on castors, the kind used by the rag trade for wheeling clothes around. Hanging from these functional frames, a large tam-tam, smaller flat and bossed gongs from Southeast Asia. On the floor, a Chinese drum and, over-exposed on the edge of the photo frame, what could be a long hourglass drum from New Guinea. A no smoking sign hangs from the wall light.

Edgard Varèse had strong reasons of his own for rejecting Luigi Russolo's inventions. Born in Paris in 1883, he connected to the vortex of French and Italian artistic action as a very young man. In 1900, his grandfather took him to the Paris Exposition Universelle; he almost certainly attended the notorious first performance of *Le Sacre du Printemps*; he sat and talked with Debussy, soaking up the fragrance of a sandalwood screen that Debussy kept in front of his fire; he made friends with Erik Satie, met Lenin and Trotsky, Picasso and Jean Cocteau. He also befriended Russolo, though personal empathy never stopped him from passing harsh judgements on the *intonarumori*. For Varèse, the noise instruments produced "material for the most part of terrifying intractability". They were the equivalent of the Ethiopian Lion's Roar: a lot of digging, then down on hands and knees to shout into your hole in the ground. But that was it.

Varèse had an insatiable appetite for material which reinforced his conviction that music should be experienced physically, rather than through the understanding and acceptance of a harmonic system. Delving into the speculations of Leonardo da Vinci, the hermetic museum of alchemical texts, acoustical studies from India, China, Egypt and ancient Greece, he absorbed Professor Hermann Helmholtz's groundbreaking study of physiological acoustics, particularly the sections on sirens. Among his many experiments, Helmholtz investigated the beating of combination tones, dissonance, sympathetic resonance, the physical nature of intervals and chords, the vibrations of very deep tones, the structure of the ear and various tuning systems, including just intonation. *On the Sensations of Tone*, first published in Germany in 1862, begins with a distinction between noises and musical tones. Wind, water splashes and the rumbling of carriages were noise, whereas the tones of all musical instruments were music. Helmholtz's distinction rested upon the idea that ambient sounds – "the rattling of a carriage over granite paving stones" – were irregular and chaotic, but music "strikes the ear as a perfectly undisturbed, uniform sound which remains unaltered as long as it exists". Just in time, science arrived at a rationalisation for art to contradict.

Critics outdid themselves in their reviews of Varèse's music. A fire in the Bronx Zoo, they called it, or saucepan banging and solos for flushing toilets. Again, the recurrent resting places of musical analogy: bowels and kitchenware.

A music supermarket called Tower. Every wretched, fourth-rate composer in history is allocated a browser bin so thick with product that browsing itself necessitates pulling out a handful of albums to make some space. Varèse, on the other hand, is represented by not a single CD.

Paraphrasing his hero, Edgard Varèse, Ruben Sano (aka Frank Zappa) printed "The present-day Pachuco refuses to die!" on the sleeve of *Ruben & The Jets*. I was never entirely convinced by the optimism of that statement: the present-day composer refuses to die. At the end of the century, when strange tunings, percussion, electronic instruments, voice and sound montages, parabolic and hyperbolic curves of sound, monstrous growling incantations, sonic earthquakes and rivers of noise are the basic stuff of music, Varèse, the seer who prophesied this future, our present, has almost vanished from the narrative. Without Zappa, this disappearance might be even more complete.

In 1967 (or was it 1968?) I sat in one of the on-stage seats of the Royal Albert Hall, London, just behind and to one side of The Mothers of Invention. They played pieces that would shortly appear on *Uncle Meat*, pieces drenched in Varèse, slimed in sleaze, a potent frothing brew of jazz orchestration, *Ionisation* percussion, improvised electronics, R&B grooves, ice-cream chords, free jazz saxophone, lyrics about hubcaps, fuzzy dice, cruising for burgers, the iconography of Los Angeles. A few condensed minutes from that concert are included on the album: the point when a man jumped on stage holding a trumpet, looking to jam. Don Preston climbed into the pipe organ loft (who would give a rock band the key to the door?) to play "the perfect thing to accompany this man's trumpet": "Louie Louie". Another incident from the same occasion, only documented on *Uncle Meat* by Zappa's acidly sarcastic request to the audience – "let's hear it again for the London Philharmonic Orchestra" – was the point when three members of the LPO stepped from the wings, dressed in what they believed were appropriately "zany" clothes, to play one of Zappa's written scores with undisguised contempt. As an oblique and misguided act of revenge on orchestral musicians, I grabbed my opportunity to steal one of the manuscript pages after the concert had finished.

Born too early to realise his ultimate visions, Varèse spent all his life envisaging instruments which could express the soundworld of his imagination. For him, music was art – science, an emotional, political and ritualistic force that should vibrate the air, resonate the human body, stir the soul. By comparison, the Futurists were literalists who doggedly searched for ways to reproduce machine sounds which already existed and would soon become obsolete. Varèse denied any direct connection between his music and the sounds of nature or industry. There were subconscious links, however. During the first performance of *Hyperprism*, his ominous, compact composition for small orchestra and sixteen percussion instruments (including siren, gongs, cymbals and lion's roar – not the Ethiopian hole-in-the-ground but a string drum sounded by the friction of resined fingers), he noticed that the audience giggled nervously whenever one particular C sharp sounded. That night, working at home, he heard the sound of a siren on the river. The pitch was identical. Without noticing it before, he had been hearing the siren play that note for the entire period of composing *Hyperprism*.

Stockhausen had his own view of the relationship between Varèse's music and his environment. In one of a series of mid-1960s' radio lectures entitled "Do you know a music that can only be heard over loudspeakers?", he added his image of a "bubbling cauldron" to a metaphor of urban living – the melting pot – that was increasingly unbelievable: "New York, that prime blueprint for a world society, is without question an indispensable experience for the contemporary artist. Ideas one might have about possible integration, about a coherent unification, or about possible syntheses of the influences issuing from all parts of the globe, all these must be tested against living experience if they are to lay claim to any truth." So New York was not simply an opportunity to jettison the classical heritage. The city also offered Varèse important opportunities to meet artists connected to a glittering variety of musical traditions: Charlie Parker, black American composer William Grant Still, Chinese composer Chou Wen-Chung, Cuban novelist, composer and music writer Alejo Carpentier (the inventor of "magic realism" who wrote of the marvellous reality of Iberian America, where anything you could imagine is always inferior to the magical workings of reality itself), Russian inventor Leon Theremin and Japanese composer Michiko Toyama, who shared Varèse's enthusiasm for *gagaku* court music. He even spoke to Frank Zappa on the telephone, telling him about the composition of a new piece called *Déserts*. They never met.

Having lived in Paris, Turin, Berlin, New York, Los Angeles and New Mexico, the furthest-reaching zones explored by Varèse were imaginary worlds. The culmination came with his *Poème électronique,* a work for three-track tape. This montage of concrete, treated and electronically generated sounds was played on four hundred loudspeakers in Le Corbusier's Philips pavilion at the Brussels world fair of 1958. The architect of the pavilion was Iannis Xenakis. Luckily for Varèse, Xenakis was also a composer and mathematician, since some support from a fellow musician was necessary to keep the objections of Philips at bay. Images of masks, skeletons, cities, human bodies and beasts were projected on every surface but one critic claimed that these images were overshadowed by the music: "By the use of moving sound they have succeeded in liberating the score from the shackles of reality."

magick paper made real

"For some traditional West African societies printed memory in the form of records or books is considered unnatural, even abhorrent. The positive and negative powers of living things, including thoughts, memories and historical events, are understood as embodied in words but, transferred in written form, are seen as trapped in an undesirable state of rigidity and permanance, a state contrary to life."

Tina Oldknow, *Muslim Soup*

Varèse struggled to deliver music that could incorporate the whole world, that obliterated the equal tempered scale, the written rules of harmony, the predominance of pitch over timbre and rhythm. The ear – not numerical systems of rhythm or pitch – was the final judge of music.

White people are conditioned out of all sense of what is true in music, Varèse thought: *"J'ai vu des nègres de l'Afrique équatoriale – venus chez moi – qui ne connaissaient rien de notre civilisation industrielle, des Indiens, des Asiatiques, et tous étaient plus sensibles à ma musique que des blancs, qui ont toujours vécu dans la ville, qui ont été à l'école, qui ont été conditionnés."* ["I have seen blacks from equatorial Africa – in my home – who know nothing of our industrial civilisation, Indians, Asians, who were all more sensitive to my music than whites, who have always lived in cities, been to school, been conditioned."] He composed with basic materials: rhythms, frequencies, intensities, blocks of sound moving and projecting in space. His first significant work – *Amériques* – he described as a symbol of "new worlds on earth, in the sky, or in the minds of men", and when critics interpreted his use of sirens as a kind of barbarous programme music, a simple sound painting of urban noise pollution, he claimed that his purpose was "the portrayal of a mood in music and not a sound picture". Mood, atmosphere . . . what do those words mean? Debussy's *Nocturnes* is an atmosphere – "the immutable aspect of the sky and the slow, solemn motion of the clouds . . . vibrating atmosphere with sudden flashes of light ... music and luminous dust, participating in the cosmic rhythm" – but so is Dr Dre's "Nothin' But a 'G' Thang" in its evocation of tyres rolling on jellied asphalt, cold beers smoking in the fridge, the lazy promise of sex, a heavy odour of cannabis. What Varèse sought to develop was the superior capacity of all kinds of music to capture emergence in complex phenomena; transient, non-articulated feelings; or what Gaston Bachelard called the Poetics of Space, whether the ambience of a room, the ribbon of a road or the boundless envelopment of oceanic space.

"One finds a bone-setting priest and he, strong in piety towards the gods, re-sets the bones so well one hears a grating noise as the bones fit into one another."

Zosimos of Panopolis, alchemist and Gnostic

Debussy believed that percussion in Europe was the art of barbarians. Listening to recordings of Varèse's compositions, I am often struck by the tame precision with which they are played. Barbarians, yes, but a hopelessly meek and fussy tribe. We hear echoes of Varèse's vision of "masses of sound moving about in space, each at its own speed, on its own plane, rotating, colliding, interacting, splitting up, reuniting". These should be star wars, battle cries, sacrificial fanfares, escaping steam, brooding earth tremors and crunching skulls, yet the executants are women and men who dedicate themselves to the minutiae of playing notes at the correct pitch and in the correct place. Imagine *Nocturnal*, *Equatorial* or *Intégrales* played by Sun Ra's Myth-Science Arkestra, particularly the one-hundred strong ensemble Ra once gathered together for a concert in Central Park.

There are stories, perhaps apocryphal, of Charlie Parker following Varèse through the streets of New York, plucking up courage to ask for private tuition. Varèse played down this not entirely innocent image of the jazzman curled up at the feet of the European master. "He stopped by my place a number of times", Varèse told Robert George Reisner, author of *Bird: The Legend of Charlie Parker*. Parker wanted to learn structure, wanted to be taught how to write for an orchestra and was even prepared to cook for Varèse in payment. "He was so dramatic it was funny, but he was sincere", said Varèse. "He spoke of being tired of the environment his work relegated him to . . . 'I'm so steeped in this and can't get out,' he said." Like Ornette Coleman ten years later, or Jimi Hendrix twenty years later, Parker struggled for escape, not only from the harmonic limitations of the blues or the conservatism of jazz, but from the expectations of promotors, record companies and the suffocating embrace of fans.

Unfortunately, the closest we come to hearing Parker's dream is "Repetition", the extended piece he recorded with arranger/bandleader Neil Hefti in 1948. Some jazz critics regard this track as an aberration. They can only bear to accept it by convincing themselves that Parker's alto saxophone was overdubbed. I hear it differently. Parker died five years after this session. Those last years of his life, often suicidal, were when he came to Varèse hoping for tuition. Time was short and Parker's options were few. His own genius for soloing over fast tempi and rapid chord changes undermined his hopes for absorption into the forests of sound invoked by Varèse. As with many aspects of his life, there were elements of his work which had moved beyond his control. After a live radio broadcast of "Repetition", compere Symphony Sid chats to Parker about the titles of his tunes. "The other side you called 'Relaxin' With Lee'. Who's Lee?" asks Sid. "I don't have the slightest idea", replies Parker. "They name those tunes after I leave the studio." So he pursued a complex relationship with the pop song and the record business, perhaps hearing beauty and potential marvels where others heard only banality. On "Repetition", Hefti's scoring for strings, reeds and brass is refined sugar, halfway between the dance band and Hollywood. Diego Iborra's congas and bongos clop along, so far back in the mix that they might have been recorded with a gun mike pointing towards Cuba. But Parker's rhythmic sophistication is awe inspiring. He plays a tumbling line, a long sculpted tendril of breath, intellect and passion, folding back on itself, stretching, freezing, kinking into weird angles and then hanging in the air over a fading chord, the last one at the party.

How could Varèse have helped Parker? As sympathetic as he was to Parker shaking the cage that enclosed him, Varèse suffered his own frustrations, particularly with the tools at his disposal. The symphonic orchestra possessed advantages of flexibility and complexity, although Varèse described it as "*un éléphant hydropique*" by comparison with the jazz band, which was "*un tigre*". He had turned to percussion, striving to come closer to his feeling in early life that music should be a river of sound, currents of sound moving in chaotic flow like the Zambezi. But ultimately, electronics held the key. Nothing, so far, had blasted music out of its prison; not Russolo's mechanical *intonarumori,* not even Leon Theremin's electrical Theremin, Friedrich Trautwein's subtractive synthesis Trautonium, Oskar Sala's Mixtur-Trautonium, Maurice Martenot's Ondes Martenot or Varèse's own experiments with phonograph turntables. In October 1964, Robert Moog and Herb Deutsch exhibited the first hand-made Moog synthesiser modules, the sounds of which would be transformed a few years later by Sun Ra into astro-blackness, a sea of sounds, the energy of distant winds, the lyric initiative of electricity, new worlds on earth.

Varèse died in November 1965. A claustrophobia sufferer in childhood, he left a request that his body should be cremated and the ashes dispersed. Inspired as a youth by Jules Verne, later by sacred texts of the Maya, the Popol Vuh, Varèse suggested, through his music, ecstatic travel in search for the magical body. "Deserts mean to me", he wrote, "not only the physical deserts of sand, sea, mountains and snow, of outer space, of empty city streets . . . but also that remote inner space no telescope can reach, where man is alone in a world of mystery and essential loneliness."

5 content in a void

*Michael Mann and Tangerine Dream; Frank
Sinatra; dead zone recordings; Alice Coltrane;
Roland Kirk; Jimi Hendrix; Miles Davis;
Karlheinz Stockhausen; Bow Gamelan; James
Brown; Brian Wilson; Lee Perry; dub; Brian Eno*

dream

Sitting in a Las Vegas entertainment lounge. Despite
being in Vegas, the room looked more like a Barnsley working
mens' club: spacious with a hint of plush but terminally bleak,
chairs lined up in long rows, bare walls, exposed stage. The
quartet that took the stage was fronted by Elvis Presley, the
only other identifiable member being ambient DJ Mixmaster
Morris. Morris was wearing his silver holographic suit, as
usual, while Elvis looked fit, tanned and surprisingly boyish. I
was amazed by his youth and the quality of his voice. The
music sounded like "Heartbreak Hotel"-era Presley crooned
over drifting electronic ambient sound. After a while, I became suspicious. Was this really Elvis? Then I noticed that his
loafers were scuffed. Elvis was a fake.

content in a void

A number of interpretations of this dream are possible. Presley's reluctance to vacate the planet has become a bit
of a bore, but his posthumous presence in supermarket
queues reminds us of how little we knew him when he was
alive. The perpetual reconstruction of celebrities through re-
visionist biographies and tabloid surrealism has an odd effect.
Post-war pop culture is so entwined in myth and yet so young,
that one major facelift or smear job can tilt the entire picture.

As a baby boomer old enough to have been aware of mid-1950s' rock'n'roll as it happened, I was misled and self-deceived into believing that the lifestyles of the rich and famous could be deduced from their music and outward image. Jerry Lee Lewis and Little Richard were wild'n'crazy guys, clearly pursuing lives without shape or restraint, and this ebb and flow, inspired by angels and demons alike, was counterbalanced by a grid of placid order and white picket fences beamed out into the universe by Andy Williams, Perry Como and Doris Day.

Naive, of course, for what could be closer to the edge of twentieth-century alienation (or more ambient, in their way) than the weird, hermetic, formless existences fashioned in late life by big shots of entertainment central USA such as Howard Hughes and Dean Martin and then imagined into print by, respectively, Michael Drosnin and Nick Tosches? "Remote control", wrote Drosnin in *Citizen Hughes*. "There was no need to venture out, not even to stand up." Jeanne Martin, Dean Martin's second wife, conjures a similar image of free fall, quoted as saying in Tosches's *Dino*: "He was always content in a void."

So did my dream resolve certain supposedly oppositional tendencies in popular music – Dionysian/Apollonian, radical/conservative, underground/populist, plugged/unplugged – only to leave me stranded with the comforting spectre of fakery and illusion? Perhaps my unconscious was transmitting cryptic prophesy. Was this how music would be in the year 2000? Future music is imagined in terms of technological hybridisation – all winking lights and digital exchanges across alien cultures. Perhaps I was dreaming up some kind of impossible virtual quartet manufactured through interactive holography, the equivalent of dream football teams, Rocky Marciano versus Mike Tyson, imaginary all-time supergroups, Charlie Parker recording with Edgard Varèse and so on, or the "lost" tracks of Prince with Miles Davis, Miles with Jimi Hendrix and other vaunted but vaulted collaborations that pub bores would contrive themselves if they only had the technology.

Techno at the end of the twentieth century may come to mean inept folksingers, lonely bigots, somnambulent fishermen and Christian monologuists on public access cable television; the global coffee house of MTV's *Spoken Word Unplugged* (poetry for the ambient TV generation); Internet conferences on dog training; or CD storytelling. Imagine the most likely use for the wired city of the future not in cyberpunk or megatripolising world music frameworks then, but as a hi-tech campfire, people plugging in to remind themselves of life as it was when they were plugged out, twisting their isolation into something resembling community.

Floating, amorphous, oceanic crooning (or crooning with attitude) seems to mirror the feeling of non-specific dread that many people now feel when they think about life, the world, the future; yet it expresses a feeling of bliss. The bliss is non-specific, also, covering a spectrum which ranges from stress management at one end to spiritual ecstasy at the other. So disquiet hovers in balance with the act of escapism or liberation. That tension between the specifics of (the) soul and the siren call of the oceanic led to strange moments in the careers of Marvin Gaye, mind torn between apocalypse, sex, personal disaster and reverie in his later work, and Nona Hendryx, whose 1989 collaboration with Peter Baumann, *Skindiver*, delivered the intriguing, ultimately depressing compound resulting from a laboratory experiment mixing Tangerine Dream with Labelle. Listening to her album now is instructive, if only to remember the ubiquity of ambient, *Miami Vice*, *Diva*, *9½ Weeks*, *The Big Blue* and *Blade Runner* style during the 1980s. Bryan Ferry, Grace Jones, Art of Noise, Sade, Vangelis – atmosphere as style; style as mood; humidity, rainfall or hue as content.

aqua

The opening sequence of *Thief* (1981), directed by *Miami Vice* creator Michael Mann: Streetlights in sharp perspective, a downward pointing V, like a runway. Night driving, a radio tuned to police frequencies. An interior, deep blue, vivid ultramarine, blackness and highlights. Technical processes, James Caan is cracking a safe. Shards of metal, drilling, hard to read what is going on, the tension wound up by unrelenting sequencer music by Tangerine Dream. Exterior. More shades of blue, the city as aquascape, nightpeople as marine creatures, the shock of redness when a car ignition fires and the rear lights come on.

Another Michael Mann film, *The Keep* (1983). Opening shots: more driving, the camera tracking across hillsides, vegetation texture and colour filling the frame. More Tangerine Dream sequencers. Surface as narrative.

Edgar Froese, Tangerine Dream founder, has this to say about the link between their music and the Michael Mann aesthetic: "He got involved in our music by listening to a studio record called *Force Majeure*, which we recorded back in '78. He was listening to a piece called 'Metamorphic Rocks' and so he put it into one of those sequences in *Thief* when they open up the roof on one of those skyscrapers. The sound mixed so well – that's what he said – that he called us and said, 'Are you interested in doing the rest?' The thing is about Michael Mann, he's an American guy but he worked for about four years in London so he was very sympathetic with the European way of making films and using cameras. That's why he chose a lot of, what I would call French, British or early German shooting sequences in his movies. Like a man like Ridley Scott, who is known as a great American film maker, but in fact is very much British. He has given a big positive push to the American cinema by using certain European visions."

Froese identifies with the idea of music unrolling in a personal mind-movie for each listener. "What your inner thoughts are, or what your subjective opinions are, you first create inside yourself, whether it's a pure brain reflection, a spiritual reflection, or whatever you wanna call it. But it's first inside you. Then, you somehow see it or feel it outside yourself and start reflecting with what you experience first inside. So through that reflection, you somehow get those inside-outside exchanges."

under my skin

A Frank Sinatra album cover – *In the Wee Small Hours* – recorded after Sinatra's breakup with Ava Gardner. Tall, grey buildings, flat and featureless, fading off into a mist of bleached aqua air. A column, floating rather than planted on the ground, like a stage set. Sinatra in the trance of emotional blankness, staring at nothing. The music revels in solitude, melancholy, quietude, night: glad to be unhappy. In the displacement of loss, buildings look insubstantial, people feel unreal, life passes in a dream.

The morning before dream #2 I had been sent a copy of Bono's duet with Frank Sinatra. More than any other duet in this era of improbable and financially motivated collaborations, "I've Got You Under My Skin" seemed to draw together two worlds which orbit in parallel universes. Buried somewhere beneath the gloss of celebrity pow-wow were distant, unspoken connections between a realm of ambient, electronic experimentation and the nice-and-easy-does-it domain of supper-club, Las Vegas, easy-listening entertainment which the mundane, fuck-off surrealism of the record does nothing to dispel. Fittingly, these worlds converged in cyberspace. "Liza was recorded in Brazil", explained producer Phil Ramone in *Audio Media,* "Bono in Dublin, Aznavour in London, Gloria Estefan in Miami, Tony Bennett in New York, and Aretha and Anita Baker were in Detroit." Through the EDNet (Entertainment Digital Network) of fibre optic lines that connect all of these cities, Sinatra's recordings, made in the Capitol Records Tower studios in Hollywood, were then

overdubbed by his duet partners in their studio location of
choice.

body snatching

Aside from a number of romantic duet albums made
by singers who never met in the studio and allegedly despised
each other – Marvin Gaye and Diana Ross spring to mind – I
was reminded of dead zone duets: recordings of dead (or
brain-dead) musicians augmented by extra instrumentation or
new vocals, as mentioned earlier in reference to Minnie
Riperton. For newspapers catering to a fortysomething read-
ership, the hot music story in 1994 was that long-awaited
reformation of The Beatles, united through technology in a
completion of the late John Lennon's unfinished song. Electronic exhumation has a rich history. A few years before The
Beatles reunion, Natalie Cole duetted with a recording made
by her dead father. More disturbing than the record was the
video, an electronic seance replete with Oedipal implications,
during which Nat "King" Cole was exhumed from the archives and montaged in seamless drifting communion with
his scantily dressed daughter. One of the pioneering works in
this field was created when Elvis Presley was raised from the
grave by a radio DJ, Ray Quinn of Baltimore's Radio WCBM,
to sing his 1956 "Love Me Tender" with Linda Ronstadt's 1978
version. Then Patsy Cline and Jim Reeves were wiggled and
wobbled in the studio, despite both of them having departed
for the afterlife after plane crashes, finally finding a mutually
agreeable key on "Have You Ever Been Lonely (Have You Ever
Been Blue)?"

In the analogue age, duets were difficult, augmentation
more common. MGM were releasing embellished Hank
Williams records by 1957, four years after his death from an
excess of booze and speed. Coral Records worked the same
electronic voodoo on Buddy Holly recordings following his
death in a plane crash, although they waited just five months
to meddle with the tapes by editing them, adding vocal back-

grounds, strings or a full band. "Ironically enough", wrote Holly biographer John J. Goldrosen, "with the passage of years and the ignorance among newer fans about the post-humous nature of these arrangements, the songs strengthened the impression that Holly had been turning decisively away from rock'n'roll or rockabilly and towards pop music."

A similar impression could be gathered from Alice Coltrane's addition of strings to recordings made by her late husband. "Living Space" was originally recorded in New Jersey in 1965 by John Coltrane. Then four violins, two violas and two cellos were added by Alice in 1972, Los Angeles. Jazz buffs regard these sweetened tracks with the same revulsion aimed at Yoko Ono by Beatles fans: the integrity of masculine art screwed up by a woman. With more justification, drummer Rashied Ali, who worked with Coltrane in the later years, told Valerie Wilmer: "It's like rewriting the Bible!" In fact, the melodramatic Hollywood mystic soup of "Living Space" could be the Bible on wax, as starring Charlton Heston or James Earl Jones.

mystery stories

Slicing strings, spooky pizzicato, ostinato creepshow organ, a snaking clarinet. Roland Kirk declaims over what sounds like a battery operated toy: "the mystery black notes that have been stolen and camouflaged for years . . . Listen!" he shouts . . . "Open your ears . . . listen!" A glass is smashed. "I tried to get the feeling of the mystery stories that I heard on the radio a long time ago", said Kirk for the sleevenotes of *Left & Right*, released in 1969. Alice Coltrane plays harp on "Celestialness", the third section of a suite entitled "Expansions", Kirk playing flute and thumb piano, bells shimmering on both sides of the stereo picture, the short piece concluded by a gong stroke and high, piercing flute note. The other side of the album, perhaps the right hand side, features Kirk's lyrical flute, tenor saxophone, stritch and manzello balladeering over lush woodwind and string arrangements. Even in this romantic context, Kirk's purpose was strategically political, his selection of tunes focusing attention on black jazz composers: himself, Charles Mingus, Willie Woods, Quincy Jones, Gil Fuller and Dizzy Gillespie, Billy Strayhorn.

earth and space

For Jimi Hendrix, who was toying with notions of bigger bands and Gil Evans or Roland Kirk collaborations shortly before his death, the orchestra signified an expansion of texture, a greater flexibility in the depiction of acoustic space. "I don't mean three harps and fourteen violins", Hendrix told *Melody Maker* in 1970. "I mean a big band full of competent musicians that I can conduct and write for. And with the music we will paint pictures of earth and space, so that the listener can be taken somewhere." Unfinished Hendrix tracks were reworked posthumously. "*Cry of Love* as the album ended up being called", wrote Mitch Mitchell in *The Jimi Hendrix Experience,* "was a real jigsaw puzzle to put together. You'd find, say, a lead guitar part in one key and then a vocal and rhythm track for the same song in a different key and one had to be speeded up or slowed down to match the other." In the mid 1970s, record producer Alan Douglas commissioned salvage jobs for two albums, *Crash Landing* and *Midnight Lightning.* Both were constructed around substandard, unfinished and extremely erratic performances. Each song had to be stripped down to Hendrix's guitar and vocals and then built up again with new overdubs and drop-ins. The drop-ins involved a session musician playing along with an original track, recorded with the same sound and style, the red record button being pushed only for those sections where the original drifted out of time. Hendrix's playing had to be copied by another guitarist in some cases, because he had started a track and then left it unfinished. "I had to vari-speed tape machines and then create little pieces to extend Jimi's notes", reconstruction engineer Tony Bongiovi told the authors of *Hendrix: Setting the Record Straight*, memories of impending nervous breakdown communicated through this professional information. "I would have to copy parts, one at a time, in increments of a quarter inch, to extend a note. This mechanical altering took forever." At the conclusion of these expensive and arduous sessions were the tightest sounding, dullest records Hendrix ever made. Death is not particularly conducive to interaction, although Mitchell claimed that his completion of *Cry of Love* was helped along by dream conversations with his former boss.

No harps and violins. Hendrix made this clear. But one fusion of rock guitar improvisation and expanded orchestration which did emerge from this period was an Alice Coltrane and Carlos Santana collaboration, *Illuminations*. At this point, both of them (along with John McLaughlin) were followers of a guru, Sri Chinmoy, and both were intent on resurrecting the spirit of John Coltrane. Despite the presence of inventive improvisers such as David Holland, Jack De Johnette and Armando Peraza, the results were closer to kitsch than deep spirituality, although sporadically enjoyable for all that. In retrospect, *Illuminations* comes across as a wish-fulfilment project. Alice would have wished to orchestrate her husband's music in this grandiose style when he was alive; Santana and McLaughlin both strived to play electric guitar the way Coltrane played saxophones, as their grimly ecstatic *Love, Devotion, Surrender* album illustrated to excess.

Through the matchmaking of Alan Douglas and the catalytic presence of Miles Davis, Hendrix had jammed with McLaughlin and organist Larry Young at New York's Record Plant just a few months before both of them (along with Holland and De Johnette) played on Miles Davis's *Bitches Brew*. Little of this fervent creativity is captured to any satisfaction, but some finished records still encourage speculation. John McLaughlin's *Devotion* album, a Douglas release wrapped in warped Mylar photography artwork by beat poet, trance aficionado, traveller and film maker Ira Cohen, touched some transcendent moments in its exploration of stoned heavy metal. Working with drummer Buddy Miles, bassist Billy Rich (from Buddy Miles Express) and Larry Young, one of the most original keyboard players of his time, on organ and electric piano, McLaughlin subsumed his virtuosity under a group sound that climbed through Escher circles of disquiet, soaring through clouds of reverb, stereo-panned echo, phasing and distortion. *Devotion* was produced by Stefan Bright, who had recorded Timothy Leary and Last Poet Jalal Nuriddin with Hendrix, as well as an exploratory jam with Hendrix and Dave Holland, regrettably derailed and abandoned after Bright and Hendrix found themselves incapably dusted on PCP. But the unfortunate Tony Bongiovi claims that the session tapes had been damaged in a fire, necessitating a reconstruction. This was the patch'n'paste job that secured him his thankless *Crash Landing* task.

Listen to *all* of this period as a patch'n'paste job and the artifice of technological assembly is reduced in importance. The fire of Hendrix resurfaces in the Miles Davis Osaka and New York concerts released as *Agharta*, *Pangaea* and *Dark Magus,* particularly in Pete Cosey's scorching fire streams of guitar. "His lines sizzle into exotic scales distorted to run subterranean channels", wrote Greg Tate in a sparkling critical revision of electric Miles, and in his sleevenotes to the CD issue of *Pangaea* Kevin Whitehead notes that Cosey was a member of the Chicago-based AACM (Association for the Advancement of Creative Musicians). Cosey worked with a table of what the Chicagoans liked to call "small instruments" – bells, water cans, maracas, sound toys, and so on.

Variants on the possibilities boiled up in this Afrocentrically wired cauldron were developed in solo work by the sidemen: Joe Zawinul's eerie tone poems – "His Last Journey" and "Arrival In New York"; Herbie Hancock's Buddhist/ African influenced albums of the early 1970s – *Sextant* and *Crossings* – neither of which sold well, so Hancock distilled their essence into the cool ethno-electro funk of *Headhunters* and *Thrust*; even John McLaughlin's unplugged (but not yet unhinged) *My Goal's Beyond*. The flexibility of the Miles Davis "insane asylums for black *and* white radicals" (as Greg Tate so aptly put it) becomes transparent in moments such as the resurfacing of McLaughlin's *Devotion* licks in "Thinkin' One Thing and Doin' Another" (*On the Corner*). McLaughlin moved on to Lifetime, initially a trio with Larry Young, led by drummer Tony Williams. This was improvisatory rock at its loosest. I saw them perform with Jack Bruce on bass at London's Marquee club at the beginning of the 1970s. My impression that night was of a music that came alight only in brief sparks. Without studio manipulation, the excitement was dissipated by misguided pitches at commercialism and the tendency of ambitious, virtuoso musicians to forget their improvising gifts in uncontrolled situations. The prospect outshone the reality.

radio reception

"... At a deeper level his attention to the upper and lower fringes of audibility suggests a further interest in exploring the two fundamental frequency areas of human consciousness: the hiss of the nervous system and the thump of the heart. *Telemusik*'s peculiar stratification of low-frequency beats, middle-frequency speech patterns and high-frequency intermodulation anticipates *Hymnen*'s adventures in memory and perceptual assimilation, and gives effective expression to the composer's frequently drawn parallel between 'stream-of-consciousness' mental processes and radio reception."

Robin Maconie, The Works of Stockhausen

Miles Davis had been listening to Hendrix, Sly Stone and James Brown, but with a little influence from Paul Buckmaster (cellist with The Third Ear Band, purveyors of quasi-Medieval ambient to UK hippies), he had been investigating the music and theories of Karlheinz Stockhausen. In his autobiography, Miles makes links between the harmolodic ideas of Ornette Coleman, Bach's counterpoint and Stockhausen's use of rhythm and space. So *On the Corner* is not a tight album, rhythmically or harmonically, nor is it meant to be. Bass or drums hold a pulse, often a very angular, irregular one, and the other instruments dart in and out of the openings. There were Indian influences too – the drone of Colin Walcott's sitar, which created a tonal centre of its own, and additive tabla rhythmic cycles – alongside West African, Afro-Cuban and Brazilian rhythms, free percussion sounds, and possibly even a deconstructing trace of UK improvisation, gleaned from David Holland in the *Filles de Kilimanjaro* period and John McLaughlin from *In a Silent Way* up until *Jack Johnson*. Tracks such as "Black Satin", from *On The Corner*, or the live tracks of that period, were microcosms of the fascinations of their time.

"It's faith music", Brian Eno says. "If you believe in it, I'm sure it will work. I can switch between minds. I can say, 'I believe and I like them' and I can say, 'No I don't, they're just unconnected rubbish, it's just guys jamming and not really knowing what they're doing'." The latter doubt can seem justifiable in times when precision and co-ordination is valued, but totally wrongheaded when falling apart is an existential imperative. There is ample evidence elsewhere that these musicians knew exactly what they were doing. As Miles Davis wrote for his brief but trenchant sleevenotes to Joe Zawinul's first solo album: "Zawinul is extending the thoughts that we've both had for years. And probably the thoughts that most so-called now musicians have not yet been able to express . . . In order to fit this music you have to be 'Cliché-Free'. In order to write this type of music, you have to be *free inside of yourself* . . ." M'tume's commercial recordings of the early 1980s, for example, were so tight, rhythmically, that they risked immobility, yet his contributions to the 1972 New York Philharmonic Hall concert documented on *Miles Davis In Concert* sound wilfully oblique. The rest of the band might be playing some kind of angular blues and M'tume is still pattering away at not quite or more than double time on his tuned drums.

Can this extreme perceptual subjectivity be explained? One

person – the classical music listener – might hear the peculiar rhythmic dislocations as expressions of Stockhausen's "moment form" – a focus on each moment "as if it were a vertical slice dominating over any horizontal conception and reaching into timelessness"; another – the funk fan – might compare it to Sly and the Family Stone and their increasing tendency to flatten hierarchical rhythmic organisation in a funk band, assigning equal importance and discrete space to each instrument (heard to perfection on *There's A Riot Going On* and *Fresh*); a third person – the jazz fan – might hear Ornette Coleman's ideas of collective blending at work, particularly the simultaneous soloing of his Prime Time band.

At the first jazz concert I attended – the Thelonious Monk Quartet – I felt baffled, then dismayed, by the audience's need to add a full stop to each solo by applauding when it seemed to be over, irrespective of merit or the flow of the music. By the mid 1960s, the perpetually fragile relationship between audience and performers had succumbed, in certain forms of jazz at least, to a sequence of stereotypical gestures. This was what Davis sought to escape with his "cliché-free" music, so he felt vindicated by Stockhausen's conceptions of "unending" duration and performance as a process. Teo Macero had begun splicing tape as early as *Porgy and Bess* in 1958. By the late 1960s, Davis was catalysing and supervising open-form improvisations which blurred the defining principles of structural organisation – improvisations were built around one chord rather than complex resolving sequences; all instruments played percussively *and* melodically; conventions such as theme and extemporisation, solo and accompaniment or head/solos/head were all thrown out in favour of textural laminates and molten fields of colour; rhythmic co-ordination became advanced maths. At times on *Miles Davis In Concert*, everybody except the percussionists seems to be playing through wah-wah pedals, a heteroglossolalic chorus of entombed wild cats. With Macero chopping up this stream of intensities, the listener might be forgiven for suffering queasy reactions to the arbitrary element that emerged as a side effect of the openness. Music that was once structured like an armadillo now took the shape of a jellyfish.

utopia I

Agharta and Pangaea were not just names pulled out of the air. Agharta was the name given to a spiritual centre of power, a land of advanced races situated, according to a bizarre collection of authorities on the unprovable, somewhere under the earth, somewhere under Asia. The theme is a familiar one from James Hilton's 1930s novel *Lost Horizon* and its filmed versions. As Jocelyn Godwin discovers in his exhaustive, clear-headed book *Arktos: The Polar Myth in Science, Symbolism and Nazi Survival*, the Agharta legend began in the 1870s with a French freethinker named Louis Jacolliot. Other writers on the subject described Agharta as a place of contemplation and good, a land of adepts, a hidden land ruled by an Ethiopian pontiff and blessed with air travel and gas lighting. A Christian Hermetist named Saint-Yves d'Alveydre described the place in terms which help to suggest why Davis was so attracted to the myth: ". . . drowning in celestial radiances all visible distinctions of race in a single chromatic of light and sound, singularly removed from the usual notions of perspective and acoustics". Godwin, a consistently rewarding scholar of esoteric musical ideas, also mentions Pangaea in *Arktos*, describing it as "the primordial continent into which all the present ones are ingeniously fitted in jigsaw fashion, its shores washed by the waves of 'Panthalassa,' the one primordial ocean. Later, the land masses are believed to have fragmented, first into super-continents with names like Gondwana and Laurentia, then eventually into the six or seven continents of today." The music on *Pangaea* is divided, probably as an afterthought reflecting Davis's preoccupations of the time, into two titles: "Zimbabwe" and "Gondwana". So, in his mind, this was music inspired by lost civilisations, united land masses, utopias of the mythical future and, as Kevin Whitehead suggests, continental drift.

utopia II

With mid-1960s' tape pieces such as *Mixtur, Hymnen* and *Telemusik,* Stockhausen depicted global absorption and transmission; the passage of organic materials into the electronic domain; music, the performer and the composer as a satellite dish (our metaphorical equivalent of the spirit medium) in the wired world. "Every person has all of mankind within himself", claimed Stockhausen. In his notes on *Telemusik*, composed in Tokyo as an electronic transformation of fragments of recorded music from Africa, the Amazon, Hungary, China, Spain, Vietnam, Bali and Japan, he wrote: "I wanted to come closer to an old, an ever-recurring dream: to go a step forward towards writing, not 'my' music, but a music of the whole world, of all lands and races." On a related theme, *Hymnen* is a work which starts with the "international gibberish of short-wave transmissions" and mixes 137 anthems from around the world. Stockhausen, who was using the term "world music" long before any rock star, broached this vision of "music of the whole world" in an essay entitled "Beyond Global Village Polyphony", written in 1973. "The possibility of telephoning Africa to order a tape recording, parts of which I then combine with electronic sounds I produce in Tokyo, is an unprecedented state of affairs, making it possible to create hitherto completely unknown relationships. In earlier times it was only possible to hear music from Africa if you travelled there – and who had such an opportunity?" Some of his prophesies from twenty years ago are extraordinary, although clearly, he was not thinking ahead to the transglobal duetting of Bono and Frank Sinatra.

the worm of Ejur

Bow Gamelan performance: London, 1990. Infernal shadow: a figure sits on a bicycle and pedals steadily. The bicycle powers a huge gramophone turntable which revolves at snail's pace, its giant stylus digging into the grooves of a four-foot-wide perspex disc. Slow music from pre-history squeals from a horn. Three crocodilian hinged baths, mated in pairs on top of each other, snap their jaws. A vacuum cleaner plays its Scottish bagpipe lament for the myth of labour-saving appliances. Whirling lights. Arrows fired at suspended beer barrels mimic the change ringing of church bells. A thunderous Burundi drum orchestra of upturned plastic barrels, illuminated from within and glowing in mentholated lime and blue like a Polynesian bar from hell. Spoons played in darkness, an echo of that odd scene in Roman Polanski's *Repulsion* when an old man playing spoons moves crabwise along the street. More vacuum cleaners, blowing smoke through corrugated whirly tunes. Alarms, klaxons, car horns, colliding metal discs, monstrous springs, musical saws attached to light bulbs, heterodyning sirens played at the low end of their range.

This episodic display of hypothetical grotesqueries from the Industrial Revolution, a homage to steam engineers and mechanics whose visions have been suffocated by our soft electronic era, reminded me of Raymond Roussel. Something of a dandy, this French surrealist writer used some of his considerable fortune to travel the world. During these tours, he would go out of doors as little as possible, preserving his imagination's sense of place from the corrupting effect of sensory input. *Impressions of Africa*, first published in 1910, depicted a number of brutal scenes, strange machines and other marvels presented at the coronation of Talu VII, Emperor of Ponukele and King of Drelshkaf. A chord is sounded by a surgical device which connects a young woman's lung to sounding tubes. In Trophies Square, Ejur, West Africa, the Hungarian Skariofszky demonstrates his zither, an instrument activated by a long worm resting in a mica trough filled with water. Undulating its body in precise motions, the trained worm allowed drops of water to fall from the trough on to the strings of the zither to play complex melodies.

animal body

A problem with utopias is that they tend to be closed systems, frozen in their supposed perfection and therefore boring, imprisoning and fanatical. Like any zealot, Karlheinz Stockhausen envisages a world changed, improved, even, according to his specifications. Body rhythms will have to go, for example, since they arise out of the "animal body" and slow down the evolution of the human race. The division of musical periodicity into sound, rhythm and form is a problem of conditioned psychological perception anyway (if we were crickets, belugas or replicants, things would be different), so Stockhausen proposed micro-rhythms as a replacement. These would tune the most gifted members of society into links with higher beings and assist in the imminent development of transportation for humans "through space on a beam of light", their bodies reconstructed, like Dr Who, on other stars.

This relegation of macro-rhythms to a low point on the evolutionary scale leads Stockhausen into profoundly suspect territory. Reading his essay, I was reminded of interviewing composer and ex-AMM improviser Cornelius Cardew, shortly before he was knocked down and killed by a hit-and-run driver. Cardew, whose diametrically opposed position to Stockhausen was underlined in his book *Stockhausen Serves Imperialism*, was talking about drawing his local community into the music he was making with the (frankly abysmal) Peoples' Liberation Music band. The problem for Cardew was living in Hackney, a solid working-class area well populated by young black reggae fans, which meant bass and drums powerful enough to steamroller flat the doctrinaire Maoism and limp music of PLM. "Those rhythms will have to go", mused Cardew without a trace of irony.

A face-to-face discussion between Cardew, Miles Davis and Stockhausen could have been very amusing. For Miles, rhythm had become the first structuring principle of his music, re-cording studio processes the second. Listening to *Bitches Brew*, most of the music evolves in a similar fashion to the Hendrix jam sessions released posthumously as *Nine To the Universe*. The big differences lie with pre-session organisa-tion (no angel dust), superb recording quality, innovative and intelligent post-production ordering of the material by pro-ducer Teo Macero, a consistently high level of musical inspiration, subtlety and discipline, a greater variety of tex-ture.

"Whoever doesn't like what I did, twenty years from now they can go back and redo it", said Teo Macero, recording col-laborator with Miles Davis. "Now there's no 'take one' etc.", he told Ian Carr, Davis's biographer. "The recording machine doesn't stop at the sessions, they never stop, except only to make the playback. As soon as he gets in there, we start the machines rolling." As Carr pointed out, additionally: "Miles wouldn't start with the idea of set pieces; instead, he would simply explore some fragmentary elements and edit them into a cohesive piece of music afterwards."

This is true of all multi-track recording and, as the Austral-ian sound restorer Robert Parker has proved, recorded music from all eras can be transformed through technological clean-ing processes. The most mutable piece of music Jimi Hendrix recorded – "1983 . . . (a merman I should turn to be)" – was mixed in various different versions by Hendrix and Eddie Kramer. An alternative, far less polished mix can be heard on a CD called *Live & Unreleased: The Radio Show,* where Kramer is heard describing the all-night mix as a "perform-ance". Jimi called the track a "song painting", but the painting was not in the song. The chords underpinned an improvisa-tion depicting the abyssal movement of unidentified submarine objects, the cries of seagulls, a descent into the maelstrom. There are lyrics, although Hendrix, who doubted his voice, might have come closer to the song painting by leav-ing them off. They outline a prescient theme: escape, via

Noah-style Ark machine, from war, environmental catastrophe (and personal chaos?), rebirthing into the amniotic fluid of the ocean.

brand new bag

Despotic control and technological deceit are regarded commonly as corrupting forces which destroy the authenticity and communality of music. I remember fondly a cartoon printed in a magazine to which I subscribed as a young guitarist: a drawing depicting Elvis Presley, seen from behind as he sang and pretended to play an electric guitar in which a radio was concealed. In February 1965, James Brown and his band interrupted their lengthy bus journey to a show by stopping off at a studio in North Carolina, for barely an hour, to record "Papa's Got A Brand New Bag". The song dragged for nearly seven minutes as the musicians, including guitarist Jimmy Nolen, struggled with fatigue. The track was meant to be hip, dance-craze R&B on the cusp, reaching back through history to the swinging, jazz inflections of Wynonie Harris, Little Willie John and Louis Jordan, looking back even further to rent parties and fish fries, but at the same time groping towards the disco cyborg future. Whatever was latent in those weary grooves, somebody heard it, for as Cliff White and Harry Weinger wrote in their notes for the James Brown *Star Time* CD box of 1991: "In a brilliant post-production decision, the intro was spliced off and the entire performance was sped up for release."

A huge pop hit was razor-bladed out of something that started as a flatfoot grind; this taut amalgam of street slang, loping beats and nervous punchy accents, arguably the first moment of modern soul. Brown's quoted reaction reflected his glimpse into a future, our present, in which songs are titles, source points, initialisations, indicating the beginning and the reference point for a process of continual transformation. "It's a little beyond me now", he confessed. "I'm actually fightin' the future. It's – it's – it's just out *there*." The peculiar aspect of the story is that most of us have only become aware of the unpromising origins of this fabulous, pivotal track more than a quarter of a century after the event. Were it not for the obsession, via CD release, for the alternate take, and hence the release of "Papa's Got A Brand New Bag" in its complete and previously unreleased, unedited, slow form, we would be none the wiser. Once amused, in a patronising sort of way, to learn that one of the guitarists from The Ventures learned to play by struggling to copy Les Paul's artificially accelerated and overdubbed bionic guitar solos, I now realise that I can be fooled just as easily. But what a privilege to be so easily deceived into pleasure, revelation, motivation. The beauty of exploitation overdubs or dead zone duets is their realisation of the potential of studio music as science fiction, the configurations which our imaginations whisper but our bodies so rarely concede. A great advantage of working with dead people is that their objections, the objections of habit or fixed identity, go unheard. In 1988, James Brown sang in that scorched earth scream of his, "I'm real", but editing equipment and tape speed controls had already (decades ago, in fact) thrown that desperate, insecure claim into doubt.

techno-glossolalia

Whilst Brian Eno and I were talking during an interview about the impact of technology on our perception of music, he began to enthuse over the enthralling sound of early rock and roll records, particularly Dick and Deedee's "The Mountain's High" and Phil Spector's production of "Be My Baby", sung by The Ronettes: "As I started collecting records I started noticing there were distinct trends in my collection. The biggest trend of all was certainly towards this fascination for things that just had their own sound picture. Like some of the late fifties, early sixties records that I had, like 'The Mountain's High'. The moment you put it on, it sounds like nothing else that you've ever heard. Within the first second of that song, you're in the place. It's sonically so distinctive. Then,

'Be My Baby', where you had this enormous, huge sonic picture with the thinnest voice you've ever heard. The voice is like a little bee inside there. I got more and more interested in that kind of thing – and then psychedelic music was an explosion of that kind of material."

In passing, he mentioned Frank Sinatra, and the "eroticism" of a vocalist singing intimately into a microphone in front of a loud big band: "I think what happened in pop music, because of electronics and recording and other cultural factors as well, was that suddenly it became possible to work with all sorts of sounds, to put together things that could never have been put together before. For instance, just the microphone enabling a singer to sing very quietly against a full orchestra. This, in itself, was an incredible revolution in eroticism. Frank Sinatra singing in an off-hand, almost introspective way against a big band was a fabulous breakthrough which could never have happened in any classical music because it's physically impossible. He would have been drowned." Brian also talked about his own production work for U2 and, coincidentally, the odd semiosis of mismatched vocal styles and social messages that occurs when seemingly incompatible singers record duets.

"Have you ever read", Brian asked me, "or seen this book, I don't think anyone could ever read it, actually, by Alan Lomax, called *Folk Song Style and Culture*?" The answer was yes, I knew about Lomax and his Cantometrics, his system for measuring social structure by vocal styles. The observations which follow are ramshackle by normal Eno standards, but a fascinating idea is hatching within. "I think it's a great book", he continued. "It's so interesting as a concept. One of the things there is that he's looking at culture and saying, one culture has very raspy nasal singing and this correlates with the pattern of such cultures being male dominated, so on and so on. He identifies those kinds of connections between singing style and cultural habits in general. But when you come to our culture, this becomes much more complex. You hear a record

like . . . Joe Cocker singing with some country singer. You
hear, on the one hand, her voice, which is very pure, very
feminine, distinctly of a culture of Western . . . almost pruri-
ence. Then you hear his voice, which is the lonely, dirty,
fucking long-haired messy hunker. In the Lomax book, there's
no provision for the possibility that you could imagine a culture that plays with the elements of other cultures like that. It
dons them like it dons masks. They're guises, really. The
whole energy of a song like that – a pretty shitty song, actually – is in playing off these two cultural pictures, which I'm
sure resonate with us in exactly the way that Alan Lomax suggested. I'm sure when we hear the Joe Cocker voice, we hear
the culture that Alan Lomax would say connects with that but
then, in the next line, we hear this other culture in her voice.
This is very fascinating to me – that we've become sonic
collagists. I think the energy of those kind of combinations
has a very long life. It outlasts melodies and rhythms and so
on. It's a very deep pattern that they're talking about."

Implicit, also, is the logical extension of these illusions and
juxtapositions. Performance can never be the same again.
One of the first live bands I saw was The Ronettes, supporting The Rolling Stones on their second national tour. On a
Ronettes record, teenage life crises were amplified by Phil
Spector's production to the scale of a major metereological
disturbance. Live, encased in iridescent sheath dresses,
stripped of Spector's awesome production, The Ronettes (and
the life crises) were reduced to human proportions. Technology has transformed us into giants, bionic superhumans,
stateless satellites, omnipresent speakers-in-tongues. We become bigger than we are, louder, displaced or multiplied or
we shrink, intimidated by the waterfall of information. We use
technology to protect and isolate ourselves, articulating desires that have been suppressed by technology, trying to
replace alienation with techno-spirituality, using contradictory messages to express confusions for which our history has
not prepared us. "Who's in the next flat? Who's in 14-B?" asks

psychologist James Hillman in *We've Had a Hundred Years of Psychotherapy and the World's Getting Worse*. "I don't know who they are, but, boy, I'm on the phone, car phone, toilet phone, plane phone, my mistress is in Chicago, the other woman I'm with is in D.C., my exwife is in Phoenix, my mother in Hawaii, and I have four children living all over the country. I have faxes coming in day and night, I can plug into all the world's stock prices, commodity exchanges, I am everywhere, man – but I don't know who's in 14-B."

living space

Is the journey of a fax as interesting as (or more interesting than) the travel journals of Marco Polo, dictated during a three-year period of incarceration at the end of the thirteenth century? Marco Polo "created Asia for the European mind", wrote John Masefield, but fax and e-mail, what mysterious zones do they create for the contemporary mind? Alienation from physical community may be disturbing, yet idealists who promote electronic communications suggest that they are being used to rebuild shattered communities, rather than complete their destruction. "Some aspects of life in a small community have to be abandoned when you move to an online metropolis; the fundamentals of human nature, however, always scale up", wrote Howard Rheingold in *The Virtual Community: finding connections in a computerised world*. "The fact that we need computer networks to recapture the sense of cooperative spirit that so many people seemed to lose when we gained all this technology is a painful irony", he admits in a chapter entitled Grassroots Groupminds.

As for flights from the body, or from rootedness in the body, these may turn out to have their positive sides also. Transcendence through chemical drugs and plant psychedelics, long stays in cyberspace via the Internet, or body-crisis films such as *Tron, Videodrome* and Wes Craven's *Nightmare On Elm Street* could be interpreted, in their various ways, as manifestations of a desire to redefine the Cartesian image of divided being. By vacating the body, losing the centre in a web of information (whether video game, electronic spectacle, audio/visual immersion, dream/nightmare, global information exchange or so-called plant consciousness), the non-corporeal part of humanness begins to question its own boundaries and to challenge the conventional belief that consciousness is housed somewhere within the head.

Ask musicians of a certain age a question: Who revolutionised the recording studio? Invariably, the response will include the following names: Phil Spector, Joe Meek, Brian Wilson, Lee Perry. At critical moments of their lives, one common link between all these studio innovators was a state of mind known, for the sake of society's convenience, as madness. During a Brian Wilson interview in 1986, we discussed The Four Freshmen and their influence on The Beach Boys. I asked one of those reflex questions that tends to pop out during a telephone interview with a difficult subject. Was it unusual for somebody like yourself to be listening to The Four Freshmen at that time? "No, it wasn't unusual", he replied. "The thing was that I had no real source of spiritual love. My parents were OK but my dad was so hostile that he kinda screwed the family up. So he messed up the family vibrations, you know? So I turned to music as my love, as a source of spiritual love. When I heard the Freshmen, I really flipped because I liked the *sound* I heard, I liked their *sound*. I analysed their sound and I learned to analyse their harmonies."

Listening back to that tape, I feel frustrated that I opted out of pursuing this disarming connection between psychic ill health and sound. Bootleg recordings of Brian Wilson studio sessions from the *Smile* era, reveal a musician completely immersed in sound: a ravishing instrumental dub of " 'Til I Die", just bass guitar, vibraphone and the gradual fade-up of distant organ, then drums, then vocal harmonies, then quiet drum machine. Another session, called "George Fell Into His French Horn", experiments with brass instruments, some of which sound like Tibetan ritual music, Varèse glissandi or free jazz, some of which fool around with cartoonish evocations of laughter. A conversation about George falling into his French horn, sticking valves and other incomprehensible stuff, is conducted by musicians talking into their mouthpieces. Sombre growlings, smears, pointilliste brass blats and hee-haws are interrupted by the serious voice of Wilson, talking from the control room: "OK, one more time please. A little bit slower moving if we could." An interesting side angle: the *Smile* bootleg LP included a Miles Davis/Gil Evans track – "Here Comes De Honey Man" from *Porgy and Bess* – claimed by the label copy as an extremely rare and unreleased Beach Boys instrumental called "Holidays".

Joe Meek was not mad. A gay man, trying to suppress all signs of his queerness in the repressive atmosphere of postwar Britain, attempting to come to terms with spiritual longings (he was a spiritualist who dubbed angelic voices on to trashy instrumentals) in the primitive context of early British rock and roll, he killed his landlady, then himself, with a shotgun. The strain of these forbidden desires pushed him beyond the point of rational constraints. And Spector, inventor of the "wall of sound", layering instrumental textures and echoes into a sweet sickness, the depth of the sound drawing you down to subterranean caves of subtle wonders. Spector became a Los Angeles recluse, like Roderick Usher, alone and hypersensitive in the House of Usher, eventually producing with a gun on the mixing desk. Not so far away was Brian Wilson, grotesquely fat, lying in bed for two years, emotionally exhausted by The Beach Boys and turned inside out by drugs. In Washington Gardens, Kingston, Jamaica, after years of producing reggae hits, Lee Perry had destroyed his Black Ark studio, first flooding it, then burning it down. Coincidence? Or did the struggle of turning the recording studio from its documentary origins to a virtual chamber of wonders push the most creative producers past the edges of self-definition, into the void? A thin line stands between the voices that torment and dominate a disordered, confused personality and the not-yet-existent sounds from nowhere which invade the imagination in daydreams, tempting the sonic explorer into finding means to duplicate them in the tangible world.

dub dream

"And he woke again, thinking he had dreamed . . . Aerol strapping him into a g-web in Babylon Rocker. And then the long pulse of Zion dub."

William Gibson, *Neuromancer*

Lee Perry sits next to me, fiddling with a small cassette recorder. Pieces of plastic are breaking off, batteries disgorged. How to offer technological assistance to a twentieth-century master of audio recording? Not master, magician. A wiry, wizened man with a mischievous look about him, he was born in Jamaica, in perhaps 1935 or '36, though nobody is sure. Festooned with coins, pendants, feathers and badges, he could be an Obeah man empowered with the trappings of Afro-Jamaican folk magic, or simply an eccentric. The ambiguity enhances his mythical status among reggae fanatics. He appears to enjoy the fact that people think he is quite mad, although confusion and unhappiness are apparent alongside the inspirational juxtapositions of his word play. "Rocking and reeling, having a ball, swinging and singing, strait-jacket and all", he sang on a tune called "Secret Laboratory".

He belonged to three different churches in his youth: the Holiness Church, the Church of God and the Ethiopian Orthodox, and tends to describe both musical motivations and the technical processes of recording with imagery that would suit an Old Testament prophet. What could be dismissed as mystical mumbo jumbo makes sense if related to Perry's music, which has consistently drawn upon Jamaican folklore and language. Some of Bob Marley's freshest work, for example, was achieved with Perry in the years 1969 to 1971; some songs that they recorded together contain hidden meanings referring to the British colonialist era and the proscribed cult practices of Jamaican slaves, including their belief in duppies (ghosts) and spirits. Later tracks transpose and collage potent Biblical, Rastafarian, Afro-Jamaican, comic book and spaghetti-western imagery: the ethereal "Congo Ashanti" chant of The Congos, "Hay Fever" chanted by Jah Lion over the sound of a squeaking door, or Leo Graham's "Black Candle" ("a warning to enemies who might seek the help of an Obeah man in order to attack the producer", writes Steve Barrow).

At its heights, Perry's genius has transformed the recording studio. If the original purpose of recording was to document a musical performance, then Perry's approach, as titles such as "Secret Laboratory", "Station Underground News" and "Musical Transplant" indicate, lifted the studio into virtual space, an imaginal chamber over which presided the electronic wizard, evangelist, gossip columnist and Dr Frankenstein that he became.

"Electricity is the eye, water is the life", he says. "In a way, electricity reach the high peak. The studio must be like a living thing. The machine must be live and intelligent. Then I put my mind into the machine by sending it through the controls and the knobs or into the jack panel. The jack panel is the brain itself, so you've got to patch up the brain and make the brain a living man, but the brain can take what you're sending into it and live. Think of music as life. When I making music I think of life, creating life, and I want it to live, I want it to feel good and taste good." This is alchemist's talk: making living matter from intractable substances. "When we smoke and feel nice," he continues, "eat cornbread with butter. Then it give you a good appetite and new vibes. The sound might be sounding sweeter. The sound might be coming from the food zone."

A substantial body of influential, extraordinary music was made in the 1970s at Perry's Black Ark studio, named after the Ark of the Covenant. Some of these – Junior Murvin's "Police & Thieves", Max Romeo's "War Ina Babylon", George Faith's "To Be a Lover (Have Mercy)" – were irresistibly, innovatively commercial. With their jump-cut edits and supernatural soundworlds, others – "7¾ Skank", "Militant Rock", "Roast Fish & Cornbread" – were more daring than anything else of their time. "I grew up reading comics", he tells me. Perhaps comics, cartoons and film (and now computer games) are more useful tools for a musician's self-education than books. John Zorn has helped to legitimize the rapid dislocations and hairpin structures of cartoon music composed by Carl Stalling for Warner Brothers' cartoons such as Bugs Bunny. In his sleevenotes for *The Carl Stalling Project* album, Zorn writes that Stalling's music "implies an openness – a non-hierarchical musical overview – typical of today's younger composers but all too rare before the mid-1960s. All genres of music are *equal* – no *one* is inherently better than the others – and with Stalling, all are embraced, chewed up and spit out in a format closer to Burroughs' cut ups, or Godard's film editing of the '60s, than to anything happening in the '40s." But listen, also, to some of Brian Wilson's Beach Boys music of the *Smile* period and after – "Fall Breaks and Back To Winter" or "Trombone Dixie" – for evidence of cartoon music and Disney influences mutating into avant-garde pop.

Lee Perry explored the potential of sound to hypnotise. "But still the Black Ark was something else," he says, "because the sound that I get out of the Black Ark studio, I don't really get it out of no other studio. It was like a space craft. You could hear space in the tracks. Something there was like a holy vibration and a godly sensation. Modern studios, they have different set up. They set up a business and a money-making concern. I set up like an ark. Studying history, I realised that the Ark of the Covenant is the top of everything. You have to be the Ark to save the animals and nature and music." The level of inspiration was very high at this point, with Perry pushing limited equipment to extremes. His attitude to the sources of his inspiration is unorthodox. "It had something to do with the location of the studio", he claims. "Because it was built on a godly plan to make holy spiritual music. I have a plan to make music that can make wrongs right. I was getting help from God, through space, through the sky, through the firmament, through the earth, through the wind, through the fire. I got support through the weather to make space music."

Lee Perry's spell

When I clap my hand, duppy appear to me from coast to coast, flying through the night post and through keyholes. Sometimes they melt the key, if the key is in the keyhole, in a puff of smoke – Pfffffffff . . . When I cut a Stench-Fart, it so loud that it bring up volcano lava, and is more dangerous than a hurricane . . . Say "hi" to the lovers of Christ, and "bye" to the lovers of the devil. 'Cause I kill the devil with my spiritual level. MXR Armagideon War. Electrical machine, computer man, the mighty Upsetter, the ghost in the machine. Mad Perry, lightning head master, breaker of doom. Dr Fu Manchu, black Fu Manchu. Boom! Boom! Boom! Boom! Boom! Boom! Boom! Boom! This is a musical curse. Blessed are the Poor, and cursed are the Rich. Hic Hoc, Hic Hoc, Yak Yak. It finish. Yak Yak.

replicant

Dub music is like a long echo delay, looping through time. Regenerating every few years, sometimes so quiet that only a disciple could hear, sometime shatteringly loud, dub unpicks music in the commercial sphere. Spreading out a song or a groove over a vast landscape of peaks and deep trenches, extending hooks and beats to vanishing point, dub creates new maps of time, intangible sound sculptures, sacred sites, balm and shock for mind, body and spirit.

When you double, or dub, you replicate, reinvent, make one of many versions. There is no such thing as an original mix, since music stored on multi-track tape, floppy or hard disk, is just a collection of bits. The composition has been decomposed, already, by the technology. Dubbing, at its very best, takes each bit and imbues it with new life, turning a rational order of musical sequences into an ocean of sensation. This musical revolution stemmed originally from Jamaica – in particular, the tiny studio once run by the late Osbourne Ruddock, aka King Tubby, in Kingston. "This is the heart of Kingston 11", Dave Henley wrote, describing the location of Tubby's studio for a reggae fanzine called *Small Axe*. "A maze of zinc fence, potholed roads and suitably dilapidated bungalows. After dark, the streets become remarkably deserted (by Kingston standards, anyway, considering that loafing on the corner is a favourite Jamaican pastime), giving the impression of an eerie tropical ghost town."

Urban, rural, tropic, aquatic, lo-tech, mystical. This was the source mix from which William Gibson drew (sentimentally, some critics think) when adding the humanising element of Rastafari and dub to his *Neuromancer* narrative of tech-Gnosis. When King Tubby first discovered dub, the revelation came, like so many technological discoveries, through an accident. There were other Jamaican recording engineers, of course: Sylvan Morris, Errol T. Thompson and Lloyd "Prince Jammy" James helped to created the sound of albums such as Joe Gibbs's *African Dub All-Mighty* series, or Augustus Pablo's *King Tubby's Meets Rockers Uptown* and *Africa Must Be Free By 1983*. But it was Tubby, cutting discs for Duke Reid at Treasure Isle, who first discovered the thrill of stripping a vocal from its backing track and then manipulating the instrumental arrangement with techniques and effects: drop-out, extreme equalisation, long delay, short delay, space echo, reverb, flange, phase, noise gates, echo feedback, shotgun snare drums, rubber bass, zipping highs, cavernous lows. The effects are there for enhancement, but for a dubmaster they can displace time, shift the beat, heighten a mood, suspend a moment. No coincidence that the nearest approximation to dub is the sonar transmit pulses, reverberations and echoes of underwater echo ranging and bioacoustics. No coincidence, also, that dub originated in a poor section of a city on a Caribbean island.

The first moment of dub has been pursued by reggae historian Steve Barrow through numerous conversations with important reggae record producers such as Bunny Lee. In *Dub Catcher* magazine, Lee conjures some of the excitement of those late-1960s, early-1970s' sessions when King Tubby began to experiment with what he termed the "implements of sound": "Tubby's, right", recalls Lee. "With all the bass and drum ting now, dem ting just start by accident, a man sing off key, an' when you a reach a dat you drop out everyting an' leave the drum, an' lick in the bass, an' cause a confusion an' people like it . . . Sometime me an' 'im talk an' me say, 'Drop out now, Tubby!' An' 'im get confuse an' me jus' draw down the whole a the lever . . . you hear 'Pluck' an' jus' start play pure distortion. Me say, 'Yes Tubbs, madness, the people dem like it!' an' just push it right back up . . . An' then Lee Perry do fe 'im share a dub too, ca' 'im an' Tubby's do a whole heap a ting . . . 'im an' Niney [producer nine finger Niney 'the Observer'] an' musician jus' play, an' 'im jus' [makes discordant noises and laughs]. 'Im drunk, drunk yunno – the engineer a go stop 'im an' [he] say, 'You no hear a vibes? Mad sound dat man.' An' when 'im come the people dem like it."

Tubby worked with equipment that would be considered impossibly limited by today's standards, yet his dubs were massive, towering exercises in sound sculpting. Legend records that he cut four dubplates – special, one-off mixes – for his Home Town Hi-Fi System at the end of the 1960s. Playing these instrumental versions at a dance, with U Roy toasting verbal improvisations over the music in real time, he was forced to repeat them all night, dubbing them up live as the crowd went crazy. Tubby worked for some of Jamaica's most creative producers: Lee Perry and Augustus Pablo, in particular, were recording increasingly exotic and distinctive music during the 1970s. On albums such as Perry's *Super Ape* and Pablo's *East of the River Nile*, the mixing board becomes a pictorial instrument, establishing the illusion of a vast soundstage and then dropping instruments in and out as if they were characters in a drama. Lee Perry was a master of this technique, applying it to all his records, whether vocal, dub, instrumental version or talkover, all of them rich in his dub signature of rattling hand drums and scrapers, ghostly voices, distant horn sections, unusual snare and hi-hat treatments, groans and reptilian sibilations, odd perspectives and depth illusions, sound effects, unexpected noises and echoes that repeat to infinity.

Dub also anticipated remix culture. In 1974 Rupie Edwards, a producer of celebrated Jamaican artists such as I Roy, The Ethiopians and Gregory Isaacs, was the first to compile a "version" album – *Yamaha Skank*, twelve different versions of the rhythm of a song called "My Conversation". Although these were not dubs, they grew out of the idea of dubbing a track, shaping and reshaping its "implements of sound" as if music was modelling clay rather than copyright property.

Prince Far I's vision

... city of nine gates, magical moon, circling clouds, marvel of miracles, twilight world, beauty unfold, in living memory ...

Suns of Arqa, "City of Nine Gates"

world of echo

After the first wave of dub albums during the 1970s from King Tubby, Lee Perry, Augustus Pablo, Yabby U, Keith Hudson and the producer stables of Bunny Lee, Coxsone Dodd, Joe Gibbs and Niney, many of dub's innovations were applied to fresh contexts in America and the UK. New York dub emerged, almost as an inevitability, from the disco tape editing and remixing of DJs such as Tom Moulton and Walter Gibbons. Moulton, whose hectic career as the pioneer of disco mixing came to a halt after a serious heart attack during a mix, restructured funk tracks with a razor blade, shaping for the ecstasies and libido release of the dancefloor; a Walter

Gibbons mix, on the other hand, entered the listener into the chaotic heart of King Tubby's "implements of sound". Although many of his mixes, particularly of material from the Salsoul label, were relatively functional, he could also play Lee Perry-style tricks with sound balance, sudden track drop-outs or perspectival distortions. His long remix of Bettye LaVette's "Doin' the Best That I Can", released on New York's West End label in 1978, redefined the logical hierarchy of instrumentation.

Walter Gibbons could make a dancefloor move to a glock-enspiel or a hi-hat. A constant collaborator with the late Arthur Russell – New York singer, cellist, percussionist and mini-malist/disco composer – he used sound relationships rather than electronic effects to create wonderfully strange music. These reach their apex on the Arthur Russell 12" singles: "Let's Go Swimming" and "Treehouse/School Bell" – songs of inno-cence and experience; convoluted slitherings of sharp sounds, chopped and dislocated; antipathetic to the modular, even-number construction of disco; formed in the eternal shape of the self-devouring Uroborus dragon of alchemy, a flow without beginning or end; contrasting/merging the de-velopmental improvisation of Indian ragas with the hypnotic, human-interlock accretions of Fela Anikulapo-Kuti's Nigerian Afro-funk.

Like Gibbons, Russell played the studio as an instrument, understanding the freedom inherent in present-day recording. For example, sound recorded in a studio live room or direct on to tape is unnaturally dry (unless recorded in special re-flective rooms), so extraordinary illusions of distance are possible through contrasting dry, forward sounds with the distancing effects of a huge range of echoes. Another point: the number of "performances" that can be permutated from a multi-track recording is infinite. *World of Echo,* Russell called one of his solo albums.

Russell studied at the Ali Akbar Khan school in San Fran-cisco, where he played cello. "Cello is Ali Akbar Khan's favourite instrument", he told me in 1986. He collaborated on projects with John Cage, Laurie Anderson, Phill Niblock, Philip Glass, François Kervorkian, David Byrne, Steve D'Aquisto, the Ingram brothers, Peter Gordon, Larry Levan, Allen Ginsberg and many others; poets, film makers, disco mixers, pop stars, soul musicians, contemporary composers. Forbidden border crossings. When Russell performed his *Instrumentals* piece at The Kitchen in Manhattan, the use of a drum kit caused a stir. "A lot of people turned off", he told me. "They thought that was a sign of some new unsophistication, a sign of increasing commercialisation. Then if you try to do something different in dance music you just get branded as an eccentric. Maybe I am an eccentric, I don't know, but it's basically a very simple idea. I like music with no drums, too. Partly, I guess, from listening to drums so much. When you hear something with no drums it seems very exciting. I always thought that music with no drums is successive to music with drums. New music with no drums is like this future when they don't have drums any more. In outer space, you can't take your drums – you take your mind." DJs told him that nobody would ever play "Let's Go Swimming". "I think eventually that kind of thing will be commonplace", he said. He was right, but neither he nor Walter Gibbons lived to profit from this new era of sound experimentation. Arthur Russell died of AIDS in 1992. Walter Gibbons died in 1994.

my life in a hole in the ground

The New Orleans torture scene conjured in hallucinogenic close up by David Lynch in *Wild At Heart*: a sloweddown Adrian Sherwood production – "Far Away Chant" by African Headcharge – adds further dimensions of hoodoo otherness to Lynch's trademark shadeworld of sexual violence, Prince Far I's warping sandblast vocals rising up from the catacombs . . . in this unholy place a steady throb of Rastafarian repeater and funde drums somehow twisted in the unconscious to draw on archaic fears, fear of voodoo, fear of the primeval occult, the old unhealthy fear of Rastas as "menacing devils with snake nests for hair".

Working with a floating pool of musicians in London, Adrian Sherwood had been pushing reggae deeper into the echo chamber for years, maybe running an entire track backwards, highlighting strange instruments, layering fugitive ambiences from the elemental simplicity of drum, bass and vocals, creating polyrhythmic ricochets, noise bubbles and chimerical voices. His mixing techniques on Creation Rebel's *Starship Africa*, the late Prince Far I's *Cry Tuff Dub Encounter* series of albums, and African Headcharge's *My Life In a Hole In the Ground* were epic explorations of mood, experiments in bass as an enveloping cloud, premonitions of the marathon dub and ambient mixes of the 1990s.

I played flute and African thumb piano on *Chapter III* of the Prince Far I *Cry Tuff* albums, east London's Berry Street studio boiling hot, air conditioning broken down, Far I (like King Tubby, soon to become a murder victim of Jamaica's random gun law) solemn and silent, sitting by the mixing desk wrapped in scarf, hat and jacket as if we were working in arctic conditions. The session was a madhouse of post-punk experimentation, indicative of the role dub had assumed as a deconstructing agent, a locus of crosscurrents from reggae, rock, jazz, improvisation and the extra-human conjectures of technological processes. Sherwood has admitted that his initial inspiration for *My Life In a Hole In the Ground* was the David Byrne and Brian Eno collaborative album, *My Life In the Bush of Ghosts*: "I was reading in the paper", Sherwood told *Dub Catcher* magazine, "where he [Brian Eno] said, 'I had a vision of psychedelic Africa' or something like that. So I had to laugh. The idea was to make a psychedelic, but serious, African dub record."

bush of ghosts
More laughter, this time from Brian Eno. In the early 1970s, he was holding forth about the genius of Lee Perry's

"Bucky Skank" to a rock journalist at the *NME*, who responded with scorn. Only a year later, Brian recalls with an allowable degree of smug satisfaction, the same journalist was sojourning in Jamaica, smoking "trumpet-sized spliffs" and filing born-again copy in praise of reggae. In *Cyberia* – Douglas Rushkoff's celebration of cyberdelic ennui – *My Life In the Bush of Ghosts* is credited as "the inspiration for the industrial, house, and even rap and hip-hop recording artists who followed". This reductive determination to prove that underground scenes (black, Hispanic, gay, whatever) must have their source in artists recognised by white media (i.e. mostly white people) is as odious and absurd as the opposite claim (heard at a hip-hop seminar in 1993) that white people have made no contribution to twentieth-century music.

Released in 1981, *My Life In the Bush of Ghosts* was an interesting record although its loose, one-chord jams, clearly influenced by Fela Kuti, have not weathered time as well, in my opinion, as Brian's supposedly less commercial ambient work of that period. Some of the musicianship sounds dated, but the last three tracks of the album sequence, predicate fruitful rhythmic possibilities – a kind of segmented, crabwise movement of unlocked rhythm relationships – along with the suggestion of a studio-generated music which explores ritual gravity (an electronic equivalent of Korean ancestral shrine music or Japanese *gagaku*). The idea of sampling radio voices and tapes of global musics in a rock context, concocting 'ethnic' forgeries or machine-age ceremonies, was nothing new. Can's bass player and short-wave-radio ham, Holger Czukay, had been doing this since his *Canaxis* album, co-produced with Rolf Dammers at the Inner Space studio, Cologne, in 1968. Moreover, when Czukay mixed this kind of source material into the music, he created integrated fictions, impossible musics from unknown worlds, rather than simply laying voice tapes on top of the funk.

The Byrne and Eno collaboration had a secret history, anyway. The project was mooted during conversations between

Byrne, Eno and Jon Hassell in New York. At that time, Hassell had formulated and was publishing advance fragments from his future/primitive Fourth World concept: "A proposal for a 'coffee coloured' classical music of the future – both in terms of the adoption of entirely new modes of structural organisation (as might be suggested by the computer ability to re-arrange, dot-by-dot, a sound or video image) and in terms of an expansion of the 'allowable' musical vocabulary in which one may speak this structure – leaving behind the ascetic face which Eurocentric tradition has come to associate with serious expression."

"At that time I had done *Possible Musics*", says Hassell, speaking to me from his home in West Hollywood. "Brian was producing Talking Heads . . . and I turned them on to a lot of ethnic music, in particular the Ocora label. After *Remain In Light* David and Brian came up with this idea that we should go off into the desert someplace with an eight-track recorder and make a record that, at that time, we were thinking would be somewhat like The Residents' *Eskimo* – that is a *faux* tribe, invented, that doesn't exist." At this opportune moment, our transatlantic telephone discussion is interrupted by a Spanish CB radio conversation. "So we conspired to do this together. They were going to go off to LA to look for a place. A month or so later, I got a cassette in the mail and it was an early version of – was it Oum Kalsoum they used [probably Egyptian singer Samira Tewfik, on "A Secret Life"]? Anyway, it was enough to send me into . . . it was enough to be quite disturbing."

Hassell is proud of the fact that Hank Shocklee, co-producer of Public Enemy with Chuck D, has acknowledged *My Life In the Bush of Ghosts* as one influence on the hectic, cut-up, collaged sound flow of Public Enemy. "We took whatever was annoying, threw it into a pot, and that's how we came out with this group", Shocklee told *Keyboard* magazine, "We believed that music is nothing but organised noise. You can take anything – street sounds, us talking, whatever you want – and make it music by organizing it."

curating the world

At the dawn of audio recording, a small boy named Ludwig Koch sat under a piano with an Edison phonograph, recording the playing of Johannes Brahms on to a wax cylinder. This document, made on the cusp of a new era of music and technology, was lost when Koch fled from Nazi Germany, but at the age of eight, he also made the first known recording of an animal – an Indian Shama thrush – in 1889.

Zoos, museums, expositions, cameras and microphones: collectors, memorisers and curators of the world. "Collecting – at least in the West, where time is thought to be linear and irreversible – implies a rescue of phenomena from inevitable historical decay or loss", writes James Clifford, professor in the History of Consciousness Program, University of California. "Since the mid-nineteenth century", he continues, "ideas of culture have gathered up those elements that seem to give continuity and depth to collective existence, seeing it whole rather than disputed, torn, intertextual, or syncretic. [Margaret] Mead's almost postmodern image of 'a local native reading the index to *The Golden Bough* just to see if they had missed anything' is not a vision of authenticity." Clifford applies the term chronotope, as used by Russian critic Mikhail Bakhtin, to New York City during World War II, a place where surrealist artists and anthropologists bathed in a "wonderland of sudden opening to other times and places, of cultural matter out of place". He defines chronotope as "literally 'time-space' with no priority to either dimension. The chronotope is a fictional setting where historically specific relations of power become visible and certain stories can 'take place' (the bourgeois salon in nineteenth-century social novels, the merchant ship in Conrad's tales of adventure and empire)."

As technology has changed, so the recording studio has become increasingly virtual. What began as documentation moved into specialised interiors. Sounds of the world were collected and transmuted at the end of the 1940s by a French sound engineer, Pierre Schaeffer, who gave concerts of noises collected from sources such as spinning saucepan lids and whistling toy tops (more instruments of darkness), steam engine and boat sounds (the Futurist noise of movement), human voices and percussion. Working with composers Pierre Henry and, later, Luc Ferrari, Schaeffer pioneered *musique concrète*: music made from sound. Varèse completed the electronic section of *Déserts* in Schaeffer's Paris studio. By 1951, electronic music experiments were taking place in Germany and America, eliminating the musical performer almost entirely; by the mid 1950s, pop-music producers were applying echo effects with such abandon that the secure physical image of a band of musicians, held in the mind during listening, began to disintegrate. Then multi-track tape and multiple microphone recording separated musicians from each other, either in time or space. Electronic effects could be applied more easily to individual instruments or vocals. Musicians were hidden behind baffle boards or shut in separate rooms. Studio performances could be corrected or updated without changing the entire song, or the song could be remixed endlessly. For the best explication of multi-track recording, the upside and downside, watch Jean-Luc Godard's film *One Plus One,* in which The Rolling Stones wrestle for eternity with the emergence of one song, "Sympathy For the Devil". Fascinating to think about, or describe, but boring to watch and listen.

With the introduction of computer sequencing and digital sampling, the tapeless studio became a possibility, though rarely a total reality. Hard-disk recording, in which all source sounds and effects – electronic or acoustic – could be stored and manipulated in the digital domain, is the current stage of this process, a point at which, in theory, the studio and its musical output can exist in virtuality, represented in our world through sound and a visual representation of sound on a computer screen. The virtual studio, then, is our chronotype, the fictional setting where stories take place. What a disappointing chronotype, though, by comparison with

Conrad's merchant ships. No saline odours, creaking timbers
or screeching steam whistles, but a facsimile of a bloodless
operating theatre, a chemist's laboratory lacking in smells or
fire.

hard/soft

Outside of playing with small dictaphones – recording
toilets flushing and similar primitive *musique concrète* experiments – my first experiences of recording took place in
eight-track studios, particularly Chalk Farm Studios, home of
one of the first eight-track machines in England. Chalk Farm
was owned by Vic Keary, a casually brilliant old-school engineer whose career began with tracks such as Emile Ford's
"What Do You Want To Make Those Eyes At Me For", one of
the earliest black British R&B hits. Keary's partner was the
extraordinary Emil Shallet, a fur-coated, cigar-chewing
East European refugee from the Nazis who fostered UK
interest in supposedly marginal musics – anything from hill-
billy, bebop and the New Orleans "Spooky Drums" of
Baby Dodds on Melodisc, to R&B and ska, via his Blue Beat
label and singles such as Prince Buster's "Al Capone", central
to the mod scene found in Soho's Flamingo club in the mid
1960s.

Shallet was a record man to place alongside some of the
American legends of the business. Notable among his business practices was the scam of selling otherwise unsaleable 7"
singles to pornographers who used them, improbably, as a
way of evading vice laws. I lived in his Shepherd's Bush house
for one week, until he threw me out in a fit of paranoia. In the
basement, I found Charlie Parker 78s on Vogue, Haitian voodoo records and Janis Joplin singles. At Chalk Farm, many
reggae records – "Young Gifted and Black", for example –
were cut, voiced or overdubbed with strings played by mid-
dle-aged Jewish violinists who had seen it all. There I met
Jimmy Cliff, Dandy Livingston and producer Lesley Kong, the
man who helped to launch Bob Marley's career and whose

heart gave out in 1971, his death rumoured to be the work of an Obeah man.

Working at Chalk Farm with percussionist Paul Burwell and a singer/songwriter named Simon Finn, I learned to add and to redo, playing instruments I had never touched before, layering arrangements with the tape machine. Eight tracks were never enough. This was the basis of so much of the progressive rock of the early 1970s. Add, add, add. For musicians and sound engineers, tape, particularly the 2" wide variety used for twenty-four-track recording, became the equivalent of paper for a writer. I remember the anxiety I felt as recording began to shift from analogue tape to computer sequencing and digital storage. Don't go into hard copy; stay soft. How sound could be printed on to tape was far from clear to me, yet this was how it was done. At least tape, curling and uncurling past the record heads of the machine, was a linear representation of music's duration. Computer sequencing packages pretended to be set up in the same way, but you would have to be stupid to think they were unreeling around the monitor screen. For a while, a psychological adjustment period, I felt the need to commit music to tape, as if this was proof that something was taking place. For musicians, this represents a paradox. Music is intangible, yet recording has added flesh and permanance, security, "continuity and depth to collective existence", as James Clifford wrote. Now musicians have to learn insubstantiality all over again. All that is solid melts into aether.

"Electric circuitry, an extension of the central nervous system", wrote Marshall McLuhan in his 1967 text/image collaboration with Quentin Fiore, *The Medium is the Massage*. "Media, by altering the environment, evoke in us unique ratios of sense perceptions. The extension of any one sense alters the way we think and act – the way we perceive the world. When these ratios change, men change." He meant everybody changes, not just men, but this was the 1960s.

So many wild, poorly conceptualised claims are being

made in this enthralling, unsettling transitional period between the era of print (from Gutenberg in 1450 to the present) and the current dawn of electronic culture, that there is a perverse temptation to reject them all. Some rejection, or scepticism, is pragmatic. Brian Eno is adamant that he will not have computers in the studio. "I don't use any programs", he tells me. "Do you know why it is? More than anything else, it's a physical reason. I've got SoundTools in my computer there, which I use as an editing system, but I get so fed up after working on it for a few hours. The only part of my finger that's engaged is my mouse finger and eyes. My body starts to feel so . . . oof, I just want to hit something or bounce around on the floor. My experience of computer mixing, which I've had more experience of than other forms of computer work, is that it creates a cautious, perfectionistic way of working. I've banned computers in the studio, actually. It isn't because I'm anti-computer. It's because nobody understands them well enough. It's happened to me so often that I'd be in the studio and there's a computer there running some sequencer aspects. You look round and the brow is knotted. Someone's saying, 'I think if we just put the SMPTE in there. Wait a minute, I've got to ID channel four . . .' and you know the session is blown. Because now the guitar player's gone off to make a phone call, the drummer's gone to the lavatory, the singer's starting reading some magazine article. The whole attention of the thing has gone. For me, the most important thing in the studio is to retain attention." In part, this must be generational. Brian is one year older than me. We grew up in an age when television was a novelty, reading was sacred, physical education was an obsession. We may be fools to resist, but then the blind acceptance of virtuality can lead to an airless, sexless world of cyber-utopia. Maybe the generational conflict can remind us of more significant struggles: the tepid image of a smart rocket floating down a street, guided to its target in a virtual world, contrasted with photographs of war horrors in the non-virtual domain.

So virtuality is not paradise. But then Eno describes a process which applies conceptual ordering in the digital domain to a random sequence of ambient sounds: "There's an experiment I did. Since I did it, I started to think it was quite a good exercise that I would recommend to other people. I had taken a DAT recorder to Hyde Park and near Bayswater Road I recorded a period of whatever sound was there: cars going by, dogs, people. I thought nothing much of it and I was sitting at home listening to it on my player. I suddenly had this idea. What about if I take a section of this – a 3½-minute section, the length of a single – and I tried to learn it? So that's what I did. I put it in SoundTools and I made a fade-up, let it run for 3½ minutes and faded it out. I started listening to this thing, over and over. Whenever I was sitting there working, I would have this thing on. I printed it on a DAT twenty times or something, so it just kept running over and over. I tried to learn it, exactly as one would a piece of music: oh yeah, that car, accelerates the engine, the revs in the engine go up and then that dog barks, and then you hear that pigeon off to the side there. This was an extremely interesting exercise to do, first of all because I found that you can learn it. Something that is as completely arbitrary and disconnected as that, with sufficient listenings, becomes highly connected. You can really imagine that this thing was constructed somehow: 'Right, then he puts this bit there and that pattern's just at the exact same moment as this happening. Brilliant!' Since I've done that, I can listen to lots of things in quite a different way. It's like putting oneself in the role of an art perceiver, just deciding, now I'm playing that role."

6   altered states I: landscape

*Brian Eno; Bill Laswell; Don Cherry; Derek
Bailey; Leo Smith; ambient; John Cage; Harold
Budd; Daniel Lanois; Japanese sound design*

The Wall Street Journal reports a worldwide crisis
amongst teachers, who claim that *The Mighty Morphin Power
Rangers* television show has colonised the imaginations of
their young charges more completely than any previous
childrens' craze. At Kedren Headstart Preschool, Los Angeles,
one teacher now plays "soothing music" to dampen enthusiasm for *kung fu* kicks in the classroom.

landscape

Brian Eno is talking to me about a man named Louis
Sarno. He describes the strange way in which Sarno apparently began to shrink after living with Ba-Benjellé pygmies in
the Central African Republic rainforest. Enthusiastically, he
describes beautiful audio tapes Sarno made of Ba-Benjellé
music, recorded by the unusual method of sitting hidden in
the trees, far away from the central sound source so that the
music was subsumed within a wider landscape of insect and
bird voices, domestic sounds from the village, the sound of air
and tape noise. Shortly after, I buy a Dutch fanzine, devoted
solely to Lee Perry. On a one-page advert for a mail-order
company selling Perry albums, four cassettes of Bayaka
pygmy music, recorded by Sarno, are advertised. Finally I find
Sarno's book, *Song from the Forest*, in one of the bookshops
lining the route between Oxford railway station and the

extraordinary Pitt Rivers Museum, home of shamanic costumes, false-face masks, fetish objects, spirit sculptures, bullroarers from Devon and twentieth-century witchcraft spells, charms and curses from deepest Sussex. The first sentence of the book says "I was drawn to the heart of Africa by a song." Sarno had turned on his radio in Amsterdam and heard the liquid polyphony of Central African pygmy singing. Out of an epiphanic moment grew a desire to travel in search of more of this music. "One quiet night the deep tones of a drum came throbbing through the forest from a great distance", Sarno writes. " '*Ejengi*,' Mobo remarked from his hut, and we lay there in the dark, listening to the faint tattoo that seemed to merge with the natural pulsation of the night itself."

For the sleevenotes to *On Land* (written 1982, revised 1986; music recorded between 1978 and 1982), Brian Eno talked about a relationship between the psychoacoustic space of the recording studio and the depiction or evocation of landscape. The potential of using SoundTools hard-disk editing software for making music out of random, ambient sounds was fomenting back then. "When I was in Ghana", he wrote, "I took with me a stereo microphone and a cassette recorder, ostensibly to record indigenous music and speech patterns. What I sometimes found myself doing instead was sitting out on the patio in the evenings with the microphone placed to pick up the widest possible catchment of ambient sounds from all directions, and listening to the results on my headphones. The effect of this simple technological system was to cluster all the disparate sounds into one aural frame: they became music." This pushed him towards a new conception of music as a soundfield, and away from the objectification of sound structures into fixed compositions. But studio technology had grown out of performance. To Eno's ears, the dominant trend in recording was towards "greater proximity, tighter and more coherent meshing of sounds with one another".

eternal drift at Lizard Point

Bass player Bill Laspell remembers those *On Land* sessions. For one whole summer in New York City, he worked with Brian on material that would be improvised, edited, then processed into a part of the album. "One by one he fired everybody and it was just me and him", Laswell tells me. "We would go to Canal Street and we'd buy junk – those hoses you twirl around – and gravel, put it in a box and put reverb on it. All these weird things to make sounds. We'd be in this bathroom with these overhead mikes, making sounds for days. A friend of mine was a photographer from Chile [Felipe Orrego]. He got these tapes of frogs and the frogs sounded like an orchestra. There was like thousands of them but they had it totally hooked up. Occasionally one would start a riff – it's like Monkey Chant [Balinese *ketjak* singing] where one voice will start and the rest will jump in. Eno really was into that tape and that's all over that record."

theatre of signs

Don Cherry is sitting on the floor of the front room of his narrow first-floor apartment in San Francisco wearing a maroon tracksuit and Chinese slippers. On the walls: a Robert Wilson poster, a photograph of the legendary Five Spot jazz club. Floor, seats and tables are covered with musical instruments – an electric keyboard, a tiny pocket trumpet, seed pods from Latin America, Indian tabla drums. Don's mind and body dart from one autobiographical landmark to the next. He talks about the Watts Towers – tall, weirdly elegant spikes of wire, scrap steel, pottery fragments built over a period of thirty-three years, from 1921 to 1954, by an Italian–American named Simon Rodia. "They said he was crazy", laughs Cherry, "then they tried to say he was a spy. That it was an antenna, you know, when Mussolini got strong. He'd work at night. I remember when I was young I used to pass there." He leafs through folders, a suitcase full of unrealised projects, notebooks, scrapbooks – photographs of Don with Dennis

Hopper, Yohji Yamamoto, John Lurie, Ornette Coleman (both of them wearing shiny Italian suits), Manu Dibango, Carlos Santana. He taps a cigarette incessantly but never lights it; then his hands flutter over the tabla. You keep up or lose his interest. In the 1960s, Don lived in Scandinavia for a while, organising communal music sessions, eating brown rice, living with Moki, who made banners. The music could sound like Terry Riley, a deep John Coltrane meditation, a SeneGambian griot's narrative, or one of Dollar Brand's (now Abdullah Ibrahim) heartlifting tunes. According to Jan Garbarek, the late Albert Ayler travelled to the far north of Norway and Sweden in search of folk music and shamanistic songs. Garbarek hears some of that music in Ayler's spirit hymns. When Don visited Oslo in 1964, Garbarek and his friends were influenced by Coltrane. The nomadic trumpet player from America made them aware of the significance of their own traditions. "We were invited to do a radio recording", Garbarek tells me, "and I remember Don was asking us to bring along a folk singer. Of course, we knew these performers and their music, but to combine it with improvisation in that way was something we had never considered."

For black American improvisers such as Don Cherry and the Art Ensemble of Chicago, and at roughly the same time their European and white American counterparts in AMM, Musica Electronica Viva, Joseph Holbrook, Music Improvisation Company, Nuova Consonanza and the Spontaneous Music Ensemble, a partial move away from the major instruments of jazz and classical music performance was an expression of politics as much as music. From the mid 1960s into the disillusioned 1970s, little instruments and non-instruments (transistor radios, contact microphones amplifying tiny sounds or surface noises extracted from tables, beards, cheese graters, etc.) became symbols of the drive to democratise music, to allow access to unskilled players (including children), draw sound from instruments rather than subjugate them to systems, open the music up to chance events and create a sense of collectively organised community as an attempted break from hard professionalism, particularly the star system that afflicted both jazz groups and classical performers.

The atomisation that took place in the wake of the early improvisation groups was interesting in itself: environmental music pursued by Alvin Curran of MEV; music for political resistance explored by Frederic Rzewski of MEV and AMM's Cardew and Rowe; ethnomusicology by MEV's Ivan Vandor; film music by spaghetti-western composer Ennio Morricone, a member of Italy's Nuova Consonanza; Tibetan Buddhism by MIC's Jamie Muir and Christine Jeffries; radical black politics and Rastafarianism by AACM's Leo Smith; open work and minimalist composing by Joseph Holbrook's Gavin Bryars; extraordinarily wide-ranging composing by Anthony Braxton, another Chicago AACM member; live electronics by MEV's Richard Teitelbaum and a dedication to improvisation from Derek Bailey, Evan Parker, Eddie Prevost, Lou Gare and Tony Oxley. It was as if the ideals of open artworks and open society converged for a moment, no matter how incompatible their specific intent, and then splintered into more focused, or in some cases more dogmatic, channels which suited the individual rather than the group.

For guitarist Derek Bailey, a participant in this early development of free improvisation as well as a documenter of its various forms in his book *Improvisation: Its Nature and Practice In Music*, improvisation is distinguished by a rare capacity to embrace such diversity. "One of the things that marks its quality," he says, "and in the right mood I might even claim its superiority as a musical activity, is its scope. It can accommodate virtually anybody. I first came to this kind of playing through working with two musicians with national and geographic similarities, but in every other way totally different characters. That was Tony Oxley and Gavin Bryars. I worked with them for nearly three years and I was struck throughout that time and increasingly as time went on, how extraordinary it was that these two guys could work together. They never have since because their approach to music was quite different. It struck me that the productiveness of that period, for me anyway, came from this disparity between aesthetic approaches. This freely improvised aesthetic seemed not only to accommodate different attitudes and approaches but it actually produced better results if you had that. When you've got ill-fitting elements, it's almost as though the rubbing together of the elements in order to make it work – the old analogy – produces a pearl."

Was it an accident of history that free improvisation, with its embrace of noise, "illegitimate" instruments, elements of theatre, non-hierarchical organisation and the chance interventions of environmental sounds, coincided with the full emergence of semiotics – the science of signs – as a recognised area of study? Roland Barthes's *Mythologies*, written in 1957 but first published in Britain in 1972, Thomas A. Sebeok's *Zoosemiotics* (the study of animal sounds, ritualisations and other communication forms), published in 1972, and Umberto Eco's *A Theory of Semiotics*, published in preliminary form in 1967 and then in English in 1976, all dwelled upon ideas that were being enacted by improvisers: Barthes's analysis of toys, wrestling and striptease, for example, or Eco's assertion – "One can hardly conceive of a world in which certain beings communicate without verbal language, restricting themselves to gestures, objects, unshaped sounds, tunes or tap-dancing; but it is equally hard to conceive of a world in which certain beings only utter words" – provided a counterpoint to the reformation of music as a field in which all sounds, silences, gestures and actions were "the music". In fact, Umberto Eco had written a number of essays on open form aesthetics in the early 1960s. These were collected in one book entitled *The Open Work*. "In the modern scientific universe", he wrote, "as in architecture and in Baroque pictorial production, the various component parts are all endowed with equal value and dignity, and the whole construct expands towards a totality which is close to the infinite. It refuses to be hemmed in by any ideal normative conception of the world. It shares in a general urge toward discovery and constantly renewed contact with reality."

The influences which led to a point where music threw aside so many conventions have been fiercely contested and often wrongly attributed. Each person's contact with reality was very different yet, for a moment, similar conclusions were being reached. With hindsight, it seems simpler to say that established categorisations of art, science, society, nature and culture, were inadequate to new needs. "One of things of the time", says Bailey, "was a dissatisfaction with orthodox forms of music making. They were OK, but there seemed to be a lot of things they weren't saying. I think that applied to other people. They were looking for ways of saying things that weren't being said. This was a time when popular music had exploded so it was a bit strange to be pursuing an alternative practice, although there was room for it as well."

Many ideas and methods from the past were interweaving at the same time, enabling certain barriers to be crossed and certain correspondences to be misinterpreted, both in their sources and their intentions. In *As Serious As Your Life*, Valerie Wilmer quotes Leo Smith's denial of any influence from John Cage. Just as Cage seemed unaware or resistant to any correspondences between his innovations and those in jazz, so musicians like Smith saw their experimentation – including his use of all kinds of sound-making devices to supplement his trumpet playing – as being part of a broader African–American tradition. "He also plays sealhorn, zither, autoharp, harmonica, recorder, wooden and metal flutes and whistles", Wilmer writes, "and one of those old-fashioned rubber 'squeeze' car-horns. He is carrying on a Southern tradition that started with children banging on washboards and tin-cans, blowing down pieces of rubber-hose and strumming wires stretched between nails on a wall, a tradition deeply rooted in Africa." Roscoe Mitchell's *Sound*, recorded in

Chicago in 1966 with a sextet that included trumpeter Lester Bowie and bass player Malachi Favors, is an excellent example of the complete departure from free jazz and its propulsive expressionism. "Sound" and "The Little Suite" both explore cries and whispers at the edge of instruments, many of the sounds allowed to develop quietly in solo space or oblique duets, rhythm used as a colour, an emphasis, part of an aural theatre of signs.

complexity

January 1975. Striated images banging up and down the screen of a portable colour television, colour layered out of register. The smell of sour milk. Too ill to stand for long, Brian Eno collapses back into bed.

My first contact with Brian came in 1974, after I had edited a small book called *New/Rediscovered Musical Instruments*, a brief survey of UK experimental instrument building featuring the work of Hugh Davies, Max Eastley, Paul Burwell, Evan Parker, Paul Lytton and myself. Madeau Stewart contributed an introduction. As a sound archive producer for BBC radio, she broadcast programmes that listeners like myself found inspiring – a survey of ritual instruments by folk-music authority A.L. Lloyd, for example. She was also responsible for items that other BBC listeners found peculiar, including talks by myself and Max Eastley, and a project of her own which involved rowing out to sea with a glum engineer employed to record broadcast quality tapes of her flute duets with seals. After the first of my talks – a twenty-minute mix of New Guinea and Brazilian sacred flutes, Balinese *genggong* frog dance music, Amazon rainforest chants, Malaysian shamanism, Korean ceremonial music, brainfever birds, beluga and bat sounds broadcast in 1972 – a letter came from Africa. A man had heard the programme, presumably on the World Service, and he and his two dogs had been greatly puzzled. I envisaged a raddled character in some remote colonial outpost, something like Almayer in Joseph Conrad's *Almayer's*

Folly, one hand on the bottle, the other twiddling the radio
tuner, hearing Korean music sent from London to the African
bush. Perhaps this stereotypical image was wildly inaccurate,
yet even as recently as the early 1970s the global mix was a
novelty.

"Suddenly we are enjoined to hear and listen to our present
environment with greater attention", Madeau wrote in her introduction to *New/Rediscovered Musical Instruments*. "From
the materials about us we are encouraged – *all* of us are encouraged – to conjure up the latent music. Some of this music
would be familiar to people on other, distant continents
whose musical life we are so successfully destroying. Where
isolated tribes used insects as buzzers attached to or trapped
in some casually cut length of local wood, so the new instrument makers – who are also composers – casually adapt a
clock spring or an ex-army shell case as a sound maker. (Incidentally, a society surrounded by disposable or throw-away
goods is not new.)."

So Brian and I talked on the telephone and then he came to
see a performance. Max Eastley performed solo on his own
sound sculptures (demonstrating, at one point, the spectral
crackling of a Purple Ray Vitalator, a device from the 1920s
which energised the skin with electrical sparks, allegedly);
Paul Burwell and I played an improvised duo on percussion,
flutes and electric guitar. Brian fell asleep, but claimed this
was a compliment.

For almost every musician searching for ways to step outside the boundaries, an interest in invented or expanded
sound technology is inevitable. After leaving Roxy Music,
Eno's approach to rock-tech had expanded beyond the VCS-3
synthesiser to embrace the notion that all devices used to create music, including the environment itself, were musical
instruments. In February 1973, for example, he had contributed a sleevenote to Basil Kirchin's second album, *Worlds
Within Worlds*. Kirchin was an oddball musician who, like
painter Alan Davie, floated around the edges of Britain's grow-

ing free improvisation scene. He had already achieved the impossible by persuading EMI Records to release the first volume of *Worlds Within Worlds* in 1971. This mixed amplified, slowed-down tapes of animal, bird and insect cries with the playing of saxophonist Evan Parker, guitarist Derek Bailey and others. "I, personally, find that it helps deliberately to induce a state of self-hypnosis by playing back somewhat louder than the norm", Kirchin suggested on the sleeve of the record. "In fact, as loud as you or the equipment can stand! In this way one can 'swim under water' in, and 'breathe in' the music." His second album was released by Island Records during a period when the company was exploring proto-New Age and ambient electronica material such as Henry Wolff and Nancy Hennings's *Tibetan Bells* and David Vorhaus's *White Noise*. The raw materials for this one included gorilla and hornbill vocalisations, noises of the docks in Hull and sounds made by autistic children. "I first heard about Basil Kirchin", Brian wrote for his sleevenote, "whilst investigating the possibility of compiling an album of music produced on hybrid instruments – handbells, steel bands, percussive voices, drinking glasses, etc." That album never appeared, but the line between rock orthodoxy and the future was clearly visible.

Then Brian was knocked down and seriously injured by a taxi whilst crossing the Harrow Road. While he was recovering, I visited him in his Maida Vale flat. Judy Nylon had visited him, he told me, and left a record of eighteenth-century harp music. He had put the album on the deck, dropped the stylus and fallen back into bed. Once there, he discovered that the volume was almost too low for him to be able to hear the music. One stereo channel was missing also, but since he was barely able to move, he left it as it was and listened. As he did so, an alternative mode of hearing unfolded. Rather than standing out from its environment, like a ship on an ocean, the music became part of that ocean, alongside all the other transient effects of light, shade, colour, scent, taste and sound. So ambient was born, in its present definition at least: music that we hear but don't hear; sounds which exist to enable us better to hear silence; sound which rests us from our intense compulsion to focus, to analyse, to frame, to catagorise, to isolate.

silence

When Death's chauffeur turns on the car radio in Jean Cocteau's film *Orphée*, a voice from the underworld recites disconnected lines of enigmatic poetry and strings of numbers. The first line we hear in the film is "Silence is twice as fast backwards . . . three times."

John Cage's *4' 33"* was premiered in 1952. The piece required a musician to present a timed performance at an instrument without making a sound. David Tudor gave this first performance on piano, using a stopwatch to time the three sections, marking the beginning and end of the piece by lowering and finally raising the piano lid without ever touching the keys. For this reason, the work is often assumed to have been composed for piano, whereas Cage instructed in his score that any instrument could be (not) played. The piano is one of the easiest options, since the exaggerated theatre of sitting and preparing to play, practised by most concert pianists and parodied to perfection by comedian Max Wall, provides a clear way of showing that something is being performed.

4' 33" is often referred to colloquially as *Silence*, on the mistaken assumption that this was a Zen demonstration of nothingness. But Cage had discovered the non-existence of silence in Harvard University's anechoic chamber, a soundproof room without any reflective surfaces where he sat and heard the high singing note of his nervous system and the deep pulsing of his blood.

Nothing happens in *4' 33"* except for a growing awareness of the immediate sound environment. I have a recorded version, performed by pianist Gianni-Emilio Simonetti and released by the Italian Cramps label in 1974. The idea seems ridiculous yet, for the first time, I listened to the surface noise of a bad vinyl pressing from Italy with interest rather than irritation. In his sleevenotes to Cage's *Variations IV*, Joseph Byrd referred to Morse Peckham's book, *Man's Rage for Chaos*; in particular, his definition of art that is consistent with the rest of contemporary life as being "any perceptual field which an individual uses as an occasion for performing the role of art perceiver". *4' 33"* directed listeners towards this situation and, in its literally quiet influence, this work in which there is no tangible work has done so ever since.

Cage's subtle awareness of the silence which surrounds sounds is at its most refined in his compositions for prepared piano, an experiment which began as an expedient way of creating a percussion orchestra in a dance space too small for anything other than a piano. "Mutes of various materials are placed between the strings of the keys used," he instructed, "thus effecting transformations of the piano sounds with respect to all of their characteristics." The brief but exquisite *Prelude for Meditation* and *Music for Marcel Duchamp*, or the longer work, *Sonatas and Interludes for Prepared Piano*, sound sometimes Javanese, sometimes Balinese. Clashing harmonics ring out, muted wood and gong sounds hang in reverberation or shadow each other in delicate pursuits which quicken and slow, tumble over themselves or abruptly stop, leaving only their decaying echo.

The *Sonatas and Interludes* were written during a period when Cage first began reading works of Japanese and Indian philosophy, so the piece was an attempt to reflect the "permanant emotions" of India and their "common tendency toward tranquility". He had also been attending the New School for Social Research in New York, where he became an assistant to composer Henry Cowell for his classes in non-Western, folk and contemporary music. It was Cowell, in fact, who had influenced Cage into preparing the piano. Cowell had played inside the piano, rubbing a darning egg along the strings, and Cage took this further by filling the inside of the piano with newspapers, magazines, plates and ashtrays. The method had precedents in Indian and African distortions of flute, percussion, thumb piano and stringed instrument sounds with buzzers or rattling objects such as bottle tops. The voice disguiser, or mirliton, extended this principle to a materialisation of the spirit world, transforming the ordinary human voice into something strange and supernatural by means of vibrating membranes or mirlitons (the instruments of darkness again). In a sense, Cage was subjecting the identifiable materials of art to a process which transported them to a sacred domain. Later, he refined the method to a point where preparation with wood screws, bolts and weather stripping might take long periods of precise adjustments. "My guess is", wrote John Tilbury for the sleevenotes of his 1975 recording of the *Sonatas and Interludes*, "that Cage simply selected his preparations from the junk he had lying about his apartment and in his pockets. He experimented and, having obtained a pleasing sound, measured the distances. I confess I work in this spirit." Tilbury also questioned the credibility of Cage's claims for the "permanant emotions of India". The claim for "permanant emotions" certainly seems false in the light of Cage's wider beliefs in chance operations and non-fixity, yet his prepared piano pieces transmit to the listener a quality that is quite unlike his other work, and powerful in its capacity to induce a calmness of being.

Variations IV was another prophetic composition. There are amusing parallels with the idea of the chill-out room, the room in which multiple signals feed into one embalming composite, except for the fact that Cage's piece, realised with the help of David Tudor, was an indigestible barrage of noise. Recorded for its 1969 record release in two rooms of an art gallery on La Cienaga Boulevard in Los Angeles, the music is a chaotic blitz of distorted conversation, distant chat, disconnected musical fragments and room ambience throughout. Traffic sounds were fed in from outside. A spoken introduction to the album advises us to: "Listen closely and you will hear the sounds of the audience as well as the tinkle of glasses as the mike over the bar was in use." (A similar idea was used to hilarious effect for *The Roxy London WC2 (Jan–Apr 77)*, the first live punk album.) "Records and previous recorded tapes," the droning voice at the beginning of *Variations IV* continues, "as well as radio broadcasts, are mixed in during the concert . . . as John Cage has said, 'Music is all around us. If only we had ears. There would be no need for concert halls if man could learn to enjoy the sounds that envelop him, for example, at 7th Street and Broadway, at 4 p.m. on a rainy day' . . ." And Joseph Byrd, writing for the album cover, added the perfect synthesis of ambient theory: "What is happening is a synthesis of the music and sound we normally hear in snatches: the elevator's ride worth of Muzak, the passing conversation, and the automobile argument all mingle freely with Beethoven and the Balinese *gender wayang*."

Cage was probably the first to use the expression "Imaginary Landscape", with his series of pieces dating from 1939. These were composed for a variety of sound-making devices: variable-speed turntables, frequency recordings, percussion, radios and, in *Imaginary Landscape No. 5*, forty-two recordings from any source, reassembled in fragments as an electronic tape collage structured according to chance methods determined by the Chinese book of changes, the *I Ching*.

The imaginary landscape, in Cage's world a place in which forms and features are allowed to emerge and coexist regardless of the personal desires of the imaginer, has come to be a central compositional device in the ambient music that has followed Brian Eno's initiative. Imaginary landscapes figured large in his work after his accident. Music, if peripheral, has the key to unlock new visions in the same way that a dream which eludes us when we try to remember its details may be retriggered unexpectedly in an unfocused moment. As Brian's songwriting fell away, so the space was filled by sonic landscapes, evocations of meteorology, natural forms and their transitional states: the second tape loop album recorded with Robert Fripp, *Evening Star*, with titles such as "Wind On

Water" and "Wind On Wind"; the electronic vignettes recorded with David Bowie on *Low* and *Heroes* – particularly "Neuköln", "Warszawa", a Steve Reich-influenced "Weeping Wall" and the Orientalist "Moss Garden"; the submarine and arboreal tracks on *Another Green World*; "Slow Water", "Events In Dense Fog" and "Final Sunset" on the *Music For Films* album; and his records with Jon Hassell, Harold Budd and Daniel Lanois.

virgin beauty

"[C]hildren, parents and grandparents gathered by the Grebe, Radiola, or Aeriola set in the radio room and marvelled at the sounds they heard transported mysteriously from faraway lands ... Radio was hailed as the world's greatest source of knowledge, the creation of international harmony, and the invention that would stop all wars. Those who had radio sets spent the better part of their days and evenings tuned in to the voices from the ether ... Listeners who bought radio sets were sometimes disappointed, though. Shrieks, grunts, groans, and cross talks ruled the airwaves, which were described by some as a hertzian bedlam."

Gene Fowler and Bill Crawford, *Border Radio*

Harold Budd was born in Los Angeles in 1936, and as children he and his brother absorbed their father's romantic infatuation with the western frontier. Subsequently, they were brought up by another family in a tiny Mojave Desert town named Victorville; a "dogwater town" is the way Budd describes it. "You could walk in any direction as long as you wanted, forever", he says. "It isn't like there aren't people around, but you're alone enough, and it's quiet enough, where you can stand and hear the sound of utterly nothing at all." What fugitive sounds existed came from a gust of wind or a radio picking up The Sons of the Pioneers from signals transmitted across the Mexican border. Some of this desertbound silence, spooked by shrieks and crosstalk from other worlds, was later bottled and resold in albums such as *Lovely Thunder* (1986) and *By the Dawn's Early Light* (1991). This was music for a saloon abandoned save for beatnik gunslingers; William Burroughs waving a Colt 45 at the ghost of Geronimo from a table in the corner; Gregory Corso shuffling cards, delivering drunken monologues at the bar; the faint echo from outside of Allen Ginsberg's harmonium drifting with the tumble-weeds. The music is saturated with memories of place, but with its myths, also. "I admit that's there", says Harold. "I get the same feeling with the music that I do in that geographical situation. But one doesn't express the other. It's not a one-to-one relationship."

Budd's landscapes were not necessarily Arcadian. Pieces like *Dark Star* and *Abandoned Cities* (both 1984), for example, were cold slabs of opaque colour: Rothko paintings as reworked by Ad Reinhardt; an ominous drift. Yet his 1978 album for Brian Eno's Obscure label, *The Pavilion of Dreams*, conjures a gorgeous, translucent mirage. Featuring Marion Brown's alto saxophone, and including compositions inspired by Pharoah Sanders's "Let Us Go Into the House of the Lord" and John Coltrane's "After the Rain", this collection of five pieces reminds us of a forgotten dimension of free jazz, the meditational point of temporary rest where sorrow, battered optimism, devotion and spiritual ecstasy melted together. Listen to John Coltrane's "Expression", Albert Ayler's "Going Home" from his 1964 album of spirituals, "Venus" by Pharoah Sanders, or a much later example, the spectral cry of Ornette Coleman's alto saxophone, floating over Prime Time's strange tunings and decomposing drum machines, along with his own slithering violin, on "Virgin Beauty". Another source for the post-minimalist improvising composer.

In the late 1950s and early 1960s Budd performed duets with tenorist Ayler when both of them served in the same army unit in Ford Ord, California. Describing himself as a jazz snob who tracked down Charles Ives or Hindemith recordings only if jazz musicians mentioned them in interview, Budd played with Ayler in the marching band, giving weekly radio broadcasts from the base. "It seemed better to me than shooting guns", he says. Two strangers in a strange land, they would make forays into the hipper clubs of Monterey and Oakland. Budd played drums, a consequence of his father's love for martial music. "My job was to make a wall of sound", he says, "and it was exhausting but of course, being in the army, I was in great physical shape. Later on, when he used Sunny Murray as a drummer, I got a better idea about what he was after, which I couldn't do." So, in a momentary intersection of seemingly opposite musical viewpoints, Budd spoke in tongues with one of the elevated spirits of 1960s' jazz: Albert Ayler, found floating in the East River, New York City, 1970, after taking his own life.

wilderness

A London hotel, 1990. Daniel Lanois and I sit at a cramped corner table in a claustrophobic basement restaurant. He claps his hands. "This would be a good place to record."

Lanois describes *The Pearl,* Budd and Eno's collaborative album, as a "chilling record". For Lanois, this is a great compliment, since his talent for creating virtual landscapes in the studio is placed at the service of strong emotional performances. "I've chosen to let people be the driving force", he says, "rather than a machine. Recording for me these days can happen anywhere, as long as the place feels good." So with Lanois producing, or co-producing with Eno, U2's *The Unforgettable Fire* was recorded in Dublin's Slane Castle, Peter Gabriel's *So* in the studio control room and The Neville Brothers' *Yellow Moon* in a rented warehouse in New Orleans. Whatever the setting, mysterious atmospheres – mystic forests, bayous and swamp, the echoes from sheer cliff walls – suffuse the finished results.

Lanois learned his trade in the basement of his mother's house in Canada. As teenagers, he and his brother, Bob, set up a studio underneath their mother's bedroom and began recording an educational mixture of local folk, gospel, country music and rhythm'n'blues. At the end of the 1970s, Brian Eno heard a tape recorded by Lanois and booked time at the studio. It was the beginning of a fruitful partnership. Eno enjoyed the cottage industry atmosphere in which the brothers worked. "It had that feeling of people doing their best with what they had", says Lanois, "which is a great quality in art." Together they worked on a number of instrumental albums, creating striking spatial effects by shrouding sounds in layered echoes. These techniques, developed to enhance such albums as *The Pearl*, Jon Hassell's *Dream Theory In Malaya* and Brian Eno's *Apollo* soundtrack (composed with Lanois and Roger Eno) to *For All Mankind*, Al Reinert's film of the Apollo space missions, later found a more commercial setting with U2, Gabriel and Bob Dylan.

The course of U2's musical evolution is interesting if seen as an integral part of the studio process. Initially, the Lanois spaces and atmospheres enhance U2's stance as a "mythical", fixed unit. For fans (though not me), the band is magisterial, epic, the essence of rock. Gradually, the full implications of opening the music up to studio virtuality erodes this epic solidity. Under the influence of Lanois, Eno and Flood, the band's *Achtung Baby* and *Zooropa* albums deconstruct, somewhat self-consciously, into lurid, lo-fi grab images of urban dissonance and media overload, closer to Bowie's *Low* than the hyperbole of *The Unforgettable Fire*.

I asked Lanois if childhood images had shaped his talent for depicting ghostly resonances and far horizons. "The railway tracks, the hydro lines, the paths that are cut through the forest to accommodate industrial power cables", he answered. "You'll be in the wilderness and suddenly you come to this open space where it's almost like God came down with a hair clipper and just cut through the forest and laid in a power hydro line. Those images are strong for me. Then hearing a train in the distance and putting pennies on the railtracks. Flattening them and going back to look at them. Kid's stuff but great images. Taking the boat out on a calm lake. Smokestacks from a distance. In Hamilton, where I grew up, in Canada, it's a steel city. It's a bit like Pittsburgh. In the dead of winter at night this area would be lit up like a Christmas tree and then the smoke would be blasting out of the furnaces. Fire and smoke. Because it's so cold, as soon as the heat touches the sky, it just bursts into steam. I love those images. Industrial, but still people images."

nature into music

In 1989, Brian Eno was invited to compose and perform a new work for the consecration of the Tenkawa Shinto shrine near Kyoto. The head priest of the monastery was an admirer of Brian's music and owned every record he had made. In his preparatory notes for the performance Brian considers musical equivalents for the shrine's significance as a receiver of spiritual energy. "It occured to me", he wrote, "that it would make sense to think of the performance as a way of receiving and digesting and then re-presenting various acoustic phenomena in the valley." He explores ideas of amplifying and mixing ambient sounds in concentric circles ranging from the very edge of the valley to the focus point of the shrine itself, proposing the use of fireworks, little instruments such as clickers and whirling tubes, steam, burning fuses, the sounds of work and the hum of lights on dimmers. Later, he mentions the approach used to record *On Land* and finds a congruence in Joseph Campbell's observations on Shinto: "[L]iving Shinto is not the following of some set-down moral code, but a living in gratitude and awe amid the mystery of things . . . it is incorrect to say that Shinto lacks moral ideas. The basic moral idea is that the processes of nature cannot be evil."

"Maybe that's why the head monk likes my records", Brian muses. "He feels there's some Shinto in there already perhaps. Certainly the notion of the continuum from nature into music is very appropriate."

continuum

In 1977, Paul Burwell and I gave a six-hour performance in a huge Butler's Wharf warehouse overlooking the
Thames. Now the site of expensive restaurants and riverside
apartments, Butler's Wharf was a warren of artists' studios
during the 1970s, where Derek Jarman filmed and musicians
ranging from Michael Nyman to Wayne County & The Electric
Chairs and The Rich Kids played at parties. The freezing cold
at the time of our duo performance slowed our actions, but
the knowledge that there was no fixed duration meant that
each sound could linger in the silence, sometimes augmented
by distant hooting from the river. Darkness closed in until the
only light came from slide projections. Paul stretched piano
wires across the empty space and suspended packing cases,
milk churns, glass rods and waste bins from them. I don't remember the sound, but in a *Melody Maker* review, Steve Lake
wrote: "Bowing and plucking the wires, or even running the
fingers along them, produces the most extraordinary noises.
Like howling feedback or the singing of sea cows (the source,
you'll recall, of the legend of the Sirens)." Evan Parker, then
increasingly investigating extended durations and continuous
music through his circular breathing and multiphonic techniques for soprano saxophone, came to listen. He proposed
an idea for a twenty-four-hour concert and this was organised,
finally, for the penultimate night of Music/Context, an environmental music festival I organised the following year. The
group – Parker, Burwell, myself, Hugh Davies, Paul Lytton,
Paul Lovens, Annabel Nicolson and Max Eastley – played for
thirteen hours before running into a wall of exhaustion and
an overwhelming feeling that there was nothing more to add.
In hindsight, I think there were too many distractions and too
many players. Incus Records released a single album –
Circadian Rhythm – edited down from those thirteen hours.

shadows

"What lies within the darkness one cannot distinguish, but the palm senses the gentle movements of the liquid, vapour rises from within forming droplets on the rim, and the fragrence carried upon the vapour brings a delicate anticipation."

Jun'Ichiro Tanizaki, *In Praise of Shadows*

A small party in a Yokohama restaurant: two sound sculptors – Minoru Sato and Max Eastley, a bass player, a theatre manageress, a traditional dancer, a Butoh dancer, two noise musicians – Masami Akita of Merzbow (as well as the brilliantly named Bust Monster and Kinbiken bondage videos) and Fumio Kosakai of Incapacitants, plus myself. "Mister David", says Mr Kosakai, the black-suited gentleman kneeling opposite me. He bows low and wrestles with a few words of English, concluding with an inconclusive "Circadian Rhythm". A question? "Incus Records", I reply, getting drunk on *sake* and beer, slightly queasy after eating *natto,* a fermented bean concoction of unsettling stickiness and smell. "What do you do?" I ask, instantly dismayed by my pathetic conversation. "Noise music", he answers, miming what could be the action of dismembering a moose with a power saw. "*Maximum* volume. But I love nature sounds too."

For Westerners, this openness to extremes of noise and quietude is regarded as a contradiction, filed under clichés: Japan, or rationalised as a consequence of the complex ethical and religious foundations of Japanese beliefs and behaviour; the Shinto belief that "the processes of nature cannot be evil"; the Confucian virtues of imitative learning and social co-operation; the Buddhist tenet that everything is Buddha. So moral judgements and oppositional categorisations imposed on noise and silence, or human and machine, are less clear cut in Japan. Trying to understand the Otaku – young technocratic fanatics who collect information for its own sake – in his *Speed Tribes* book, Karl Taro Greenfield concludes that "the Japanese maintain a different relationship with their technology than the West. They simply view their PC or television as another object, like a rock or a tree or a kimono, which is of nature and hence of themselves." This is why encounters with such apparent oddities as shrines piled up with lavatory brushes are not uncommon in Japan, or why Buddhist priests pray for worn-out microchips. Everything is Buddha.

Sound design plays an important role in the constant movement that characterises Japanese street society and public spaces, but nature is encoded within microchips and the vaporous world whose passing was lamented by Jun'Ichiro Tanizaki is blasted by noise levels of striking insensitivity. Traffic signals chirp ornithologically or play synthesised folk tunes; water sounds rush along tunnels; sliding gates on the Shinkansen "bullet train" platforms play computer game melodies; deranged loops of hard-sell hysteria blare from the doorways of electronic discount shops; brief cycles of background music repeat endlessly in food supermarkets, as if to create a subconscious time limit between the moment of picking up a basket, shopping and then arriving at the check-out to pay; in hotel rooms, easy listening muzak plays until silenced and in the corridors, Mantovani's "Charmaine" floats in ancient clouds of sleeping gas.

Not all Japanese greet these fractures and earsores with approval. At NADI sound design laboratory in Kobe, Yoshihiro Kawasaki records ambient sounds, collaborating with sound artists such as the American Bill Fontana and Germany's Rolf Julius, as well as participating in a remarkable radio project called St GIGA. "I made sound systems for public spaces", says Kawasaki, explaining his entry into the sound world. "At the time I thought, how about sound? Music has power or force, or it says something. Environmental sound has some kind of force, but not so strong. I started to think about the sound surrounding me. In Japan, there are a lot of spaces where music plays, like the Muzak system. It's a kind of masking. Now I think it's too much. Now we must start to think again about environmental sound. In the big station at

Osaka, in the morning they play bird singing. Sometimes it is very strange. People rush to their companies. They don't speak, they walk like robots. It's a kind of surrealistic scene. For me, I am thinking always about sound. When we talk about sound, most people think only of music. But for me, there are many, many kinds of sound. We are surrounded. I want to keep my consciousness at a kind of flat level so I can catch sound." A number of Kawasaki's nature recordings have been released on a Japanese CD series entitled *Sounds of the Earth*. "It's very interesting", he says, laughing. "When I'm making those CDs in the studio, most people fall asleep. Some sound causes alpha waves. A young assistant had to check for digital noise so he tried to listen very carefully with headphones, but every time, he fell asleep for thirty minutes."

Among the tapes made by Kawasaki for St GIGA are hours of Buddhist chanting made in Nara, the seat of Buddhism in Japan, and Koya-san mountain, centre of the Shingon-Mikkyo sect of Buddhism. John Cage and Karlheinz Stockhausen both heard Buddhist chanting in situ and found much in these prolonged sound events that confirmed their opposed philosophies. In the Dai Hannya ceremony of the Shingon sect, for example, the chanting of the *sutra* will be modified according to seasonal influences. The *sutra* is six hundred volumes in length, and so a part of the reading is symbolically accomplished by the monks opening out their folded prayer books and then shutting them noisily. Evil spirits are driven away with other noises, such as door banging, hitting the floor with wooden staffs, the clatter of running, crackling fire and the blowing of conch shells. Kawasaki recorded the ancient Shunie (also known as Omizutori) ceremony, which heralds the beginning of spring in March each year. "It's a very long ceremony", he says. "For the monk it's very hard work. It's about fourteen days. No meat, no fish. No one can enter this space, only monk." He draws a diagram. "This space is only selected people – you ask permission, maybe you come. Woman cannot. Here they have screen. You can hear the sound. They walk around. At that time, they put on wooden shoes, so it's a very special sound. They sing, and sometimes silence, sometimes ring a special bell. Sometimes they sing very fast, singing all names of the gods, including Shinto gods. At that time, it's very, very fast. It's like Superman. Maybe they are in trance. People have only imagination: 'What are they doing?' That screen, they only use candlelight, so only silhouettes come through. When they come into the space they bring some very big torch. The sound causes many imaginations."

amniotic fluids

Devised in 1990 by Hiroshi Yokoi, a pioneer of twenty-four-hour FM radio transmission in Japan, St GIGA was the first Japanese satellite station. The concept was inspired by a Kurt Vonnegut story called "The Sirens of Titan", in which cave-dwelling creatures called Harmoniums eat beautiful sounds and shine with light. The only words they know are "I'm here" and "I'm glad you're there", the perfect distillation of radio's most basic principle. Programmed according to tidal patterns, sunrise and sunset and the changing phases of the moon, rather than Greenwich standard time, the station works upon principles which would be regarded in the UK as symptoms of delusional mania.

"The cyclical patterns created by these various natural forces are combined to form a single line which is used as the guiding line for programme scheduling", writes Mr Yokoi in the radio station handbook. "The movements of this 'guiding line' are irregular and, rather than conforming to the Greenwich time line, form a cyclical pattern based on the natural rhythms that synchronise with human behaviour and emotions. Sounds and music which match the wave patterns of this guiding line will be selected and transmitted to harmonize with each cycle. By matching the wave patterns of nature and the melodic patterns of music in this way, a powerful and deep world of sound will be realised. This world of sound, filled with the vibrations of nature, will draw people into an unusual mental space where they can experience the sweet beginnings of life itself, reminiscent of the start of existence as an embryo within amniotic fluids . . . We are about to enter a period of major historical change not often witnessed in the long history of mankind. I believe that people involved in media have an important obligation to fulfil. That is to truly grasp the spirit of the period. And at the same time to use their imaginative powers and practical skills to create a 'dream tide'." Those who understand the St GIGA programme best, and thus its main target audience, Hiroshi Yokoi claims, are "unborn babies sleeping quietly in amniotic fluids".

A Japanese doctor was the first to release a commercial album of womb sounds (track titles included "Aorta" and "Aorta and Vein") mixed with the soporific end of the classical repertoire – *Air on a G String* and so on. The intention of Dr Hajime Murooka's *Sleep Gently In the Womb*, released in 1975, was to pacify crying babies. Electronic lullaby tapes designed to calm new-born babies or ease birth pains for women are now common, both in Mothercare and in the tape sections of New Age bookshops; Mickey Hart of the Grateful Dead, for example, has released a birthing tape of his own. Anecdotal evidence suggests that if rhythms and beats derived from heartbeat recordings are transmitted to a foetus in the womb throughout pregnancy, then this stimulation may increase the child's learning capacity after birth. Coincidentally, the music my daughter heard, or felt, just five nights before she was born was a loud performance by Daniel Lanois, with guest vocal on one song by Brian Eno. The consequences are as yet unknown.

water streaming
"In the silent meditation, the sound of the gong can be heard several times. Then the sound of a cloud-shaped metal gong as well as a wooden drum telling the end of the morning meditation can be heard in a unique rhythm. The sound of gongs

and drums not only awakes sleepy novices or young monks, but also it helps to awake the insight of monks to lead them to the state of enlightenment or *Satori* in Japanese. All monks start to chant a scripture in unison as a part of the morning service. Circumstances and atmosphere are so silent that one can hear sounds of the wind and water-streaming very clearly."

> Shoyu Hanayama, *Zen: Sound & Silence* (Nippon Phonogram LP booklet)

John Cage was influenced profoundly by the lectures of Daisetz Suzuki, who gave classes in Zen at Columbia University, New York City, from the late 1940s through most of the 1950s. Cage's biographer, David Revill, wrote in *The Roaring Silence* that "the teachings of Suzuki had a startling effect on Cage. He felt that they catapulted him into conceptual and emotional adulthood." As for Cage's own thoughts on the matter, the influence is apparent from his description of the lectures: "Suzuki never spoke loudly. When the weather was good, the windows were open, and the airplanes leaving La Guardia flew directly overhead from time to time, drowning out whatever he had to say. He never repeated what had been said during the passage of the airplane."

Whilst sound sculpter Max Eastley and I are staying in Yoshihiro Kawasaki's Kobe apartment, he plays us his tapes of an Edo-period (1603–1867) garden sound maker called the *suikinkutsu*. This is a large stone basin mounted over an even bigger inverted pot. The pot is sunk in the earth, set in an underground drainage system of stones. Drips collect in the basin, fed from a bamboo pipe, and then fall into the resonating water vessel below. "People can hear the silence", says Kawasaki. "That's the point." Anxious to experience the point, I travel to Kyoto in the company of Kawasaki's assistant, Kana Kobayashi, who takes me on a whirlwind tour of Zen temples, stone gardens, moss gardens and patisseries. In Ninomaru Palace, originally built by the first Tokugawa Shogun Ieyasu in 1603, we leave our shoes on racks at the door to pad softly around the famous chirping *uguisu-bari*, the "nightingale floor". Designed to reveal the presence of *ninja* assassins, this artful construction of cramps and nails under the floorboards seems to squeak only when somebody else is moving, leaving me with the eerie impression that I am floating on Hiroshi Yokoi's dream tide.

But the highlight of this Kyoto daytrip is the garden of Zuishun-In and its *suikinkutsu*. Swapping our shoes for green garden sandals, we walk through the garden to the water chime. The sound is minute, so quiet in fact that we deafened creatures of the contemporary world must be provided with a bamboo listening pole. This bamboo adds the typical phasing drone of resonance in a cylindrical tube (the "sea" we can hear by putting an ear to a seashell); after a short period of listening to the pure, sparse bell tones of random drips ringing in their underground chamber, all auditory experiences are heightened. We sit for an hour in the garden, eating a green jelly sweet, drinking Japanese tea, watching fish being fed. The tranquillity switches open a calm state of mind. Bodily receptors tune in to a flickering microsphere: a butterfly landing on moss, intermittent water droplets, insect drones, reflections of water ripples on bamboo poles, the scrape of an old woman digging weeds from a path. Giant carp jump, then flop back into the ornamental pond. Birds flutter loudly as they weave through the bamboo platforms erected to train tree branches and foliage into pleasing shapes. A crow squaws. The environment has been carefully designed to draw this state of mind into becoming. A few minutes ago, we were walking along a noisy city street. But the garden is an aesthetic, meditational construct, an enabling tool which relegates foreground clutter to the edges of the picture for a brief period and focuses instead on fleeting patterns of light, shadow, colour, smell, sound and silence.

The *suikinkutsu* was often built near the outside toilet. To complete the meditation on nature and bodily functions, when you came out you could wash your hands in water collected within the stone basin and listen to its delicate sound.

Earthy as well as ethereal in his appreciation of fugitive beauty, Jun'Ichiro Tanizaki, the author of *The Secret Life of Musashi*, described the pleasure of sitting in an old-fashioned Japanese outside toilet and absorbing nature: "There one can listen with such a sense of intimacy to the raindrops falling from the eaves and the trees, seeping into the earth as they wash over the base of a stone lantern and freshen the moss about the stepping stones." This reflection is one of many delights contained in his essay on aesthetics, *In Praise of Shadows*. Written in 1933, the book captures a moment of crisis before such extremes of subtlety, already wilting under the glare of technology, were almost completely crushed by the consequences of aggressive Japanese nationalism, post-war American influence and the brute commerce which followed economic recovery. Tanizaki believed that recording technology, originally developed in the West, was unsuited to capturing Japanese music, "a music of reticence, of atmosphere". In an uncomfortable fit of his own nationalistic tendencies, he none the less shows an acute appreciation of technology's inability to capture and reproduce the substance of silence, or the elusive aether talk of quiet sound and acoustic space. Ironically, Japanese concentration on mass market hi-fi and musical instrument technology has done very little to redress this balance or indeed protect the special qualities of non-Western scales and tuning systems against the uniformity of the octave. Quite rightly, Tanizaki felt that the loudspeaker diminishes certain aspects of sound by emphasising others. Even the most secluded spots of Kyoto are not immune. At a moss garden temple, a *shakuhachi* flute plays on tape, and in the tea house of Zuishun-In garden, a cassette player is set up to play Kawasaki's recording of the *suikinkutsu* during the tea ceremony.

Writing about the aesthetic sensibility of Japan's Heian era (ninth century) in *Zen Culture*, Thomas Hoover says: "Beauty was all the more arresting for the certainty that it must perish." In the land of hardware that Japan has become, this attitude still exists, paradoxically, but only in small pockets of forward thinking that project into a speculative, post-consumerist future. Hiroshi Yokoi's St GIGA project is one example. Xebec Hall, sited on Kobe's Port Island, is another. Here, John Cage's absorption of Zen has come full circle. There are other centres for sound exploration – IRCAM in Paris and STEIM in Amsterdam – but Xebec is unique in its visionary linking of sound art and consumer research.

In the 1980s, the TOA Corporation, a company specialising in PA systems for public spaces, celebrated its fiftieth anniversary by building a corporate headquarters on Port Island. Given that such buildings are required to incorporate a public space, TOA had considered the idea of including an equipment showroom in their plans but eventually decided to build a concert hall, digital studio and café (serving typically excellent coffee) with exhibition space – all equipped to present experimental music and the kind of sound art pioneered by post-Cage composers such as Pauline Oliveros, Alvin Lucier, Max Neuhaus, Akio Suzuki, Alvin Curran and Annea Lockwood. So the Xebec Corporation, along with its unique relationship with a parent company, was born.

Travelling on the Shinkansen train between Kobe and Tokyo in April, 1993, Nobuhisa Shimoda, planning director of Xebec's concerts, workshops and exhibitions, explained to me the unusual workings of this sound centre. For him, the presentation of sound art, installations and music concerts (experimental, jazz, Asian classical music, Fluxus art and so on) is the most effective and rewarding way to communicate models of a less product-orientated society, a society which directs income more towards time-based enrichment than solid packages of entertainment technology. At the time, the ailing Japanese economy was dedicated to exaggerated demand-creation for such packages. Shimoda's position seemed radical, yet Japanese economists and policy analysts were asking fundamental questions about so-called consumer fatigue (make houses bigger in order to allow more room for consumer durables, suggested Yukio Ohnuma, a general manager of Itochu Corporation) and the collapse of Japan's bubble economy (create more life-satisfaction for workers and more original products for consumers, suggested political writer Taichi Sakaiya). Xebec has something of a head start in this reinvention of the relationship between culture and the economy. Its parent company, TOA, is not a musical instrument manufacturer, but a specialist in the more intangible field of designing for optimum deployment of sound in space. The TOA motto is: "We sell sound, not equipment."

"CD consumption doesn't make people think how to create something inside themselves", says Shimoda. "Maybe about five or ten years ago in Japanese society it looked as if people chose goods by how good they are - goods should have a certain level of ability, plus good design. But it turned to the next phase. I imagine people would like to have rich life by buying or using some goods to make their life rich. When I use the word rich, it's not only for physical things but mental or spiritual. So we have to shift." How this possible trend connects with Xebec and its parent company remains nebulous. The event which opened Xebec in 1989 - a Brian Eno light sculpture installation - required an enormous amount of explanatory liaison between Xebec and TOA. But the principle of this particular work exemplified a speculative area which distinguishes between what people customarily do in the present and what they might benefit from doing in the future, given the opportunity. "This space urges people to be calm," wrote Eno for the first Xebec document. "Regular people almost never sit motionless. This is one of the problems of modern society - there are no situations, without actually going to sleep, where people can sit quietly."

Although there are specific situations which require the technological expertise of TOA itself - the performance of complex digital works, for example - the brief is open. "We should think about art, sound, people, society", says Nobuhisa Shimoda. "That will bring our parent company

something new. I feel a typical point of many artists is they are
not only making a package of sound – they are making a kind
of system. The people who encounter that system will be reminded that there is another rich world there, or inside them.
Like John Cage did. He made people listen to the world."
Where all this would lead, particularly at a time when Japan,
Europe and America were deep in economic recession, is another matter. Clearly, the sound work itself, along with its
usually delicate, refined aesthetic, connects to Japanese cus-
toms and devices, such as the *suikinkutsu* or the insect sound
sculptures of which Lafcadio Hearn wrote at the end of the
nineteenth century in *Insect Musicians*: "But even today, city
dwellers, when giving a party, will sometimes place cages of
singing-insects among the garden shrubbery, so that the
guests may enjoy not only the music of the little creatures, but
also those memories or sensations of rural peace which such
music evokes." As Yoshihiro Kawasaki says, "Especially after
World War Two, most people forget those kind of things. Recently, I have talked about these things with sound artists from
foreign countries and I saw their performances. I find that
Japanese essence in their performance. Maybe young people
in Japan don't know those old things but they find that essence in sound artists of foreign countries. It's a kind of
circle."

Packaging is a high art form at every level in Japan, but the
intangible qualities of a process or ceremony, the substance
of memories and experience, have equally deep roots in Japanese society. Imagining a possible future for TOA, Nobuhisa
Shimoda says, "They might find that they don't have to manufacture products any more. They have to think about the
design of space for sound. That's just one possibility. To make
this kind of thing happen, only this kind of movement like in
Xebec can change the company thought. Maybe the company
will change, we will be changed, society will be changed."

7 altered states ii: fourth world

Jon Hassell; Pandit Pran Nath; Duke Ellington

> *"Peeling to the lethargic beat of tumescent music, she wore vivid makeup, glitter in her hair and crystalline clothes, all hooks, straps, sequins and secret snappers. The stripper's art needs special garments made to tear away like the husk of a pomegranate. So you do not notice the woman as she is, because you are looking for fulfilment of the mind's eye. You are examining an idea – depravity or pleasure, or their perilous symbiosis."*
> David Thomson, *Suspects*

In a creeping, convoluted trail suggestive of plant growth, David Thomson constructed a novel, or a lattice of biographical sketches, from the imaginary web of lives as they might have been lived by cinematic characters outside the frame of the cinema screen. These characters – Walker from *Point Blank*, Norma Desmond from *Sunset Boulevard*, Evelyn Mulwray and Noah Cross from *Chinatown* and so on – their previously unknown pasts and futures, snag and pull at each other in this web, implying an invisible world occupied by the ragged stories of every fictional identity ever invented.

A similar process of dragging icons and overlaying them, sliced translucently thin, on to fictional histories, has been one of the key devices of technological music. Feasibly, you could extrapolate a novel from the interweaving stories buried within John Cage's *Variations IV*, but richer possibilities unfolded in the early 1980s when Jon Hassell began to capture, loop and laminate fragments of sampled sound on albums such as *Aka-Darbari-Java*. A student of Stockhausen who had recorded with Terry Riley (*In C*), La Monte Young (*The Theatre of Eternal Music*), Brian Eno, Talking Heads, David Sylvian and Peter Gabriel, Hassell formalised that process by naming his 1994 band Bluescreen, after the cinematic technique of filming foreground action against a blue background, "adopting this metaphor in musical ways, creating magical textures in sound, making something familiar sound fresh and exotic by separating it from its background and combining it with something new and startling". Finding a review of David Thomson's *Suspects* in the *LA Weekly*, he hit on this as another metaphor connecting to his own search for a music which was almost psychotropic in its capacity to activate alien worlds in the imagination through strange juxtapositions.

Previous Hassell albums, particularly *Earthquake Island*, *Vernal Equinox*, *Possible Musics* and *Dream Theory In Malaya*, along with his collaborations with Gnawa trance musicians from Morocco and the Farafina percussionists from Burkina Faso, were made in the spirit of creative anthropology exemplified earlier in this century by the surrealist writer, traveller, critic and documenter of dreams Michel Leiris. Writing on ethnographic surrealism in *The Predicament of Culture*, James Clifford offers an outline of the territory: "I am using the term *Surrealism* in an obviously expanded sense to circumscribe an aesthetic that values fragments, curious collections, unexpected juxtapositions – that works to provoke the manifestations of extraordinary realities drawn from the domains of the erotic, the exotic and the unconscious."

That could be a précis of Jon Hassell's *œuvre*. But with *Aka-Darbari-Java* the perfume of ethnopoetics was supplemented by parallels with literature and the advanced technology of hyperreality, indicated through affinities with Latin American magic realist writing and the video technique of keying in. As for the sound, sluggish shapes undulated in the depths of a

liquid fog formed from particles of air passed through metal >
electronic transformations > the pitches of an Indian raga >
slowly turning variations of a drum cycle from Senegal recorded in Paris > glittering spirals of noise lifted from gamelan
music and an Yma Sumac record (already a repository of colonial myths) orchestrated in Hollywood Exotica style by one of
the inventors of the exotica genre, Les Baxter.

This was a form of music, Hassell suggested, which would
leave behind "the ascetic face which Eurocentric tradition has
come to associate with serious expression". Taboos were
transgressed, notably in the music's sensuality, and its free use
of source material, but this was not untutored montage. The
raga – Darbari – can be heard as interpreted by one of Hassell's
teachers, the great *kirana*-style vocalist Pandit Pran Nath. Recorded in New Delhi by Alan Douglas, this was released
eighteen years later on *Ragas of Morning and Night*.

Though hampered by age and Parkinson's disease by the
mid 1990s when he recorded with the Kronos Quartet, Pran
Nath's approach to teaching was formidable. "It is necessary
to remain one hundred years with the guru, then practice for
one hundred years, and then you can sing for one hundred
years", he has said. The first time Hassell and I talked, back in
1989, he tugged and worried at the contradiction between
lengthy (though not quite *that* lengthy) study and the instan-
taneity of Xerox culture. "It's a quandary for me", he said,
"because I did develop a physical dexterity when I studied
Indian music with Pandit Pran Nath. I decided at that point I
wanted to walk into a room and have something that was in
my nervous system which I could activate and bring with me
wherever I went. It's a problem to know what to do with that
in the age of sampling and audio sleight of hand, because the
audience is looking for the final result, basically. They don't
care if it took you twenty years to arrive at it or whether somebody sampled it off of a record and used it."

He had just released *City: Works of Fiction*, an album produced with a lot of digital editing, a strong influence from

Hank Shocklee's Bomb Squad productions for Public Enemy and a vocal sample from P.E.'s "She Watch Channel Zero?!". *City* set an industry standard for digitally sliced soundtracks of the city twitching in delirium tremens: chicken sacrifices and dog fights in the basement, bullroarers on the bridges, camcorders at the murder scene, TVs in the lamp posts, sex temples, knock-down kidneys at car-boot sales, fake breasts, fake Cartier, the smell of a thousand cuisines. As Japanese bass player and composer Motohiko Hamase wrote for the sleevenotes to his *Technodrome* album: "*City* . . . provides a thorough expression of city music in one of the most remarkable accomplishments of recent years." The reference points for this album were characteristically broad, mostly extra-musical, ranging from Ben Okri's *City of Red Dust*, Italo Calvino's *Invisible Cities* and Jean Baudrillard's portrayal of America as "the primitive society of the future", to Federico Fellini's custom-built celluloid city of Reggiolo, Salman Rushdie's tropicalised London and Ridley Scott's Los Angeles 2019. In a long version of *Blade Runner* screened in San Francisco, a scene later excised from the commercially released director's cut version showed two women, like Japanese Butoh dancers, moving slowly on a nightclub stage to the liquid techno-throb that Vangelis envisaged (prophetically, yet still miscalculated by more than twenty-five years) as music of the next century. A fertile texture of images: body, machine, global, intimate, expressive, emotionally withdrawn.

Like Terry Riley, playing saxophone in an electronic hall of mirrors in early recordings such as "Poppy Nogood and the Phantom Band", Hassell had created an otherworldly studio sound that had become recognised as his signature. This use of digital delay, combined with pitch shifting, created its own problems. "When I started studying with Pran Nath", he said, "I realised that the basic art of raga is, as he says, the music between the notes. That's to call attention to the fact that if you have a grid and each one of the lines on the grid is a pitch level, the art is in drawing precisely a beautiful curve between one level and another level. It's like calligraphy. Trumpet's a lonely instrument. It's one voice. When I realised I could have a replica of the trumpet playing with me, then it was as though instead of drawing the curves with one pencil I could hold a handful of pencils and draw the curves. In trying to make these curves in raga, a very breathy, vocal-type sound resulted. Basically, it's playing the mouthpiece, not the trumpet. I blow it like a conch shell – that's the most primitive, fundamental aspect of what I do. This is the only instrument other than the voice that works that way. The sound is strange to start with, so when I add the electronic eye-shadow, the mistaken conclusion is that it's all done with mirrors, not meat." So a voice within seemed to be saying – as it does to most trained musicians from time to time – to bare the expertise behind the plug-in mask. His next project was planned as a solo album, untreated, unadorned, unplugged.

But the album that emerged, eventually, was far from the naked intimacy of a solo acoustic trumpet. There was a naked intimacy, or should I say provocatively dressed nakedness, but this was absorbed into the associated imagery of the music rather than the instrumentation. As the title – *Dressing For Pleasure* – indicated, this was a further footstep in the move away from ascetic aesthetics, into hip-hop, jazz, ragga and the ritualised sex of the modern primitive movement. *Dressing For Pleasure* can be placed next to all the younger hybrids of hip-hop, jungle, trip-hop and so on, linked by a connecting thread which has little to do with age or geography. That thread was tenuous, yet it constituted a sonic assault on musical fundamentalism.

An avid Internet user, Jon Hassell has some interesting observations on fundamentalism, pertinent to the tensions between nationalism and transglobalism. Click yourself on to the Internet and you can find electronic discussion sites devoted to heraldry and folk dancing. "Maybe it will become convenient to redraw a map of the world according to interests and who wants to live in which era", he says from his home in West Hollywood as we talk on the telephone. "We could have wars between the fifteenth century and the twenty-first century . . . In the past, having been coming from the abstract, instrumental side of things, music was metalanguage for performing. I always felt that music took off where words stopped. Hip-hop changed that, because hip-hop allowed a new relationship between words and music, one that I felt more comfortable with. At the same time, every record I've ever done has always been some sort of a fantasy, an erotic fantasy. They've always been in this same constellation of sensuality, where the Gil Evans sound equals this sense of feeling good at a certain place at a certain time – maybe post-orgasmic music as opposed to pre-orgasmic. I keep asking the central question: What is it I really like? What is it that I really want to hear? And both in the personal realm, the sex fantasy realm, and the musical realm, it comes down to shockingly simple things. I love lush sensual atmospheres. I love beautiful chords. I'm in love with harmony. Strangely enough, I've taken the path of disciplines which didn't have a lot to do with that – at least in the sense of traditional chord changes – like studying raga. Although there are vast harmonic implications. It is, in fact, very covertly harmonic, but I'm talking about the beauty of having one note and you've got these chords changing underneath. Within each chord, that note takes on a different kind of character. It's a different picture each time, but using the same foreground. Brazilian pop music seemed to pick up on that right away – 'One Note Samba' et cetera.

"Why did Brazilians choose this, or why did Gil Evans choose those harmonies out of the repertoire that existed at that point. There is something going on there, some deep essential drive towards the beautiful. The beautiful is defined here as being that which drags you most profoundly without any abstract constructs. Without talking yourself into what's beautiful." At the heart of our emergent sense of beauty in the present is a new tonality, which Jon sees as a development of samples being detuned and overlaid, particularly in hip-hop, to create dense, strange harmonic dissonances. To people who don't insist that music must be Eurocentrically in tune, these are very pleasurable, but to those whose first and formative listening experiences are hip-hop, this new tonality is normal.

Jon sends me an essay from *Skin Two* (issue 14), written by Pat Califia and entitled "Sex Magic: Modern Primitives, Latex Shamans & Ritual SM". "Modern primitives live, for the most part, in urban enclaves in the age of the machine", she writes. "We have to find a way to synthesise the rhythms of nature with our electronic lives. A fuzzy-headed, sentimental longing for a bucolic utopia will not save us from toxic waste or nuclear weapons. We need a world where we can have both computers and campfires." In condemning misguided appropriations of pre-industrial, communal ritual for the post-industrial, private theatre of sex, this brilliant essay illuminates some of the murkier areas of Fourth World theory.

And in *Dressing For Pleasure*, there were musical developments of the Fourth World idea also. "Destination: Bakiff", for example, sampled and chopped snatches of Duke Ellington's recording of "Bakiff". Composed by trombonist Juan Tizol, the original tune is a heady piece of exotica. "When Ellington and Strayhorn composed the *Far East Suite* in 1964", wrote Mark Tucker in his notes for the *Duke Ellington: The Blanton-Webster Band* boxed set released in 1986, "they may have been inspired by their recent visit to the Orient, but surely they drew upon memories of Juan Tizol's earlier studies in musical exotica, among them 'Caravan', 'Pyramid' and the atmospheric 'Bakiff'. Tizol's Puerto Rican origins seem to have little to do with a piece like 'Bakiff', where musical impressionism is the product of its composer's imagination, not his first-hand experience with indigenous Caribbean idioms." And for Ellington, these explorations were stimulated by an interest in Africa and the diaspora. "As a student of Negro history", he said, "I had, in any case, a natural inclination in this direction."

In the Fourth World, nothing is simple. "Possible musics, possible cultures, possible architecture, possible lifestyles, etc.", Hassell says. "This is an idea that boils down to the range of possible relations between individual, tribe and nation in the mass electronic age. Imagine a grid of national boundaries, and on to those project a new, non-physical communications-derived geography – tribes of like-minded thinkers. Since a situation like this has never before existed, it follows that old, narrow-band approaches can't work and that new approaches must be creative. That means intuitive and improvisational. I would like the message of Fourth World to be that things shouldn't be diluted. This balance between the native identity and the global identity via various electronic extensions is not one that can be dictated or necessarily predicted. One should be very humble and respectful of our lack of knowledge about how those things combine, and be informed by knowledge of the way things used to be in smaller numbers – that's where it becomes very useful to look at other cultures, small cultures, and try to develop a modus operandi for the new age, not New Age."

Fourth World

The stairwell of a Tokyo department store in Shibuya. Clean. Hi-tech. Deserted. A disembodied voice transmits information over the public address system, the words echoing in the exit shaft. A man and a woman are kissing hard, pressed against the wall. Time is frozen.

A downpour in Ikebukuro, rain sheeting down. Milky neon *kanji* glow dimly through the mist, floating in a night sky that has scrubbed out the buildings on which they sit.

In Atlanta, subterranean cities extend out from under the hotels. In Lake Tahoe, the half of the town that lies in California is dark and spooky at night; the gambling half that lies in Nevada throbs with insomniac, halogen, polyvinyl, slot machine lust. Just beyond Tahoe city limits, birds of prey hover over the ochre ripples of the desert.

Itsukushima Shrine on Miyajima Island near Hiroshima, a famous Shinto site where *gagaku* music and *bugaku* dance are performed in the open air on New Year's day, ultramarine sea running over the huge O-Torii grand gate, then passing under the vermilion posts of the stage. A Shinto priest wearing stiff white robes walks along carrying a shiny black briefcase. En route to the shrine, some of the souvenir and cake shops are equipped with voice chips, activated by electronic eye, which say "hello" when you enter and "thank you" when you leave. At closing time within the shrine, the tranquillity is blasted apart by deafening martial synthesiser music.

The Caracas rubbish dump. A graveyard for hundreds of lorries which have been driven to death, finally abandoned at their destination, rusted, collapsing onto their own axles, sinking into shit. The poorest of the poor pick amongst the waste, looking for saleable scraps. Huge black vultures gather wherever a human has passed, wings spread in cruciform.

A cardboard box lies unattended on one of the backstreet pavements behind Akihabara's department store cornucopias. Inside the box, six mechanical dogs, luminous eyes protruding on stalks, their bodies transparent plastic, their heads the colour of blood-drained skin, tumble over each other, scrabbling at the sides of the box.

A Mexican restaurant in Hong Kong. A group of Filipino musicians dressed in ponchos and sombreros move from table to table, singing Mexican songs to white people who yell drunkenly through "Guantanamera", shake maracas out of time and throw food. Outside, the roads are gridlocked by taxis flying black pennants from their radio aerials in protest against the Chinese government killings in Tiananmen Square. In the night market, eels writhe in neon-lit water tanks. Tough guys preside over fold-open card tables inlaid with magazine photographs of fake Rolex, Cartier, Louis Vuitton, prices scrawled underneath in felt tip. Tokyo Cat The Disco Tailor is making up suits at midnight. I buy a Chinese pirate copy of a Japanese T-shirt. On the front is printed:

PEACE AND LOVE WORLD TRAVEL
Avant garde, sephlsticated and a little evolution of the colonial retro-mediapolis' urban plaids and adventure-seeking worl

London's Cavendish Square: almost deserted, a Saturday evening during the hot, rainless July of 1994. Humidity and electrical pressure are intensifying by the second. The air is thick with petrol, the sky darkening to a leaden blue haze of surreal clarity. Heavy raindrops fall in isolation, like the last drops squeezed from a dirty rag. As I walk around the square, I sense at first, then hear, a grinding drone rising out of the underground car park. Sitting on a bench in the middle of the square, a man is screaming a tirade of immitigable harshness to an absent subject:

"Yaaafuckingaraaaghafuckineeearakafuckinagaafauogh. . ."

Candi Dasa, near Cape Bugbug, southeast Bali. Paradise, basic model, optional drawbacks. Televisi Stasiun Denpassar begins its evening transmissions: first a static, fixed-camera studio performance of Balinese dance-drama, then an American sit-com: *Alf* (the one about the cuddly alien adopted by the all-American family). Study this programme and use it to improve your English, advises the TV announcer. The following morning, as the tourists begin another day's sunbathing, a posse of young men gather at one end of the beach. Wrapped in black woollens and head scarves, they push huge concrete octagons along the sand in broiling heat, then push them into the sea. Periodically, they stop to rest and catch sneak glances of bared breasts.

On Kobe's Port Island, Japan, the neon logo of the Portopia Hotel dominates the skyline. After dark, the lobby is a phantasmagoric scene from an improbable future. Water cascades in silver darts and runnels down a wall of steel; set on a platform in front of this synthetic Niagara is a transparent grand piano. Pouring from the basement theatre comes a crowd of Japanese ragga and rasta boys wearing baggy jeans, high tops, tams for non-existent locks, mingling with another crowd of body-con girls in leather skirts, flares, high heels and see-through tops. Across the street, a Mini Cooper is parked at an angle, doors and windows wide open. Sitting on the pavement outside the Lawson late-open convenience store, a bunch of reggae obsessives drink from cans and listen to Buju and Shabba on the booming system of a black Banzai jeep. A warm spring night. Sensuous bass, strange hybrid language, strange dreams.

8 altered states iii: crystal world

La Monte Young, Marian Zazeela; Velvet
Underground; Yoko Ono, Richard Maxfield, West
Coast jazz, Indian vocal music, Terry Riley

A theatre restaurant in London. La Monte Young and Marian Zazeela sit together, both dressed in a strange composite of Indian and New York boho-wear circa 1950. Having listened to loud music for so long, La Monte is obliged to use a hearing aid. At one point during our conversation, he turns it down as the background opera muzak rises to heights of ecstasy. The conversation goes like this: I wait, pent up with my question, until a brief chink of light parts the eternal flow of La Monte's fascinating, humorous but somewhat unyielding discourse. The conversational style – fluid, detailed but heavy on conjunctions – fits the music, since for more than thirty years, this has concentrated on long durations of sustained pitch relationships. In *Composition 1961*, he gave the following instruction: "Draw a straight line and follow it." These are points on that line.

rain, wind, blues

A photograph, taken in New Jersey in 1963. La Monte Young sits crosslegged under a tree, wearing dark glasses, black shirt, tight black jeans, playing sopranino saxophone. An axe is buried in the tree just behind his head. Bottles are hung from the branches.

The Theatre of Eternal Music, La Monte called his performing groups. Always involving Marian Zazeela's light and

colour installations, her singing and gong bowing, these also
included Jon Hassell, playing trumpet in the early 1970s,
trombonist Garrett List and, in the mid 1960s, Angus MacLise
playing percussion, Tony Conrad on bowed guitar and
mandola, John Cale playing modified viola and, passing
through, Walter De Maria and conceptual artist Henry Flynt
(who coined the term "concept art" at the end of the 1950s).
So La Monte has some right to claim a proprietorial interest in
huge swathes of subsequent music. MacLise, Conrad and Cale
were members of The Primitives, The Warlocks or The Falling
Spikes, all forerunners of the Velvet Underground. Interviewed for *What Goes On*, the Velvet Underground
Appreciation Society magazine, Tony Conrad described promotional gigs for "The Ostrich", a single written and recorded
by Lou Reed: "The song was very easy as they explained it to
us because all the strings were tuned to one note, which blew
our minds. We couldn't believe that they were doing this crap
just like in a sort of strange ethnically Brooklyn style, tuning
their instruments to one note, which is what we were doing
too (in Young's group), so it was very bizarre. In fact we were
tuning to two notes and they were tuning to only one."

Musicians from the Theatre of Eternal Music can be heard
together on an unissued tape from 1964 called "Sunday Morning Blues", a looping, exultant trance improvisation on which
Young plays sopranino saxophone (influenced by composer
–saxophonist Terry Jennings as much as by John Coltrane).
John Cale and Tony Conrad play drones which sound uncan-
nily similar to the first Velvets's album, particularly "The Black
Angel's Death Song" and the intro to "Venus In Furs". Marian
Zazeela bows a gong and Angus MacLise drums in wild, complex polyrhythms.

La Monte Young has written that MacLise claimed the rain
as his main rhythmic influence. This cemented a connection
between them, since La Monte composed according to
Debussy's maxim: "Listen to the words of no man; listen only
to the sounds of the wind and the waves of the sea." MacLise

was sacked from the Velvet Underground by the irascible Lou
Reed. He recorded trance explorations with his various bands
– Dreamweapon, Joyous Lake, The Tribal Orchestra – and
wrote poetry, made books, acted as the green mummy in a
Jack Smith film called *Normal Love*. But tapes tended to be
sold for immediate money. Little survives. In 1979 MacLise
died in Kathmandu, aged 41, of hypoglycaemia and drug com-
plications. He belongs with a shadowy group of New York
bohemians, shapers and shape-shifters of art movements in
the 1960s before they became mass movements: poet and
photographer Ira Cohen, painter Mati Klarwein, electronic
music pioneer Richard Maxfield, vocalist Meredith Monk, film
maker and composer Phill Niblock, film makers Jack Smith
and Ron Rice, and all of the Fluxus performance artists, some
beginning to enjoy recognition three decades later.

Before the issue of a French album in 1973, La Monte's
music could only be heard on a 7" flexi-disc issued with *Aspen*
magazine and a limited edition LP extract from *The Tortoise,
His Dreams and Journeys*. In recent years, CDs have been
released of *The Well Tuned Piano*, *The Second Dream of The
High-Tension Line Stepdown Transformer from The Four
Dreams of China* and, strangest of all, the just intonation raga-
blues of *Just Stompin'* by The Forever Blues Band. Not even
these relatively high-profile works have dented mass public
consciousness, however, so the links which can be made between his pioneering work and various forms of so-called
minimalism, ambient, Fourth World hybrids, the guitar noise
symphonies of Rhys Chatham and Glenn Branca, the isolationist drones of Thomas Köner, Faust's Kraut rock and the wide
variety of guitar bands stemming from the Velvet Underground's explorations of distortion – Sonic Youth, Band of
Susans, Jesus & Mary Chain, Main, Spiritualized, Spectrum,
Verve, Slowdive, My Bloody Valentine, and so on – are indi-
rect, often disputed, invariably unwitting and unwritten.

dream house

In 1962, he conceived of the Dream House, an environment in which his music could be played continuously, eventually mutating into a "living organism with a life and tradition of its own".

La Monte's dreams and journeys

"The concept of the Dream House was very much related to my work, *The Four Dreams of China*, which I composed in 1962 and which is the first work in which I thought about the possibility of no beginning and no end. I began to think of the silences as including the beginning silence and the ending silence so that musicians could take it up and if they worked with the same pitches and the same key, let's say, then we could think of each performance as a continuation of the bigger work. To facilitate that approach I somehow came up with this idea of a permanant location where a work could grow and develop and evolve a life and tradition of its own. This was before I had begun working very much with electronics. So with my various groups – various sets of performers who comprised The Theatre of Eternal Music – I worked towards longer performances within an evening and towards bigger installations until it reached the point where we were going on tour in the early seventies with six to eight musicians, two slide projectionists, a technician, a road manager and two tons of electronic equipment, taking a week to set up, being on location for a week and taking three days to take it apart. It was really a big thing."

In 1973, Young, Marian Zazeela and Pandit Pran Nath were invited to the first of a series of Italian festivals called East West. La Monte proposed a Dream House performance of his piece of the moment (i.e. the previous seven years), called *Map of 49's Dream The Two Systems of Eleven Sets of Galactic Intervals Ornamental Lightyears Tracery*. The promoter asked for something new, so La Monte laid out the deal. "This is not a supermarket", he told him, "where you can one day buy tomatoes and tomorrow you buy lettuce and the next day a quart of milk. This is really what I'm working on and this is really what I want to do." OK, said the promoter, but I can't afford it anyway. Then La Monte played him a tape of a piece that needed a week for setting up, tuning the piano and installing Marian's light environment: *The Well Tuned Piano*. Fine, said the promoter, who enjoyed the three-hour-long Rome premiere so much that he commissioned two more concerts and bought a piano which La Monte tuned (for perpetuity) and then signed. "Then, I became completely absorbed in *The Well Tuned Piano*", he continues, "and for a while, it was less expensive to produce than Dream House had been. The way we looked at it, it was just the piano and sort of, maybe four of us – me to play, Marian to do the lights, the tuner and a recording engineer."

As the piece developed in performance, the duration of each concert crept past three hours to four. Preparation time expanded to a month of tuning and practice in the performance space. "If you want to talk about what the pattern of some planetary body is, the frequency of its orbit, you not only study it for five years or ten years, you look back into history and see what ancient astronomers were saying. Somehow, through the *Trio For Strings* and, just before *Trio For Strings*, in the middle section of *Four Brass,* I became very inspired to begin writing long sustained tones. I was definitely hearing Indian classical music and Japanese *gagaku* music. When I got to UCLA I was a musicology major. They had a student *gagaku* orchestra and also, some time at that timeframe, I heard this first recording of Ali Akbar Khan on Angel Records with Yehudi Menuhin announcing, and when I heard that on the radio I literally ran out and jumped in my car and drove down to the record store called Music City in Hollywood and bought the record and listened to it for hours and hours. Actually I was living at my grandmother's house in Los Angeles and she used to get very upset. She used to call it opium music.

"When I was a child I used to love to stand and listen to power plants. Before I was four years old my father had a job in Montpelier, Idaho, working for my mother's father, Grandpa Grandy, who owned a gas distribution centre and they would deliver gas all around that area in big trucks, you know? But right next to this gas plant was a power station. It was just humming. I used to love to stand there and listen to it and I remember even playing up on top of the big gas storage tanks, sitting there in the hot sun and listening to this thing hum. I remember standing by other high tension stepdown transformers in Bern, Idaho, the town where I was born, and I also used to like to listen to the sound of crickets. Of course, the first early sound experience was the sound of the wind blowing up off Bear Lake around the log cabin I was born in. I think what really happened was a coming together of all this information which was, I think, then set into place by my hearing of Eastern music and by the fact that the world had begun to shrink because of the electronic age.

"As an ethnomusicology minor at UCLA I got to listen to a lot of recordings from places like Siam, pygmy music from parts of Africa, *gagaku* music, Balinese and Javanese music. Then, only years later, the world was becoming smaller in many other ways. When you think of what it meant to Debussy when the gamelan orchestra came to Paris and what an enormous thing it must have been for him and then when you think how easy it is to travel today and that I've been to India seven times and we went with Pandit Pran Nath to Iran. I think that apart from whatever uniqueness there may be about me, I came from a time when it was possible to absorb all this information and to bring it forth into a new manifestation in which the whole was really much more than the sum of the parts. By letting my inspiration guide me, the way I work, I try to not let my mind get in the way of my inspiration. It's curious that money gets tied up with this kind of really extraordinary spiritual and learning experience about the nature of universal structure. God created the body so that the soul could come to earth to study music so that it could have a better understanding of universal structure. Music can be a model for universal structure because we perceive sound as vibration and if you believe, as I do, that vibration is the key to universal structure you can understand why I make this statement."

minimalism

"Often, I'm asked to define minimalism and I have my own definition which is that which is created with the minimum of means. I guess I like to think in those broader terms. If one thinks of minimalism according to my definition, it's able to include the works of Rothko and Barnett Newman, as well as the works of Webern and *haiku*, and a great deal of my work."

crystal world

"Just as the so-called post-Webern movement was reaching a ceiling of complexity with flocks of notes", Jon Hassell tells me, "I was trying to figure out where all those notes came from, so I went to the centre of it – La Monte Young. As a matter of fact, Stockhausen was the first person who ever played La Monte Young for me. I'd never heard of him before. La Monte highlighted the point where it's a matter of listening to yourself. If you have a constant background like a drone, you can project your own nervous system against that background. You become aware of listening high, listening low, listening foreground, listening background. That was the beginning from which Terry Riley, Steve Reich, Philip Glass, and that whole minimalist thing – and me to a certain extent as well – came from. I got a lot from being around La Monte. When you're playing for four hours and you're trying to tune up perfectly on various intervals, occasionally it happens that out of those four hours you might get ten minutes when everybody's in tune. Then you feel the floor begin to lift. You hear this wonderful crystalline world happening in the overtones. People are slightly off, and then you're getting these combination tones as they struggle to reach the same pitch, so there's this incredibly silvery world going on out there. Some music is not recordable."

"From the beginning of recorded time", says La Monte, "people have always wanted to understand their relationship to universal structure and to time. Even in as simple a way as where do we come from, why are we here and where are we going? I point out that our entire concept of time is dependent on an understanding of periodicity. Time is depending on night and day, the periodic rotations of the planets, the stars, the periodic functions of our bodies and the seasons, all of these various periodic events, and without them we really have no concept of time. Time is really a very important aspect of universal structure. What I have learned is it goes very slowly."

a swarm of butterflies encountered on the ocean

1968. A psychedelic club called Middle Earth, Covent Garden, London. An event called Float. Yoko Ono is performing, along with a number of other London-based "happening" artists. The only memorable performance, however, comes from artist John Latham. He is hunched over a large, floor-standing electric saw, the kind you see used by timber merchants. This is connected by contact microphones to an amplifier and he is passing books through the saw blade, slicing them into chunks. A monstrous, chaotic, exhilarating drone batters the air.

1994. Disobey Club, Islington, London. For forty minutes, Richard James, the Aphex Twin, plays two highly amplified "records" made of sanding discs. The sound is augmented by the noise of an amplified food mixer. Sometimes the noise is so loud that it blots out all conversation in the room.

1960. A loft on Chambers Street, New York City. Yoko Ono, the occupant of the loft, is approached by electronic composer

Richard Maxfield with a view to collaborating on a series of new music concerts curated with La Monte Young. For the first, John Cage and David Tudor turn up. The following year, Yoko performs at Carnegie Hall. Maxfield provides electronics and technical assistance. "Performers with contact microphones taped to their bodies hauling heavy objects across the pitch-black stage", wrote Robert Palmer for his booklet essay accompanying the CD *Onobox*.

If Richard Maxfield had not committed suicide in 1969, and if his electronic music pieces were not so difficult to find or to hear, then our ideas of how music has changed and opened out during the past thirty-five years might be very different. His influence permeates the psychedelia of Joseph Byrd's rock band, The United States of America, released on CBS in 1968. He worked with Yoko Ono, and although most rock critics attribute a Stockhausen influence to the Lennon/Ono tape experiments of The Beatles' *White Album* and after, they are far closer to the work of Maxfield. In 1960, La Monte Young presented Maxfield's work to a group of Bay Area composers which included Terry Riley. Riley's 1960 piece called *Amazing Grace* sampled and treated the voice of a revival preacher named James G. Brodie; Steve Reich's far better known tape loop pieces – *It's Gonna Rain* and *Come Out* – both of which sample black voices, were composed in 1965 and 1966 respectively. In 1960, Joseph Byrd and La Monte Young enrolled in Maxfield's electronic music classes at the New School in New York. At the heart of avant-rock, hybrid electronics and plunderphonics, yet completely obscured by the vagaries of history, is Richard Maxfield.

steam

Maxfield's *Steam IV* (1961) was created by tape processing manipulations of steam, recorded from radiators in Maxfield's New York apartment. [1994. Mick Harris, ex-drummer with Napalm Death, now recording unsettled, unmoored electronic pieces under the names of Lull and Scorn, sends me a letter describing his working methods: "My sounds are source sounds from fridges to radiators (I'm a big fan of *Eraserhead* etc etc that type of radiator drone drift sound)."]

night music

Created from the interaction of an oscilloscope and a tape recorder. "I noticed that the electronically generated sounds I had produced", wrote Maxfield, "were identical in feeling to those made by birds and insects on summer nights in Riverside and Central Parks in New York City. After this discovery, I then assembled a small portion of the material which I had made into a multi-channel composition intended to evoke this antiphonal chirping of birds and insects on a summer night." [1994. Michael Prime, ecologist and performer of live electronics, sends me his CD – *Aquifers* – and a manifesto. "In my music", he writes, "I try to bring together sounds from a variety of environmental sources into a performance space, particularly sounds which ordinarily would not be audible . . . traffic sound may be filtered so that it resembles the sound of surf, while actual sea sounds may be transformed to conjure up images of an interstellar dust storm . . . I am especially interested in organic sound sources, such as plants, fungi and the human nervous system . . . Short-wave signals interpenetrate our bodies at all times, and provide a vast musical resource . . . Many of the characteristic effects of electronic music (such as ring modulation, filtering, phase-shifting and electronic drone-textures) were first heard in the interaction of early radio broadcasts with the earth's magnetic layer. Perhaps Gaia was the first composer of electronic music . . . At a given location, plants, fungi, animals and humans could be used to drive sound sculptures, and receivers could be tuned to radio, gamma and cosmic rays. . . live musical interactions in a new ecology of sound."]

bacchanale

Maxfield's most remarkable piece, created in 1963. A surreal mix of spoken poetry, read by Edward Field, who also plays clarinet, drum and typewriter; live violin scraping noise; Korean *kayagum sanjo*; Spanish flamenco; treated violin sounds; treated saxophone played by Terry Jennings; underwater clarinet sounds; live jazz recorded at the Five Spot. This eight-minute montage appears to begin in an overlapping series of rooms, then fall through space into a subterranean, slow-motion zone.

the blues according to ...

Terry Riley, who is speaking on the telephone from his home in California, his voice strangely reminiscent of Henry Fonda ...

In their search for absolutes, a number of music critics have looked to Riley as the definitive starting point for various trends: minimalism, extreme repetition, all-night trance improvisations and tape-delay systems. Pieces such as *In C*, *A Rainbow In Curved Air* and *Poppy Nogood and the Phantom Band* were important in their time because they signalled two important changes in the way the worlds of music and commerce worked. One: a composer was writing pieces which had grooves and improvised around modes (just like John Coltrane, Miles Davis, Frank Zappa and half the rock bands in psychedelia), that sounded as if psychotropics had been involved at some stage of the compositional process, and that explored new technology and studio processing. Two: the albums were packaged by Columbia as rock albums, despite being on the Masterworks series, so implying that the razor wire dividing so-called classical, rock, jazz, art and commerce had been cut in a few places. Never mind the embarrassing occurrence of hippie-speak on the *In C* sleevenotes – "No preconceptions, you just dig it" – the sort of thing that Oliver Stone might exhume for another chapter of his 1960s revisionism. The music, as musicians and sleevenote writers love to say, spoke for itself. Essentially modest, Riley downplays all of this. After all, his contribution to the late twentieth-century mix emerged out of collaborative work and improvisations with La Monte Young, Pauline Oliveros and Chet Baker. After the first flush of enthusiasm for minimalism and systems music, Riley and Young tended to be dismissed as old hippies, past their peak, while Philip Glass, Steve Reich, John Adams and Michael Nyman slid with varying degrees of compositional credibility into a new orthodoxy of avant-garde populism. But as Riley says, life goes in cycles. Suddenly, the open works of Riley and Young seem more expansive, more useful to the fractured nature of music in the 1990s than all that knitting-machine repetitiveness and its mutations.

I am asking Riley about a 1960 composition called *Mescaline Mix*, mentioned in passing in the explanatory notes for a recent piece, *Cactus Rosary*. Was there any great significance in the title? "Oh yeah, the psychedelic movement was just beginning then", he says, "but it was definitely happening. I remember Richard Maxfield brought me my first psilocybin mushrooms in '62 or something like that. He was very into psychedelic drugs before he died. Well, all kinds of drugs, unfortunately. He took some very strong things and maybe his death could be explained by that." Riley met him at Berkeley, where Maxfield impressed everybody with his resourcefulness, using simple tone generators and spliced tape to create imaginary landscapes. He patiently edited pieces for Riley, displaying the obsessive, perfectionist nature that goes hand-in-hand with the skill like a curse. "He would make several splices per inch", says Riley. "He was a very top notch editor at CBS. That's what he did. He spliced together performances of Horowitz and all these classical artists. That's where he developed his technique."

Mescaline Mix was a piece made when Riley was music director for the Ann Halprin dance company, and was used to accompany a dance called *The Three Legged Stool*. "It was recorded tape loops that were all mixed from people playing the piano, laughing, different sounds I'd collected here and there, explosions. I did it all by overlaying tape loops", he explains. After a lengthy period of composing solo piano works in just intonation and string quartet compositions for the Kronos Quartet, Riley's 1993 recording of *Cactus Rosary* seems a return to his sources: jazz, blues, electronic keyboards, ritual. Towards the end of the piece, a blues emerges, like a microtonal, instrumental version of John Lee Hooker's "Boogie Chillun", a trumpet peeking out from the shuffling rhythm every now and again. Riley tells me about the piece. "I've been a very close friend of Bruce Conner, the artist, for many years", he says. "He sent me this magazine which had an interview with him and Robert Dean. Bruce started out the interview with Robert Dean by holding out two peyote rattles. They were both made by an Indian shaman. One was made with a pepper shaker, an aluminium can, and one was a traditional gourd type rattle made by the same shaman. He said that something would be signified by shaking each rattle, instead of him giving an answer sometimes, which I thought was a very nice way to structure the interview. Then I started writing this piece and I thought of making the peyote rattle the centrepiece and having the piece kinda having the feeling of what it would be like to be at a peyote ritual, or at least some kind of experience like that. I notated it differently and I put it in a special tuning, using the time-lag effect, which I used to use in some of my earlier music. I was thinking of a pyramid shape when I wrote it. The conducter shakes the peyote rattle. He's sitting in the centre in a transparent tent, which is lit theatrically, and then the other players are gathered around him."

Fond of the music of Bach, Debussy, Ravel, Bartók and John Coltrane, Riley was a piano player originally. "I started out learning honky tonk and ragtime with Wally Rosen," he says, "a very good dixieland player." He played solo piano in bars, learning how to engage an audience and expand outwards from familiar themes into flights of imagination, taking the innocent listener with him without causing too much discomfort in the process. "Improvisation is important", he insists. "Being able to create music on the spot and to keep it open. That was the message that kept coming through to me from John Cage: keep it open." His contemporaries – Terry Jennings and La Monte Young – had both played saxophone since their youth. Riley wrote a piece for a player named Sonny Lewis but then felt the need to learn the instrument just to play his own composition. Under the influence of La Monte Young and John Coltrane, whose soprano playing in the mid 1960s persuaded many tenor and alto players to add the instrument to their repertoire, Riley took up soprano to play *Dorian Reeds, Poppy Nogood and the Phantom Band* and, later, film soundtracks such as *Les yeux fermés*. The straight horn has close affinities to the Indian double reed *shehnai* and *nadaswaram*, or the Middle-Eastern flute, the *ney*, all of which are played with strong vocal qualities. "When I started studying Indian music", he says, "I abandoned the saxophone because I wanted to sing."

With his *Persian Surgery Dervishes* album, two live solo performances for electric organ and tape delay system recorded in Los Angeles and Paris in 1971/72, Riley became the guru of trance improvisation and meditative music. "You can get high by getting in one groove", he says. "You can get high by staying on one note, there's different ways but that's definitely a way to ecstasy. Things come around in cycles. I'm sure this has happened other times in history too, even in the West, when people try to organise their music so it can be experienced in a different way. For instance Satie and *Vexations*. It probably happens every once in a while. It's a real need to experience music in a deeper, more continuous way, rather than as wallpaper, or a very quick hit. I've been having young kids come up here to talk to me who are involved with the rave, full-moon events here in California. They seem to think there's a big connection between the things I did then and the things they're doing now. I think it's fine. I think there is a connection." In the repetitive keyboard figures of UK acid-house records by Baby Ford, A Guy Called Gerald or 808 State, back in 1988, Terry Riley's influence seemed to have located itself in an arena of machine-trance and circadian ecstasy which was not always conscious of his existence. Mixmaster Morris was well aware of his all-night concerts, however, and claims them as a central influence on his campaign to make listeners "lie down and be counted".

Riley recalls this brief but notorious period of all-night performances: "The first one I was asked to do was at Philadelphia College of Art. Before that I hadn't thought about even doing it myself but after I'd had this experience of playing for people over a period of eight hours and having them bring their sleeping bags and hammocks, people brought food and spent the whole night. It felt like a great alternative to the ordinary concert scene. It was '67 and '68. By '68 I didn't do any more. I was playing *Poppy Nogood and the Phantom Band* and *Keyboard Studies*. Then later on, *Rainbow In Curved Air*. It was always the same pieces, but very long, long versions of them. It takes a sense of urgency out of music that you have performing over a short period of time. This way, you could have long periods where the music could be saying not particularly anything, just waiting for a chance to develop. I also felt very comfortable with the audience in that situation, because they came there to hang out for a long time and they weren't coming to get a hit and then walk away and go someplace else. This was going to be the whole night's event so you developed a kind of feeling, like you were a sort of channel for the energy that was coming in from the space. You were all joining together, which was more of a ritual experience." Later, during the first half of the 1970s, he played lengthy solo concerts in France and Italy, but none of these lasted all night.

Tansen's enemies were determined to ruin him. "Make him sing

Deepak Raag. He will burn himself to death!" ... "!!" ... "That's a brilliant idea!" ...

"This time I'm done for. The heat of Deepak Raag's notes turns the body into ashes!! No wonder the courtiers look triumphant.

"Megh Raag brings rain and cools the heat. If someone sings this raag simultaneously I have a chance to survive ... but who?? ..."
      Dolly Rizvi, *Tansen* comic

"At that time, about 1970s," Terry Riley says, " I got really seriously involved with Indian classical music, which goes on all night anyway, so by that time I had transferred interest into that. Indian classical music was doing the kind of thing that I was trying to produce on my own, this kind of deep modal effect that each raga has, the psychological effect and spiritual effect that the ragas carry, I was starting to sense in the music I was producing. When I found Indian classical music, there was a great tradition already developed over several centuries by artists. There was a large body of work I felt necessary to become acquainted with and find out how they did this and just how the music worked, because it seemed to assimilate what I was trying to do anyway."

calligraphy

The Royal Albert Hall, summer 1994. Bidur Mallik and his two sons, Ramkumar and Premkumar, can be linked to a time when the *dhrupad* singing style to which they have devoted themselves was credited with supernatural powers. They claim that their family can be traced back to 1790, when Radhakrishna and Kartaram Mallik averted a drought by singing *Megh* raga, the magical raag which brings rain and cools the heat. Those who have never seen this austere, abstract music performed can find the experience almost comical, yet the beauty of tone is profound. Though a small man, Bidur Mallik swooped down to very low-pitched, sustained notes without a safety net of vibrato, jumping through outlandish intervals as if he was engrossed in an arcane form of audible mathematics, inscribing the physicality of his notes in the air with graceful hand movements. The hands seem to coax the notes, draw them out, hold them in one spot for incredible sustains or float them on their way. Otherworldly in its unadorned beauty, the *dhrupad* style is the closest that vocal improvising comes to calligraphy. After hearing this group, I feel that there is nothing else in the world I need to experience. But then Rajan and Sajan Misra explore a single raag in *khyal* style for more than one hour. *Khyal* means fantasy. This style is lush, developed in shaded increments that seem calculated to bring an audience to intense levels of perceptual awareness, opening in ravishing slow motion like the birth of a butterfly, rich in harmonic sensuality. Thickly composed of two tambouras, electronic drone, harmonium, supporting vocals and plucked zither, the drone implies a universe of possibilities over which Rajan and Sajan sustain perfectly tuned notes, holding them in the air with their hands until every molecule has dissolved into the infinite sound pool. Tabla drums patter in raindrops. Another world wheels into view, an aesthetic just as enticing as the *dhrupad* which preceded it.

"The note: a taut bow. Syllables: true arrows. Their target: ecstasy", Haridas Dagar has said. The virtuosity and grace of allowing pure simplicity to flow in unbroken streams. Many years ago, I saw the Dagar brothers, Mohinuddin and Aminuddin, the exalted exponents of *dhrupad*, singing in two very different settings. The first, Golders Green Unitarian Church, was attended by a predominantly Indian audience. Disturbingly, they squirmed, gesticulated, sighed and called out with every exquisite parabola, every held note, every tremolando and daring ornament. Despite the severity of the *dhrupad* style, this physical, vocal appreciation was the response they expected. The Dagar brothers could trace their family back to Vrija Chandra, or Daguri, a rival of Tansen, singer to the court of the emperor Akbar in the sixteenth and

early seventeenth centuries. I saw them sing again in a more
New Age setting in Hampstead. Here, the non-Indian audience
was rapt, silent, physically inert and dutifully lotus-posi-
tioned, hungry for higher consciousness. At half-time, the
Dagar brothers slipped out for cigarettes, smoked fervently in
the open doorway.

resonant intervals

For Terry Riley, along with La Monte Young, Marian
Zazeela, Jon Hassell, Don Cherry, Lee Konitz, Jon Gibson,
Henry Flynt and dancer Simone Forti, Pandit Pran Nath was
the teacher. Riley explains the distinction between *kirana*
style and other forms of Indian classical vocal music: "*Kirana*
is the most lyrical. It has the attention to the notes that
dhrupad does, but it has the imagination and lyrical effect of
khyal. Pran Nath himself is a synthesis of styles he observed
and studied. He has a unique place." Riley reiterates Jon
Hassell's view of Pran Nath's core teaching. "He always said
the first lesson was you go inside the tone. You're in the tone
and the tone is in you. To really feel, when you're singing, like
you are that note. It has a physicality about it. That was a very
big thing for me, because it was something I was approach-
ing anyway."

This concern with tone and accurate pitching dovetails
with Riley's and Young's move away from twelve-tone equal
temperament – the system by which semitones are slightly
adjusted in order to make all the intervals of the octave equal.
Written for all the major and minor keys, J.S. Bach's *The Well-
Tempered Clavier* was one of the earliest works to explore
and publicise the possibilities of equal temperament. Allowing for modulation between keys, the system has dominated
Western music since the beginning of the eighteenth century.
Fixed-pitch modern instruments such as the piano and organ
are tuned to equal temperament, although many synthesisers
now allow retuning; increasingly, both software writers and
instrument builders are exploring alternatives to the out-of-

tune instruments with which Westerners (and anybody else in the world who accepts European musical standards) have become accustomed. The American composer and instrument inventor Harry Partch, having himself rejected equal temperament, devoted a large section of his weighty but witty book *Genesis of a Music* to the subject. "With this tuning", he wrote in the mid 1940s, "the musician could rosy around all day long with completely satisfying, undeviating monotony." Retuned keyboards can sound strange on first hearing, despite the fact that they have been returned to an accord with the physical laws of nature. But the popularity of blues, or the musics of Africa and Asia, along with the odd tunings that can arise when detuned digital samples are overlaid, has ensured a growing openness to music not played in equal temperament. "The practice of singing resonant intervals, the intervals that are really in tune," says Riley, "is probably more prevalent in the world than equal temperament. Just in the Western world in the last hundred and fifty years. It's not strange really. We've sorta got into this black and white movie and the colour just for a minute there shocks us. And it is very colourful. In the coming years, the frontier will be tuning."

Before recording the albums which established his reputation, Riley worked with jazz trumpeter Chet Baker in Paris. In the early 1950s, Baker had played in the Gerry Mulligan Quartet, a piano-less group with Mulligan playing baritone saxophone, Chico Hamilton on drums and Bob Whitlock on bass. Recorded in Los Angeles and hugely influential on the West Coast "cool school", Mulligan's group now sounds interesting, if slightly tepid, for its exploration of melodic cycles, circling and weaving in improvised counterpoint within the format of popular songs. "Jeru", for example, can be imagined as an acoustic precursor to Riley's dervish improvisations. Like Terry Riley (and The Modern Jazz Quartet's John Lewis), Mulligan was inspired by Bach. "I consider the string bass to be the basis of the sound of the group," Mulligan wrote, "the foundation on which the soloist builds his line, the main thread around which the two horns weave their contrapuntal interplay. It is possible with two voices to imply the sound of or impart the feeling of any chord or series of chords, as Bach shows us so thoroughly and enjoyably in his inventions."

This emphasis on the formal possibilities of jazz, whether small group or orchestra, resurfaced continually among white musicians, adding another tension, often a racial opposition, within the music. As Miles Davis complained in his autobiography: "What bothered me more than anything was that all the critics were starting to talk about Chet Baker in Gerry Mulligan's band like he was the second coming of Jesus Christ." As is still the case, the problem was not so much the music (though that could be bloodless), or the musicians, but the critical hype which surrounded it. Davis himself, George Russell, Andrew Hill, Chico Hamilton, John Lewis, Ornette Coleman and Eric Dolphy were all exploring areas of vaguely common interest. Dolphy, for example, recorded tapes influenced by Indian and Japanese music before his untimely death in 1964; his *Out To Lunch* album is an enduring example of how eclectic interests can be integrated into music which sounds at once utterly familiar yet from another dimension. And Ornette Coleman's interest in Third Stream, evident on a number of compositions for supposedly non-jazz instrumentation, has made a lasting impact. His playing with Dolphy, Scott La Faro, Jim Hall and The Contemporary String Quartet on Gunter Schuller's *Variants On a Theme of Thelonius Monk* can be instructively compared with the Coleman/ Howard Shore soundtrack to David Cronenberg's film of *Naked Lunch* (the best thing about the film incidentally). What was considered an aberration, a heresy, in 1961 becomes the main theme to a major motion picture in the 1990s.

Yet the list of cool school and so-called Third Stream white musicians whose music could gravitate towards a kind of polite, formal experimentation, as opposed to hard bop's self-conscious blues-rootedness, or the more open expression of free jazz that emerged at the end of the 1950s, is extraordinary:

Claude Thornhill, Gil Evans, Lennie Tristano, Lee Konitz and Warne Marsh, cellist Fred Katz, Jim Hall, Dave Brubeck and Paul Desmond, Paul Horn, Stan Kenton, Bob Brookmeyer and Jimmy Guiffre, Bill Evans, Scott LaFaro, Gil Melle (soundtrack composer for *The Andromeda Strain*), Clare Fischer (later to arrange strings for Prince, The Family and Jill Jones at a time when Paisley Park was at a creative peak), Gunter Schuller and Don Ellis all leaned, with varying degrees of artistic success but a generally high level of commercial acumen, towards colouration, impressionism, counterpoint and self-conscious rhythmic experimentation. This period of jazz, or this sector within this period, has given birth to some interesting developments: film composer John Barry studying by post with Bill Russo, a Stan Kenton arranger, shortly before composing *Beat Girl*, "The James Bond Theme" and his first Bond scores; Gavin Bryars's admiration for the precise, mathematical bass playing of Scott LaFaro in the Bill Evans Trio; the influence of cool school alto saxophonists such as Paul Desmond, Lee Konitz and Bud Shank on John Zorn; Jon Hassell's extrapolations from Gil Evans and the Evans, Mulligan, John Lewis, Miles Davis *Birth of the Cool* sessions; Harold Budd's fascination with pianist Lennie Tristano; and the aforementioned collaboration between Prince and Clare Fischer.

Some of these players touched upon areas later developed into full-blown movements. Don Ellis was using sitars, clavinets and strange percussion in his orchestra, playing trumpet through a Conn Multivider with loop delay, Antonin Artaud's Theatre of Cruelty name checked on the album sleevenotes and *still* sounding corny. And Lee Konitz, who later experimented with electric saxophone and over-dubbing, participated in Lennie Tristano's free improvisations – "Intuition" and "Digression" – in 1949. "We had rehearsals at Tristano's home", Konitz told me in 1987. "We'd try some of that", he said, forming his fingers into a joint-holding position. "Have a little taste, you know, and just start playing. We'd hit it right away. We did some of that at the concerts and it was thrilling." In his booklet notes for Ornette Coleman's *Beauty Is a Rare Thing* boxed set of Atlantic recordings, Robert Palmer assesses these early free improvisations as failures. "It was an intriguing experiment", he writes, "but without a firm grounding in the blues the music tended to simply meander in counterpoint; without a basis in vernacular rhythms, it failed to really go *anywhere*." True enough, although passion existed before the blues and besides, music not *going anywhere* is one of the most fertile developments of the twentieth century. Perhaps the problem lay with Tristano's style (and the style of his disciples). When deeply moved, Tristano's most expressive response was "Wow". His playing was gripping for being so fluently obsessive, rather than open-heartedly expressive. Without a channel for that obsession, the fluency became aimless and introverted.

Not that introversion is such a bad thing either. Chet Baker's introversion was integral to his appeal. Like Bill Evans, a pianist whose pellucid tranquillity made melancholy sound like a Zen state, Chet Baker had qualities which shone through the hype. "Chet was a wonderful master of understatement", says Riley. Despite the style-fixation romanticisation of Baker's heroin addiction through the 1980s, the still clarity of *Chet Baker Sings* and *Chet Baker & Strings* survives. "He has a relationship to Pran Nath in my mind – deep lyricism, a lot of depth in the music, but immediate appeal to the listener. Chet Baker could have been a pop star; was to a certain degree a pop star. We came together in a very strange way. I was working as a kind of arranger of his music, but the ideas that I had, I started developing these looping ideas. We were working on a theatre project together with a director named Ken Dewey. When I worked with Chet I recorded his quartet in Paris at that time individually, and then I put it all together electronically and then they played against it. It's a very different form but when you listen to it, you can still hear it's Chet Baker."

Rainbow In Curved Air, recorded in 1968, seemed like a

rock record at the time, although CBS also marketed Don Ellis's big band albums – *Shock Treatment* and *Electric Bath* – along with Walter Carlos's Moog showcase, *Switched On Bach*, in the same way. But *Rainbow In Curved Air*, in particular, exemplified the transition from music which is interpreted from written instructions on a score to music which emerges from a combination of composed melodic and rhythmic elements, improvisation and sonic manipulation through technology. Riley played electric organ, electric harpsichord, rocksichord, dumbec drum and tambourine on the album. "The recording was made on the first eight-track machine at CBS", Riley explains. "That was a chance to do a lot of stuff that I had been trying to do in my home studio on my little stereo machine. I could expand much more in the studio with overlaying and overdubbing the ideas that before had been a little bit one dimensional. I remember they just wheeled the eight track in. We were going to do it on four track but the technology hit so fast, from stereo to four track to eight track. Eight tracks at that time seemed like the universe, you thought you'd never run out of tracks." He laughs at that naivety. "But I ended up feeding some live tracks into the master. I brought my organ into the mixing room so we fed a couple of tracks in and mixed them live."

the machine
becoming part of the work; encroaching on performance in
real time

9 altered states iv: machine

Ryuichi Sakamoto; Erik Satie; Kraftwerk

Technology can reduce live performance to an anachronism. In the past decade, computers have delivered cybernetic music into realms which reach beyond human capabilities. For example, a concert stage in London: Ryuichi Sakamoto is faxing messages to friends around the globe during "Rap the World", a song in which machines do more of the work than the humans. But any sense of diminishment which may come from this new role of redundant operator, tends to be compensated by the satisfaction of feeling connected across great distances to like minds. Sakamoto, a founder member of techno-pop pioneers Yellow Magic Orchestra, is driven by the idealism of this connectedness. "I'm not a representative of Japanese culture", he insists. "I hate to divide the world – east and west. Where is the edge? My music is much more melting. All the different things are layered at the same time. It represents a sense of utopia. My view is always looking outside of Japan. One of my friends, he's a philosopher and critic. He made a word: outernationalism. Internationalism is still based on nationality. Being outernational is like Moses in the desert. There's no country. There is just trade, transportation, communication and merchants, but there's no nationality. It's a utopia and I like it. I don't want to be Japanese. I want to be a citizen of the world. It sounds very hippie but I like that."

mad computer

A hi-tech studio in west London: blond wood, perforated metal screens, the black padding and chrome rings of a chic S&M dungeon. A Mitsubishi TV screen, seven computer monitors. A lead connecting mainframe to memory is malfunctioning. Technological ennui. The black ice, as William Gibson called it, meditates. On one screen, moirés, pyramids and lozenges mutate; on another, devolving linear rectangles flick clockwise around the frame. The only sound is the soft rattle of computer keystrokes. Outside the control room, the chef is playing table tennis with the programmer. Inside, Ryuichi Sakamoto plays a loud distorted version of Erik Satie's *Gymnopédies* (a recurrent obsession with the Japanese: a swaggering bouzouki version turns up during a walking scene in Beat Takeshi's film *Violent Cop*). Later, observing the creation of music for his film of *The Sheltering Sky*, Bernardo Bertolucci walks into a practical joke. In the live room, a computer-linked Yamaha grand piano is playing all by itself, the ghost of a machine. Seeing the keys rising and falling, seemingly without human intervention, Bertolucci appears spooked. After the laughing has died down, he sits with assistant director Fernand Moszkowitz, both looking glum and creased on a charcoal couch. "*C'est monstrueuse, cette computer*", says Bertolucci. "*C'est fou*", Moszkowitz agrees. They both lapse into a grumpy silence. Moszkowitz's head drops back in sleep.

awkward silences

Composing music in 1917 for *Parade*, a ballet collaboration between Erik Satie, Jean Cocteau, Pablo Picasso and Léonide Massine, Satie scored for typewriter, pistol shots, steamship whistle and siren alongside more conventional instruments. "Satie caught the harshness of contemporary life", wrote a Satie biographer, James Harding. "He mixed ragtime and music-hall in a blend which expressed both the ugliness of a mechanical, commercialised age, and the spirituality that is crushed beneath it."

Thanks to the concise melodic charm of the *Trois Gymnopédies,* his best-known piano work, Satie has been embraced by advertising, his first *Gymnopédie* used in television commercials for Cadbury's chocolate and Strepsils throat lozenges. But despite his accessibility and the seemingly direct (though often ironic) humanity of his music, I think of Satie as the first machine composer. In certain respects, he lived like a machine: wearing the same grey velvet suits every day, then replacing these with a uniform of black-suited respectability. He drank beer, cognac and calvados steadily in Parisian bars and cafés until cirrhosis of the liver killed him. He even devised a precise timetable with which artists could regulate their lives – ". . . inspiration from 10.23 to 11.47 . . . I only eat white food . . . I only sleep with one eye shut . . . I wear a white bonnet, white stockings and white waistcoat . . ."

His virtuosity with such jokes and satires has left a residue of ambiguity. Now that some of Satie's most affecting works – the *Gymnopédies* and *Trois Gnossiennes* – veer dangerously close to being appropriated as clichés of middle-class easy listening, his elaborate, deadpan jokes resonate as blueprints for the music of our time. His *Musique d'ameublement*, for example, is cited often as a visionary precursor of ambient music, Muzak, dinner party music, interval music, Walkman music, elevator music and all the other functionary fill-ins and backgrounds, highbrow and lowbrow, that now accompany our lives. This "furnishing music" was devised after Satie and his friends had been driven from their lunch by loud restaurant music. As always, Satie weaved dangerous speculations with barbed wire. With such a self-protective, vulnerable man, disengaging satire from serious purpose is virtually impossible. But in building a theory of furniture music, a neutral and utilitarian background for all spaces and all activities, Satie suggested the second of two opposing characteristics of ambient music. On the one hand there was *Parade*, a hybrid of

new styles, sounds and technologies which drew the environmental into itself; on the other there was the furnishing
music, a style of composition which blended into any environment. In the former, the environment is transmuted by the
composer; in the latter, the composer is transmuted by the
environment. "I imagine it to be melodious", Satie wrote of
his *Musique d'ameublement,* "softening the clatter of knives
and forks without dominating them, without imposing itself.
It would fill up the awkward silence that occasionally
descends on guests. It would spare them the usual common-
places. At the same time it would neutralise the street noises
that tactlessly force themselves into the picture."

But even the furniture music, when Satie came to present
it, did not conform to my binary formula. During the interval
of a Max Jacob play staged at the Galerie Barbazanges in the
Faubourg Saint-Honoré, Satie organised an experiment in neu-
trality with Darius Milhaud (later to become a friend of the
Modern Jazz Quartet – a group that some might see as the ultimate in highbrow furniture music). In this instance, the
compositional method used by Satie and Milhaud invites
various descriptions – postmodern, for example, or plunderphonic – since the music consisted of snatches taken from
works by other composers. These were repeated over and over
by musicians scattered around the room. The idea of neutral-
ity was ahead of its time, however, since in an irony worthy
of his own sarcastic wit, Satie had to rush around the room,
commanding the audience to ignore what they were hearing.

i feel good

Del Webb's High Sierra Casino, Lake Tahoe, Nevada,
1986. At the epicentre of the casino, a shrill nightmare of
slots, blackjack, video sports betting, craps and all known and
legal forms of American financial haemorrhage, is a small circular bar. In the centre of the bar is a tiny stage revolving
around a thick pillar. Inexorably circling, trance-like, in torture of blandness, of slug-like tranquillity, of morbid cynicism,

are Kenny and Wayne, who play a thin, barely recognisable counterfeit of James Brown's "I Feel Good" on electric keyboard and Fender guitar. The bar is ringed by losers, drinking to oblivion, their dead eyes registering nothing as Kenny and Wayne pass and vanish, pass and vanish. Nobody hears a thing.

vexations

Satie used the device of repeating short, neutral fragments of melody for his soundtrack to René Clair's short film of 1924, *Entr'acte*. Discontinuous, pounded ostinato cells of repetitive material which go nowhere before giving way to the next theme, they clearly prefigure the strain of minimalism represented by Steve Reich, Philip Glass and Michael Nyman. In his 1974 book, *Experimental Music*, Nyman quoted Roger Shattuck on Satie's *Entr'acte* music: "Satie merely uses eight measures as the unit that most closely matches the average length of a single shot in the film . . . The transitions are as abrupt and as arbitrary as the cuts in the film." In another Satie piece, *Vieux sequins et vieilles cuirasses*, Satie instructs the pianist to repeat the final passage 380 times, the early equivalent of a locking groove at the end of a vinyl record. His most notorious (and vexed) exploration in repetition, boredom and ecstasy, however, was *Vexations*.

John Cage discovered the piece in 1949 during a Parisian sojourn. Composed in 1893, this brief passage for piano was accompanied by an instruction: "In order to play this piece 840 times the performer should prepare beforehand in deep silence and serious immobility." James Harding takes this as "exhibitionism", a "laboured joke", despite the fact that so much of Satie's work explored extremes of simplicity or repetition, and despite the fact that Satie's jokes invariably concealed a serious purpose. Cage certainly regarded the piece highly, as did London-based experimental composers like Gavin Bryars, Christopher Hobbs (a member of AMM during the late 1960s) and Michael Nyman. Cage premiered

Vexations in 1963, in a performance played in shifts by eleven pianists, lasting from 6 p.m. on 9 September to 12.40 on 11 September. Among the performers were John Cale, working that year in La Monte Young's group. Bryars and Hobbs gave their own performance of the piece in Leicester in 1971, writing comments during their rest periods. "Like falling asleep while driving on the motorway", is a note made by Hobbs and quoted by Nyman. Another strong argument to set against sceptics is the immediate awareness, as soon as the repetitions begin, that the psychological effect of these phrases intensifies as the music repeats. A strange lack of resolution brings the listener back to zero at each new beginning. Where the number 840 came from is anybody's guess, but to listen for a long time is more effective than listening just once.

Satie had certain interests in common with Varèse. He studied alchemy, the occult and Medieval music forms such as plainchant. *Vexations* turns out to be a heading from a work written by Paracelsus, the sixteenth-century alchemical philosopher and physician who wrote repeatedly about "the natural light of man" and the tranquillity of mind that would come at the conclusion of the alchemical process. In one respect Satie's preparatory instruction suggests a meditation through which the ability to play this arduous piece will shine through and be rewarded by illumination; in another respect the demands of immobility followed by a need for inhuman self-control and sustained repetitious action suggest an assumption of machine characteristics, a meditation through which the body becomes robot. By composing a work which few humans would feel capable of undertaking, Satie gazed one hundred years ahead of himself to a time when music of all kinds could not be played by humans without the assistance of machines.

ch-ch ch-ch-ch

1987. Halfway through the eighth bar of a brisk cover version of Kraftwerk's hit tune, "The Model", available on a lime-green cassette published by the Saha Kuang Heng Record and Tape Company, familiarity is shredded beyond repair. The tempo is dragged down by about thirty-four beats per minute, the rhythm turns Latin, a beat that in the hands of a vocalist such as Cheo Feliciano might be a smouldering salsa *montuno*. The electric organ slips back a few decades from quasi-Kraftwerk to the pop-psychedelia of The Seeds or ? and The Mysterians. Then the singing starts. The singer wears a white blouse with leg-o'-mutton sleeves and a mandarin collar, a white skirt, one black earring and one white. She sings in Thai, so the reason for this drastic segue from Kraftwerk 1978 into Thai pop 1985 via Latin garage-psychedelia 1966 is something of a mystery.

Kraftwerk's Ralf Hütter wears a black leather coat. When he takes it off he reveals a black jacket underneath. Black shirt, black tie, black trousers, black shoes. The socks are white. The hair was once all black but now it's going grey on top. He leans forward attentively in order to hear this singular version of his composition a little more clearly. "It's very good", he says in amused and clipped English. "I like it. We should go to Thailand."

Kraftwerk: the original power station, the conductors, the operatives, the sound fetishists. For something like a decade and a half before this interview they had been creating Düsseldorf dance music by allowing machines to speak for themselves. "I remember we played a dance party in some arts centre in Düsseldorf in '71", says Ralf. "We were not a fixed group in the beginning and the drummers were changing all the time because they were just banging and they wouldn't do any electronics. 'No! Don't touch my instruments.' One day we had this gig at the arts centre and I had this little old drum machine. At a certain moment we had it going with some echo loops and some feedback and we just left the stage and joined the dancers. It kept on going for an hour or so."

Kraftwerk: sexual, pure concentration, edible. Constraint with humour. Camp. Boys in uniform. Expression through proportion. Emotion through detachment. Inspiration through work. "Machines dance, so to speak," Ralf muses, "and repetition, rhythm, builds. But that's more an artistic fiction." Minor qualitative differences do differentiate the Kraftwerk of *Trans-Europe Express* in 1977, *The Man-Machine* in 1978, *Computer World* in 1981, *Tour de France* in 1983 or *Electric Café* in 1986. With devout classicism, the band aligned and realigned a miniature collection of melodies and pulses.

"La Côte d'Azur et Saint-Tropez, Les Alpes et Les Pyrénées, from station to station, Düsseldorf City, meet Iggy Pop and David Bowie, Business, Numbers, Money, People, I am adding and subtracting. By pressing down, a special key plays a little melody, *ein, zwei, drei, vier, fünf, sechs, sieben, acht, ichi, ni, san, shi,* computer love, computer love, I call this number for a downtown date. The number you have reached has been disconnected. Boing Boom Tschak, Boing Boom Tschak." The subject matter was the philosophy but deeper still was the obsession with pure sound. Like Fragonard painting satin, Kraftwerk indulged their appetite for the sensuality of surfaces and their depths in a setting that was contemporary, social and slyly ingratiating. Are you ever seduced by sound so much that form gets lost? I ask. "Mm", agrees Ralf. Your main problem, I suggest. "No, not problem. Aim," he counters, "because form we don't care for too much."

Is that the reason for the "travelling" form? "Autobahn", "Musique Non Stop", "Europe Endless", "Trans-Europe Express", "Tour de France". "Ja, ja", he agrees. "Letting yourself go. Sit on the rails and ch-ch ch-ch-ch. Just keep going. Fade in and fade out rather than being dramatic or trying to implant into the music a logical order which I think is ridiculous. The flow is much more . . . adequate. In our society everything is in motion. Electricity goes through the cables and people – bio-units – travel from city to city. At one point they meet and then – *phwiit*. Why then should music be at a standstill? Music is a flowing artform."

This is benign futurism, returning us to a post-war version of Marinetti dreaming about energy of distant winds, electrical power and the Danube running in "a straight line at 300 kilometres an hour", anticipating the deification of sporting speed stars such as Juan Fangio, Ayrton Senna and cyclist Bernard Hinault, prophesying travel manias and the fetishisation of communication regardless of content: on the ground – the destruction of homes to make way for roads and airports; in the aether – the intangible information infobahn, the so-called superhighway. For their stage show, Kraftwerk's visuals deliver a deadpan celebration of technological utopia, a deadly efficient parody and confirmation of Germanic efficiency. For "Autobahn", the screens display grainy monochrome films of a golden dawn of motorway driving when roads were clear and happy nuclear families made picnics on the grass verge to break their journeys.

In the late 1980s, Atlanta International Airport was, the brochures crowed, "the world's largest passenger terminal and second busiest in the world. The airport is the largest private employer in Georgia, pumping a billion dollars annually into the local economy." Its internal transportation (as America describes anything that moves) was particularly striking to the Kraftwerk fan. While the little electric train burrowed its way from Concourse C to Baggage, a voice droned instructions and information in a Vocoded monotone. As the doors opened, another computer voice of a higher and less authoritarian pitch joined in for a minor symphony of sound poetry.

When the American composer Alvin Lucier wrote his *North American Time Capsule* in 1967 for a Vocoder (described by Lucier as "designed by Sylvania Electronic Systems to encode speech sounds into digital information bits for transmission over narrow band widths via telephone lines or radio channels"), the results made for difficult listening. Like much of Lucier's music, the theory was fascinating but the sound seemed to be an inconsequential, unengaging by-product of a conceptualisation. In the same way that

Kraftwerk appropriated the doomed art of sound poetry or evaded theory and transmuted the base metal of German electronic music into gold, so they successfully took the new technologies and baptised them in the mainstream of culture. "Industrial societies are today worldwide", says Ralf. The ideal, he suggests, is to have "artistic presence also. Not just big corporations, business, numbers, money, people, but art, music." Using the innovations, both profound and trivial, of the proliferating technological society was part of their aim to create a new *Volksmusik*.

January 1984. I'm sitting in the bar of New York's Copa Cabana with The Fearless Four, a now long-vanished electro-hip-hop band. Their most enduring record, "Rockin' It", now sampled for mid-1990s' rap records, was a shameless and highly creative reconstruction of Kraftwerk's "The Man-Machine". "Kraftwerk – that's our soul group", mumbles The Great Peso over the muzak that mixes into the Copa's air conditioning.

Ralf Hütter's response to Kraftwerk's popularity in hip-hop reveals another aspect of machine-age thought, a reversal of the received dictum that art should elevate us above our surroundings and transcend functionalism. "I'm not a musicologist", he says, "but I think black music is very environmental. It's very integrated into lifestyle. You can do your housekeeping . . ." He scrubs the table energetically and suggests that Kraftwerk music is also good for this function. "When we started", he says, "electronics were either science-like – university, big academic titles – or space programmes. Our thing was always to incorporate from everyday life. On the cover of 'Autobahn' is my old grey Volkswagen and the sounds also – it's the noise from two hundred or a thousand kilometres of the autobahn." He beeps the pulse code on his black digital watch and laughs. To an extent, this was a reaction against bourgeois academic culture and the tyranny of theory. "For us it's something that's called in Germany the *Intellektuell Überbau* – the intellectual building, so huge,

Kafka-esque. For us that was never a problem. We came from little train sets and *Elektrobaukasten* – the post-war generation with these little electric toy boxes. You immediately become child-like in your approach."

Ralf Hütter and Florian Schneider first met at a jazz and improvisation course organised by the Düsseldorf Conservatory, Ralf with his electric organ and Florian with electric woodwinds and an echo unit. They were fellow members of what Ralf describes as the fatherless generation. "We were born after the war", he says. "It was not much of an incentive to respect our fathers." The Austrian/German heritage of Beethoven, Mozart, Wagner and Brahms was weighty, yet the pop world of the late sixties was also restrictive, particularly for non-English speakers. "Well organised", Ralf recalls. "Woodstock-like. You had to look a certain way. It was very strict and pre-programmed. We sneaked in through the back door." The two of them played for parties after art gallery openings in the industrial area of the Ruhr – the Cologne, Dortmund, Essen, Düsseldorf beat. Sometimes they linked up with the emergent free jazz movement: musicians such as Karlheinz Berger, Gunter Hampel and Peter Brötzmann. "We didn't play three-minute singles", says Ralf, unnecessarily. "The music would be long – building and vibrating." They also encountered the American avant-garde then touring a similar art gallery circuit: La Monte Young, who in 1969 constructed a non-stop sound environment of sine wave oscillators for thirteen days at the Galerie Heiner Friedrich in Munich; or Terry Riley, whose *In C* had attracted attention in many areas of music and who was playing concerts of lengthy duration in Europe. It was possible for them to watch Stockhausen at work in Cologne, as Ralf and Florian once did after taking LSD, live-mixing performances of his own work.

This was the period when everybody began to talk about world music. One of the lavish sideshows at the Munich Olympic Games of 1972 was a vast exhibition – World Cultures and Modern Art – devoted to the "encounter of 19th and 20th century European art and music with Asia, Africa, Oceania, Afro- and Indo-America". So, La Monte Young in one room, Javanese court gamelan musicians in another, with some sport and international terrorism as the main event. For Hütter and Schneider, the opportunity to see and hear performing musicians from Asia or Africa led them to ask themselves some vital (though problematic) questions: "What is our ethnic culture? . . . Was it bombed? We even included bomb sounds in our music at one time. What's our sound? What's our environment? Am I mute?"

In the Kling Klang studio in Düsseldorf, seemingly unproductive for many years now, there are storerooms of historic technology. Kraftwerk '70, Kraftwerk '75, Kraftwerk '81, Kraftwerk '87. "We call it a garden situation", says Ralf. "New things coming in, rebuilding. The old mixing with the new depending on the weather. We have a nearly organic mix. We are still using that old cocktail music rhythm box and then, on the other hand, we have the Synclavier. Our instrument is the studio. It's our little laboratory, our *Elektrospielzimmer*, our toyroom. Post-computer is the new primitivism. Over the last five years you can print or design more low frequency sculpture which before wasn't possible. It would just be one big boom . . . or glue. That's the art of studio technology. You can sculpture the sound from 20 to 20,000 Hz. We might hammer into granite one particular sound for an enormous amount of time but then later we think more in terms of film. With certain sounds we are fetishistic. One special *kling* then somebody else *klang*. Modelling this to the utmost." Voice recording he describes in terms of physical impact. "They melt. It's like talking drums. Percussions. More can be done. I feel like we're just about to start." In retrospect, this was rather sad, since nothing new emerged from the Kling Klang studio other than an album of remixes.

My last question: Do you listen to other music? "No", replies Ralf. "Maybe when we wander round. Sometimes when we go out to dance. Sometimes radio. I don't have a stereo at home. We listen to silence. We listen to fictitious music in our head. Think music."

10 altered states v: lucid dreaming

dreams, electronics; Aphex Twin; global techno

The Marquis d'Hervey de Saint Denys, author of *Dreams and How To Guide Them* in 1867, used mechanical music as a dream technique. He would dance with women he desired during tunes which he knew were available on musical boxes. Then he would have the music box play that piece of music as he slept, an apparently successful method of inducing the woman to appear in his dream. What happened, once they had appeared, is unrecorded.

bedroom bores

1992. I interviewed Richard James over the telephone. Still living in Kingston Polytechnic's halls of residence, he admitted that his electronics studies were already slipping away as a career in the techno business began to take precedence. He had released "Analogue Bubblebath 1", a conversation between simple breathy chords and a selection of rich squelches, and the follow-up, "Digeridoo", a fast, metallic piece of electronic minimalism built around the overblown upper tones produced by a didg' (as this native Australian voice tube is now known among legions of neo-hippie didgeridoo players and drummers). The legend was this: Aphex Twin was a mad inventor from Cornwall who built his own synthesisers. Surfing on sine waves, he would lead a pack of young boffins out of the computer screen glow of their bedrooms into the public domain of clubs, shops and charts, then back in and out of more bedrooms in a feedback loop of infinite dimensions. So far, all true. "One of my hobbies is looking into old analogue synthesisers", James told me then. His enthusiasm for the music of other people was restricted to acid, hard techno and experimental ambient from impeccably underground sources: Underground Resistance, Jack Frost and the Circle Jerks, the New Composers of Leningrad. "I just like music that sounds evil or eerie", he said. His biggest problem in life was the challenge of moving his instruments to club PAs. "They haven't got cases", he said. "They're just circuits. If I took them out at the moment they'd all bust up."

Fast-forward to January 1994. We sit in a King's Road restaurant drinking coffee. Despite the cold, a fan sweeps the air above us and, when I listen back to the tapes two days later, I hear periodic rumbles of distortion as the circulating air is blown over my microphone. "If you're into wild stuff, it sounds better if it's dirty", Richard said, back in 1992. Working under a variety of label-hopping pseudonyms, The Dice Man, Polygon Window, Aphex Twin, he had made a virtue of distortion. Not since the days of Throbbing Gristle or the earliest, crudest Chicago house tracks of Farley Funkin Keith and Sleezy D had tape overload been redeemed so thoroughly or celebrated so fruitfully. With their visceral twitter, clubbing percussion and stone-age moans, tracks such as "73 Yips", "I Keata", "Phloam" and "Flap Head" sounded like reasonably conventional dance tracks that had been sabotaged in the cutting room by a driller killer. *Selected Ambient Works Volume II*, on the other hand, was a serene, disembodied, episodic collection, the aural equivalent to a photo album filled with Polaroids of sunsets and seascapes. James compared them with "standing in a power station on acid". "Power stations are wicked", he says. "If you just stand in the middle of a really massive one so you get a really weird presence and you've got that hum. You just feel electricity around you. That's totally dream-like for me." The Cornishman comes out in him. "It's just like a right strange dimension."

Broaching this subject of dreams, he becomes animated. "This album is really specific", he says, "because 70 per cent of it is done from lucid dreaming." To have lucid dreams is to be conscious of being in a dream state, even to be capable of directing the action in a dream. The subject has been explored intensively by Celia Green, Director of the Institute of Psychophysical Research in Oxford. In her book *Lucid Dreaming: The Paradox of Consciousness During Sleep*, produced in collaboration with Charles McCreery, she confirms that composing music or hearing music and environmental sounds are not uncommon in lucid dreams. Green's relevance to musicians exploring so-called ambience, musics aimed at stimulating ecstatic states and generated by highly speculative machine–human relationships, was underlined by her agreement to record CDs outlining her theories for the emit series released by Nottingham-based Time Recordings, specialists in post-dance technological music. She has also written on the subjects of apparitions and out-of-body experiences. In the latter, a person can look down on her or his own body as if consciousness had located itself suddenly outside the physical boundaries of the body. All of these hallucinatory manifestations challenge consensus views of human perception. Ultimately, they realign us in the environment of ourselves; in turn, they must affect our conception of environment and ambient.

"I've been able to do it since I was little", James explains, talking in a way which indicates either a serious person who has never been taken seriously or a practical joker who has been taken too seriously for too long. "I taught myself how to do it and it's my most precious thing. Through the years, I've done everything that you can do, including talking and shagging with anyone you feel that takes your fancy. The only thing I haven't done is tried to kill myself. That's a bit shady. You probably wouldn't wake up and you wouldn't know if it had worked anyway. Or maybe you would. I often throw myself off skyscrapers or cliffs and zoom off right at the last minute. That's quite good fun. It's well realistic. Eating food is quite smart. Like tasting food. Smells as well. I make foods up and sometimes they don't taste of anything – like they taste of some weird mish-mash of other things."

This contributes handsomely to the Aphex Twin myth of the mad inventor, rarely sleeping, lost in boyish obsessions with combat, voyeurism and the internal workings of non-sentient, scientifically explicable machines. It also appeals to a new generation of teenage mutant phobic white (game)boy screenies. Judged in a more positive light, the Aphex Twin is staying true to his intuitive sense of the world. This is a world in which words and writing are overshadowed by more fluid, ambiguous media. His reason for playing live, which he no longer relishes, is to hear his music loud. Soundchecking, he locates the resonant frequencies of a room in order to ripple floors with sub-bass and shatter glass with high pitches. The reason for not naming some tracks is related to his synaesthetic ability. Whenever he hears music he enjoys, he sees one of his least favourite colours, which is yellow. Rather than fix music with words (even invented nouns or numbers), he is searching for a way to identify compositions with colour.

"About a year and a half ago", he says, "I badly wanted to dream tracks. Like imagine I'm in the studio and write a track in my sleep, wake up and then write it in the real world with real instruments. I couldn't do it at first. The main problem was just remembering it. Melodies were easy to remember. I'd go to sleep in my studio. I'd go to sleep for ten minutes and write three tracks – only small segments, not 100 per cent finished tracks. I'd wake up and I'd only been asleep for ten minutes. That's quite mental. I vary the way I do it, dreaming either I'm in my studio, entirely the way it is, or all kinds of variations. The hardest thing is getting the sounds the same. It's never the same. It doesn't really come close to it. When you have a nightmare or a weird dream, you wake up and tell someone about it and it sounds really shit. It's the same for

sounds, roughly. When I imagine sounds, they are in dream
form. As you get better at doing it, you can get closer and
closer to the actual sounds. But that's only 70 per cent of it."
Before he leaves, Richard explains his fondness for electronic
musician friends such as Michael Paradinas, otherwise known
as μ-ziq. "They've all got these strange personalities you've
never seen in the pop stardom world, people in their bedrooms all day long. They make four tracks a day", he says.
"People like me, bedroom bores, coming into the public eye.
That's quite amusing."

virtually muzak

For the sleevenotes of his first album – *Tango n' Vectif*
– μ-ziq cribbed liner notes from an album of Dutch low-to-
highbrow sci-fi electronic music from a 1962 album, *Song of
the Second Moon*, by Tom Dissevelt and Kid Baltan. "It sounds
quite good," says Paradinas. "It's not cheesy. It's really jazzy.
There's really long tracks, and short poppy ones which sound
a bit like Thunderbirds theme tunes but more jazzy. It's a bit
like Joe Meek. That's what Richard James said when I lent it to
him. I haven't heard Joe Meek." In *Incredibly Strange Music
Volume II*, Jello Biafra describes the record as "avant-elec-
tronic-exotica" with an "ethereal '50s sci-fi mood" which sums
it up comprehensively. Most people who read these
sleevenotes took them at face value, an indication of some
actual connection between 1990s' techno recordists and the
early pioneers of *musique concrète*, tone generator and tape
experiments. "No longer valid is the old music-hall joke about
the man who, on being asked what musical instrument he
plays, replies, 'the gramophone'!" the notes begin. "The
cheerful melodies . . . are served up with an accompaniment
that is a fascinating stream of tapping sounds, hisses, bubbles,
bumps, rattles, squeaks, whistles, moans, sighs, twitters,
clanks, muffled explosions and unmuffled explosions. This
may appear to be a cosy little chaos, but these works are in
fact as highly organised as anything conceived by Schönberg."

True to form, Paradinas in person is painfully reserved. "I'm not too into this old electronic stuff", he says. "Kraftwerk have got some good melodies. Tonto's Expanding Headband – that's all right. It is a bit cheesy. Cabaret Voltaire and stuff like that I could never get into. Human League, New Order, Depeche Mode, I used to listen to that stuff in my bedroom." Barely a flicker of reaction crosses his features when I pass on James's damning new category of techno music: the bedroom bores. He knows that all of these musical categories – intelligent techno, intelligent dance music, electronica, electronic listening music, artificial intelligence, ambient techno – are senseless and divisive, more representative of the pretentious aspirations of fans and critics than the motivations of musicians. What they do reflect, however, is an upsurge in domestically composed and recorded electronic music, thanks to the increasing affordability of compact, user-friendly sequencing software and digital audio recorders during the late 1980s. Atari manufactured a computer – the 1040 ST – fitted with in and out ports for MIDI leads, the communicating channels that carry information to and from computer, electronic keyboards and drum machines. It was cheap, so Atari became a standard, both for the bedroom bores and for the studios which they frequented at times when the limitations of the bedroom were unavoidable.

For Paradinas, the prospect of being incarcerated in a professional recording studio with a trained recording engineer is a nightmare. "You can't distort", he says, his body cringing even as he imagines the prospect. I encountered a similar reaction in 1991, visiting the home studio of LFO – Jez Varley and Mark Bell. Set up in the attic of a parent's home in Lofthouse, near Leeds, the studio was full of drum machines, digital samplers, synthesisers, a mixing desk, tape machines, all racked and stacked alongside a personal computer. After making a hit single called, with typical economy, "LFO", Bell and Varley tried recording in Sheffield's Fon studio. Home studio hum was annoying them, but at Fon, the results were intolerable for being "too polished". So the purview of electronic music, its stereotypical conceits of coldness, detachment, mechanisation – the attributes of robot-mindedness and laboratory clinicism in old-fashioned hard sci-fi – were displaced by a determination to transmute machine sequencing and electronic sounds into organic, changeable, "soft" substances. Speaking in 1989 to Manchester's 808 State, the first UK post-acid-house act to make a long-term pop career for itself, I found the same attitude. "Some of the best records are shoestring", said Graham Massey. Then, later in the interview, key words defined the difference between the emerging techno generation and most of its predecessors from the 1970s and early 1980s – Gary Numan, OMD, Jean Michel-Jarre, Tomita and Vangelis. Key words and phrases such as "alchemy", "getting your hands in the mud", "accident".

night drive thru babylon

But techno's machine-age coldness has a basis in mass production, mass consumption and the human – machine interface of Henry Ford's assembly line, an urban workforce marshalled and entrained by heavy industry and then left stranded by its relocation in Asia. The central inspiration for European techno came from the black housing projects of Detroit. In the late 1980s, Kirk DeGiorgio, a London-born techno musician who has recorded under the names of Future/Past, As One and Esoterik, travelled to Detroit as a record buyer. Anxious to meet his idols – Derrick May, Juan Atkins, Carl Craig – he experienced a shock of realisation. "I remember driving in from Chicago", he says, "and seeing the hi-tech headquarters for Ford and then I was in the most extreme poverty I've ever seen in my life, five minutes later. There's just no hope at all. It's just complete despair. Young girls on the street. You can really understand the melancholy feel of a lot of those early Detroit records, the coldness people associate with them. You can imagine Derrick May sitting up in his flat and looking out on Detroit. You can really see a city shaping a music."

Having grown up with the latter-day effects of Fordism, the Detroit techno musicians read futurologist Alvin Toffler's *The Third Wave* and found that Toffler's soundbite predictions for change – "blip culture", "the intelligent environment", "the infosphere", "de-massification of the media de-massifies our minds", "the techno rebels", "appropriate technologies" – accorded with some, though not all, of their own intuitions. First came the George Clinton-inspired electro-funk of Cybertron, a duo of Juan Atkins and a Vietnam vet named Rick Davies who called himself 3070. I am a number, not a name. Their music was explicit in its cold precision and roboticism. Track titles – "Clear", "Techno City", "Cosmic Cars" – dwelled on familiar Futurist themes of transcendence through movement and immersion in the smart city, the wired megalopolis. After Cybertron came another Atkins recording pseudonym – Model 500 – as well as Derrick May's Rhythim Is Rhythim and Mayday, Kevin Saunderson's Reese & Santonio, Carl Craig, Kenny Larkin, Stacey Pullen, Mark Kinchin and Underground Resistance. This was the canon, and tracks such as Derrick May's "Strings of Life", Carl Craig's "Crackdown" or Model 500's "Info World" and "Ocean To Ocean" established an intricate, subtle aesthetic that was difficult to match.

The repercussions of this music rippled out to European musicians, labels and DJs, particularly in Britain, Belgium, Germany, Holland, Scandinavia and Italy – A Guy Called Gerald, Orbital, The Black Dog, Moody Boyz, Future Sound of London, Dr Motte, Jam & Spoon, Carl Cox, Bandulu, Autechre, Redcell, Speedy J, Aqua Regia, Dave Angel, The Irresistible Force, C.J. Bolland, Frank De Wulf, Source, Stefan Robbers, Sun Electric, Thomas Fehlmann, Global Communication, Higher Intelligence Agency, Sweet Exorcist, Seefeel, Bedouin Ascent, Mouse On Mars, Sketch, Oval, and then the next generation of UK jungle producers, whose innovations in rhythm programming and edit experimentation swept aside the astral melancholy of techno – L.T.J. Bukem, Goldie, Foul Play, 4 Hero, Omni Trio, Roni Size, DJ Crystl. This tidal wave of software surfers expanded regardless of the market or major-label indifference, their growing numbers, pseudonyms and productivity rates precluding any possibility of keeping track. Cottage industrialisation in the digital world seemed to be generating its own needs, its own pace, its own channels of communication.

In Frankfurt, Peter Kuhlmann worked under the name of Pete Namlook and ran an independent record label called Fax, releasing a series of mostly limited-edition CDs at the rate of two a week. These were either lengthy electronic solo pieces or collaborations and solo albums from musicians such as Tetsuo Inoue, Ritchie Hawtin, Dr Atmo, Jonah Sharp, Robert Musso, Bill Laswell, Geir Jenssen, Mixmaster Morris, Deep Space Network and Daniel Pemberton. By fax, I asked Namlook about the transition from an earlier musical phase, when he had played New Age music with a band called Romantic Warrior. "I'm basically not interested to talk too much about what you call 'Ambient' music", replied Namlook, assuming that this categorisation was accepted by everybody but himself. "I never had an intellectual approach towards this music and I was never inspired by any other musician to do my kind of music. This music comes from my 'heart'. My musical experience was more focussed on jazz and Oriental music. What you call 'Ambient' was there when I learned to play my first two chords on the guitar in 1974. I went out with my father to a journey through Turkey and sat near to the water and 'played' along with it. I tried to pick up the noises and give back my feelings to the environment through my instrument. I never stopped doing this kind of music, which for me was very emotional and melancholic. Nature was my main teacher."

11 altered states vi: nature

bionics, shamanism and nature; singing sands;
the Orinoco; holy minimalism and whales;
Pauline Oliveros; reverberation; Alvin Lucier and
sound art

> "I'm going up on the mountain, find me a cave and talk
> to bears if it takes me years"
> "Wildlife", Captain Beefheart

In an essay of film criticism called "Technophobia", Michael
Ryan and Douglas Kellner argue that technophobic films such
as *THX 1138* and *The Terminator* use technology fear to af-
firm traditional social institutions. Such institutions declare
themselves as a part of nature, the antidote to technological
threat, yet technology – from virtual reality to genetic engineering – is in the process of reconstructing nature.
"[T]echnology represents the possibility that such discursive
figures as 'nature' (and the ideal of free immediacy it con-
notes)", they write, "might merely be constructs, artificial
devices, metaphors . . ."

The hard-body roboticism of Arnold Schwarzenegger (machine impersonating nature or human in machine form?)
embodies this supposedly unstoppable technological jack-
boot march. But with *Predator*, not referred to in the Ryan and
Kellner essay, the picture morphed into a new shape. The
predatory creature at the centre of John McTiernan's film gen-
erates maximum fear when integrated into nature, a flickering
presence distinguishable from the jungle vegetation into
which it merges only as an interference pattern at the edge of

perception. Not until the end of the film, when it reveals it-self as alien beast/machine in order to go *mano a mano* with Schwarzenegger, does it slip into the comforting realm of or-dinary horrors. And after that revelation, Schwarzenegger permits himself to unveil a brief glimpse of his own human side. About to crush the predator's head with a rock, he is stopped by a mixture of compassion and curiosity. In that pause, the predator taps out a code and blows himself to pieces. Confused messages here: Never allow the hawk in you to be weakened by the dove, perhaps; some suggestion that humans are equally frightened of nature and machines, de-spite being part of one and symbiotically entwined with the other. Reading too much into Hollywood films is an intellec-tual party game that can shed darkness on an infinite variety of subjects.

This uneasy relationship between nature and technology was given a positive boost in 1958 when a US Air Force major named Jack E. Steele coined the word bionics. Steele defined bionics as the science of systems whose function is based on living systems, or which have characteristics of living sys-tems. The principle can still be found in contemporary research, particularly in the development of smart technolo-gies and biomimetic products, some of which are based on the muscular movements of sea creatures such as starfish and sea cucumbers. But scientists have always learned from ani-mals. Early examples of bionic engineering would include Leonardo da Vinci's sketch of a flying machine based on a bat, or the post-Titanic disaster suggestion by Sir H.S. Maxim, the inventor of the Maxim machine gun, that the echo-locating ability of bats could indicate ways of avoiding a similar calam-ity in the future.

The origins of radar date back to 1793. A professor at Padua University, Lazzaro Spallanzani, was fascinated by the fact that bats can fly and hunt in darkness. He began to investigate and concluded correctly that they must emit sounds and then find their way by hearing the reflections bounce back off objects in their flight path. These sounds are ultrasonic, however, so radar development was delayed for more than a hundred years, partly because later researchers believed that many of the experiments performed on bats were cruel, and partly because they refused to believe in sounds that they could not hear. So they dismissed the poetic theory that bats see, or maintain spatial awareness at least, with their ears. Until the development of an ultrasonic detection system in 1938, the sounds made by bats remained secrets of the aether.

Technology has made us a party to many of the sounds which surround us, as well as adding many more of its own. A question posed by Donald R. Griffin, an American researcher into the use of acoustic orientation by sight-impaired humans, bats, moths, marine mammals and cave-dwelling birds, offers another angle on the human fear of nature's alien otherness. "Twenty years ago", he writes in *Listening In the Dark*, "bats seemed from any ordinary point of view to be miniature monsters . . . Yet there can be no doubt that questions of the most arresting sort were already clearly posed by the simple fact that these little creatures spend their active lives in rapid and skillful flight through varying degrees of darkness. Why until so very recently did these intriguing questions attract so little interest? Was it because of the superstition that surrounds the popular image of a bat . . . ?"

"Matthew, think what it would mean if I could talk to the animals . . ."
    Rex Harrison, *Doctor Doolittle*

The desire to learn from animals and communicate with them is as old as paradise and the hellish underworlds that counterbalance it. The ancient Chinese seven-string flat lute, the *ch'in*, sometimes appears as a passing symbolic reference to magic and antique refinement in Hong Kong martial arts films, particularly costume dramas such as King Hu's *Touch of Zen* and Ching Siu Tung's *A Chinese Ghost Story*. Finger techniques for playing the instrument included touches described as "a crane dancing in a deserted garden", "the Shang-Yang bird hopping about", "a swimming fish moving its tail", "white butterflies exploring flowers", "echo in an empty vale", "a cold cicada bemoans the coming of autumn" and "cold ravens pecking at the snow". Admittedly, the *ch'in* was a repository of élite esoteric lore. One touch – *ting-yin* – consisted of pressing the fingertip heavily down on a string without moving it. According to some handbooks, vibrato was produced with the pulsation of the player's circulation. Strict rules which dictated when the instrument should or should not be played were formulated in Ming period handbooks. Sitting on a stone, in a high hall or boat, resting in the shadow of a forest or, rather ambiguously, meeting a suitable person were all considered good situations. Markets and shops were considered to be unsuitable, and playing whilst drunk, sweaty, wearing strange clothes or after sex was forbidden. But, as detective novelist, diplomat and *ch'in* scholar Robert Hans van Gulik has written, these rules of constraint were "much more precise and severe, and therefore the least observed".

Unity with nature and the uncluttered mind that came with this unity were fundamental to the appreciation and proper playing of the instrument. Cranes, the Chinese symbol of longevity and, by extension, immortality, were regarded as psychopomps, messengers which guided souls to the domain of the dead. This shamanistic motif figured large in the symbology of *ch'in* music, particularly during the period before magical associations were overridden by literature and aesthetics. One story, quoted by van Gulik in *The Lore of the Chinese Lute*, illustrates the connection between music, altered states and shamanistic flights to the heavens: "Chang Chih-ho loved to drink wine, and when inebriated used to play his lute all night long without resting. One evening there suddenly appeared a grey crane, which danced round about him. Chang then took his lute, and riding on its back, disappeared in the sky."

Why do shamanistic images appear as survivals in so many forms of music? Perhaps because music is so often a gateway to unusual or ecstatic states of consciousness and because shamans were (and occasionally still are), as Mircea Eliade put it, technicians of ecstasy. Shamanism flourished in animistic hunter–gatherer societies, in which a comprehensive survivor's knowledge of the natural world was indivisibly linked to the magical technique of nature mimicry. In every hallucinatory journey, shamans would transmute into animal forms. Travelling to spirit regions and dead zones, often carried by an eagle or riding a drum, they would speak their own secret language – a mixture of arcane vocabulary, strange noises and wildlife sounds – in order to communicate with spirits and animal familiars. In his classic study of the subject, *Shamanism*, Eliade finds many examples of this inter-species skill, interpreting it as a symbolic return to the primordial, paradisiacal time when animals and humans spoke in a common tongue and lived in harmony together. Like the Chinese Taoists, shamans heard spirit music in running water. "According to the Carib tradition", Eliade wrote, "the first *piai* (shaman) was a man who, hearing a song rise from a stream, dived boldly in and did not come out again until he had memorized the song of the spirit women and received the implements of his profession with them." But as this story's imagery of death, rebirth, the abyssal unconscious and inspirational female knowledge also suggests, shamans' songs and language were demonstrations of the fluidity and fearlessness with which the shaman could negotiate zones of remote consciousness and profound experience.

nature

December 1994. A news agency reports a significant find by Chinese archaeologists: two *xun* wind instruments, estimated to be 6,500 years old, used as decoys by hunters to attract birds and animals.

echo beach

> I drew a nine foot treble clef in the sand with
> my feet and recorded the sound on tape.
> The beach comprises clean, evenly spaced Quartz
> granules and emits a musical note when walked on.
> Paul Burwell, *Island of Eigg 1977*

"Singing sands are susceptible to changes in atmosphere", Annabel Nicolson wrote in *Musics* magazine in 1978. "On a hot dry day walking over the singing sands of Eigg can be noisy. When it is damp the sands are silent and it is hard to believe they could ever be otherwise . . . On the cliffs of Beinn Bhuidhe, facing away from the singing sands, we overlooked another stretch of coast from which came strains of music at sea level. The purity of tone was sustained over some distance from the source. The sea was transparently green, reflecting the light from the surface onto the sea bed. There were rocks in the water which seemed to be close to the source of the sand but not the cause of it."

January 1995. Singing sands are reported to be disappearing. These beaches, scattered around the world, actually chirp as a person walks across them, making a sound that has been likened to Japanese *koto* music. Walking across a chirping surface also recalls the Nightingale Floor in Kyoto. Maybe these associations explain the fact that vanishing singing sands (*nakizuni*, as they are called in Japan) have been investigated by a Japanese researcher, Shigeo Miwa. An analysis of a sample taken from Florida's Pensacola Beach by Dr Miwa revealed a high proportion of pollutants mixed with the 99.7 per cent pure silica quartz sand, but forty minutes of boiling in water restored the sand to full voice. Dr Miwa's sample is now displayed in the Niwa Sand Museum in southern Japan.

In *Oriental Magic*, Idries Shah claimed that the ancient Egyptians took oracles from singing sands. Desert people of the Middle East also believed that singing sands were portents. Just after World War II, Shah was told that a Libyan dervish had foretold war in 1937, advised preparation for the Western Desert campaigns and predicted independence from Italian colonisation, all based on oracular interpretations of singing sands.

dreaming up nature

1972. I am keeping two small alligators in a small tank in the garden. A loud shrieking noise breaks out. The alligators are mating, but at the same time they are eating a large sea snail. Other sea snails, monstrous and white, leap in panic across the lawn.

chasm

In 1950, a French explorer named Alain Gheerbrant played a Mozart record to Venezuelan Maquiritari Indians during an expedition along the Orinoco, Ventuari and Amazon rivers. A photograph in Gheerbrant's book, *The Impossible Adventure*, is captioned "Listening to Mozart". This striking portrait shows a man listening with his eyes closed. His mouth is relaxed, blissful, but his eyes seem squeezed shut, as if the experience is as painful as it is pleasurable. "I do not know if music is really the universal language people often say it is", wrote Gheerbrant, "but I shall never forget that it was the music of Mozart to which we owed our rare moments when the chasm which centuries of evolution had dug between us, civilised white men of the twentieth century, and them, the barbarians of the Stone Age, was almost completely bridged."

In 1978, a similar scene was replayed. Pulled up at night on a shelf of flat land at the edge of the Orinoco, Nestor and I dragged out the suitcase that contained our tape recorder, microphones, tapes, batteries and bags of silica gel. Setting it up, ostensibly to test the equipment, more truthfully to ground ourselves for a few minutes in a memory of life in London, we played a track from one of our favourite albums, Marvin Gaye's *I Want You*. The Maquiritari Indians with whom we travelled listened, giggled and then turned away to continue discussing the forthcoming Venezuelan election.

By the late 1970s, the racial encodement of Europeans and Indians into a neat opposition of civilised, individualised city dwellers (culture), set against an abstract mass of Stone Age barbarians (nature) was no longer the kind of sentiment to be expressed in books. Having said that, every American missionary we encountered in Amazonas talked openly about the devil-worshipping Indians as children, calling their shamans witch doctors, an expression I don't think I had heard since the 1950s. The Maquiritari often referred to their neighbours, the Yanomami, as banana-eating monkeys. As for the Yanomami, yet to be lauded as gentle forest people, they ate earth, drank soup made from the ashes of dead people, played humiliating practical jokes, walked miles along a river to find a crossing place rather than sweat over building a boat, engaged in perpetual warfare and spent afternoons consuming strong plant hallucinogens which made them vomit and drool. I rather liked them.

Writing about Debussy's archaeologist and writer friend Victor Segalen, James Clifford places him in a turn-of-the-nineteenth-century milieu described as "a post-symbolist poetics of displacement". Also locating artist–travellers Paul Gauguin, Arthur Rimbaud, Blaise Cendrars, Michel Leiris and Antonin Artaud within this milieu, Clifford goes on to say that "the new poetics rejected established exoticisms" and "the new poetics reckoned with more troubling, less stable encounters with the exotic". I had read Artaud's account of his search for magic and collective myth in Mexico, along with a number of "impossible adventures", all of which luxuriated in dire warnings of sting rays, piranhas and strange little barbed fish which could swim up a stream of urine and lodge in a man's urethra. Nothing prepared me for the surrealism of Amazonas, however.

a journey sideways

2 November 1978. We tied up our hammocks under a roof with no walls at the edge of the Orinoco. The night noises are intense, the sky lit by flashing tracers of light. I sleep fitfully. In the morning, I am woken by a loud, eerie siren chorus of frogs, a sound like lost souls calling to tempt unwary travellers: "Oy, oy, oy, oy." I knew this strange call from a record of Venezuelan wildlife sounds released by French bioacoustic recordist Jean C. Roche, who wrote: "The unusual musical volume of this tropical country [Venezuela] made its impact on my arrival in town, where the unbelievably shrill chirping of the cicadas overwhelmed me each time I passed under a tree. At nightfall, around even the meanest of ditches filled by the daily rain, myriads of toads and frogs struck up a concert, which, through its sheer intensity, muffled all other surrounding noises. When I penetrated the forest, I could hear bird species literally by the dozen and individuals by the hundred, all calling and singing together at dawn and at dusk." I never thought I would hear this chorus in situ, one of the weirdest sounds in nature, let alone on the first morning of our journey. Its extra-human quality is reinforced by the character of each individual voice – a single descending note with no front attack, which gains in volume over its brief duration. The effect is quite psychedelic then, like a recording played backwards, but with an added perspectival element. As one frog calls, another answers in the distance, so the overall sonic picture gives the illusion of swelling forward, but then constantly falling away into the void. I lay in my hammock, sticky and stupefied. With the dawn, the sound gradually fades.

The name of the Maquiritari, or Yekuana, as they are also known, means "dugout canoe" or "river people". Setting off from Puerto Ayacucho, on the border of Venezuela and Colombia, we travelled on a craft seemingly devised for a Terry Gilliam film: three dugout wooden boats lashed side by side, driven by two motors and loaded with a metal filing cabinet and a large cupboard, thirty school chairs, two huge glass-fibre water tanks, ten drums of gasoline, a Yanomami teenager named Pompeo, two Maquiritari families with their luggage and a dog, and us – myself, Nestor and Odile, the photographer – with our two enormous trunks full of food and equipment. The only shelter is a pitched roof woven from leaves. The bottom is awash with water, often writhing with foot-long thread worms.

4 November. Night falls and the gorgeous colours of a protracted sunset wash across the sky, then melt away slowly, as if to tantalise and seduce by degrees. The river is still and dark as oil, birds flitting over its surface in their hunt for the insect nightshift. A man in a canoe paddles past us very quickly. We have trouble finding a place to camp, since the jungle is very dense. Eventually a place is found, and as we stop, Indians appear on top of a ridge. We cook in the dark, and Simon Garcia, our guide, makes a frame from which we can hang our hammocks. Simon is a Maquiritari, a protégé of a famously liberal priest, Padre Cocco, who took Simon and Pompeo's father to Rome to meet the Pope. He tells us about the time when he took a German woman to the mouth of the Orinoco. The work was too hard, he jokes; she insisted on sleeping in a bunk which had to be constructed every night. As we eat, we hear flutes from a nearby Jaiyibo village drifting through the forest. Simon plays us a cassette tape of harvest and house-building songs recorded in his own village. Once we fall into our hammocks, the night noises of frogs, cicadas and insects build to a swarming complexity, but enjoying this symphony is impossible due to the itching of countless swollen mosquito bites.

9 November. "Oh, there are sting rays everywhere in the water", says Simon, "but they're all right if you don't step on them." We take the Ventuari river for a while, in order to avoid a difficult section of the Orinoco. Lianas hang down into the water. Birds skim the surface of the river, sometimes making contact in tiny glittering splashes. Silence, then a section of the jungle will come alive with the malevolent hissing of

insects. After very heavy rain, the day is overcast, the atmosphere like an evening of supernatural green light. Pompeo sits in the prow of the middle boat, singing quiet guttural songs, voicing bird sounds into his cupped hands, pulling faces and making hand signs, barking, pointing his bow and arrow towards the jungle. We stop at a break in the trees and pull up to a cluster of rocks buzzing with bees. Pompeo, Simon and his uncle fish and catch five piranhas, their tiny razor teeth jutting from bulldog jaws. Shortly after we set off, the boats run aground. We jump out into the shallows and push but then jump back in as piranha fish gather around our legs. At night, we stop at some huts. Fruit drops in a soft tattoo from the palm trees. Simon decides to catch a crocodile. First, he shoots one from our boat, impaling it on an arrow tipped with a harpoon. Then he takes Nestor and I on to the river in a small canoe, gliding up close to the crocodile, shining a torch on its eyes, then striking with an improvised spear armed with the harpoon head and dragging it back to land, still alive, where Pompeo hacks it to pieces, kneeling on the claws as they push his knife away. The river is narrow here, and the trees high. Every sound echoes in the tense silence of the hunt, as if we had drifted into a cave in another time.

11 November. Our ninth day on the boat. Mist trails on the surface of the water. We arrive at Tama-Tama – an American Evangelist Missionary training camp – soon after setting off. Deep in jungle, the scene might be transplanted from a Georgia suburb. Artfully arranged: mown grass, flowers, a wheelbarrow, a bicycle, a little stone lavatory. By six in the morning, the temperature is unbearable. Clouds of tiny mosquitoes bite any patch of flesh they can find, wrists, ankles, tips of ears, lower face and neck being particular favourites. I am reminded of the ghost in Lafcadio Hearn's *Kwaidan*, which tears off the ears of a musician named Hoïchi after his body, save the unfortunate omission of his ears, is painted with the text of a holy sutra. A loud water pump at the hydrology station is mounted a few yards from a corrugated iron

building, so the equilibrium of the scene is shattered by a cascade of sharp, fast echoes. The following night, we drink the last of our rum and I record night music: a bird which whistles sporadically in a descending glissando; huge moths which flap close to the microphones, their wing beats registering on tape as a low-pitched flutter.

13 November. Nine large predatory birds circle above us. We stop at a small village, where we see the local malariology representative. In his boat are two large turtles, both alive, and an executive briefcase. We meet the first Yanomami group we have seen on the river. One of them whistles a greeting, the sound bouncing off the trees on the opposite bank. At Ocamo, we meet a Spanish anthropologist and ethno-botanist named Emilio Fuentes, who agrees to help us with recording the shamans of the Yanomami village where he is living. Three days later we reach Continamo Falls after an arduous morning of unloading and reloading the boat every time we reach rapids. Our time sense is changing dramatically. By watch time, each of these stops takes one hour, yet our subjective reckoning is fifteen minutes. Yellow and blue butterflies, their wing spans close to five inches, land on our arms and heads and sit there until disturbed. At the Falls we find a big caterpillar which has wrapped itself in a leaf sealed with saliva. This improvised house is dragged along and the caterpillar withdraws inside if danger threatens. Yellow and black mosquitoes abound here. We set off in a small boat, heading into rapids, the sunset behind us. The river narrows and mist rises from the surface. Groups of turkeys take flight from the trees and flocks of small birds skim the water in front of the boat. As mist envelops the river completely, the perfume and colours of this place rise to a high pitch of intensity.

17 November. Another overcast day. My nausea and giddyness is not helped by an overpowering awareness of the aliveness of this place. Small biting ants and huge spiders are everywhere. Every surface is wet, parasitic, almost visibly moving through states of decay and regeneration. We walk

upwards through the jungle for four hours at speed in dehydrating heat, crossing log bridges and looking out for snakes. By the finish, I feel closer to death than life, shooting pains in my chest and my heart threatening to burst. That night in Continamo village, high in the mountains overlooking the Sierra Parima, we drink thick beer made from fermented yucca. Simon and his uncle make clarinets from two large bamboos and reeds. The duets they play on these honking *tekeyë* symbolise the songs and movements of a pair of mythical animals.

19 November. A Yanomami shaman arrives in the village, the lower half of his face painted black for fierceness, the upper half painted red, the life colour. He agrees that we can tape his hallucinogenic *ebena* visions so we follow him with our recording equipment. On the way, we cross a river in a boat but the boat sinks so we wade the rest. On the trail I see a fly the size of a fir cone with a five-inch span of red wings. When we arrive, the man is lying in his hammock. Somebody has stolen his *ebena* out of jealousy, he claims. A later counter-claim suggests that his family hid it from him, frightened by our tape recorder. Nothing to do here, so after ten minutes we leave. On the walk back to Continamo, the rain pours and Simon's uncle cuts us umbrellas from huge leaves. Wet through from the storm and wading two rivers, we collapse into our hammocks and fall asleep. Waking up in the afternoon, we hear a commotion. A young Yanomami man is chanting in the village, snorting *ebena* from a tin plate, dancing with his arms outstretched, making sounds of animal spirits. That night, I dream that animals are living in my skin.

21 November. After a day of fishing with poison plants, we leave Continamo, Simon shooting birds as we go, me carrying the two *tekeyë* clarinets, Nestor carrying a long blowpipe. After nightfall we are still in the boat, now divested of its strange cargo and outriders. The rain is pouring and a thunderstorm looms overhead. No moon this night, the impenetrable darkness of the sky split vertically by fork lightning. We shoot two sets of rapids in this theatrical scene, a wave engulfing us

as we pass over the second set of rocks like a funfair ride, followed by internal waves of energy and elation which only subside when we reach Toki. The next morning, I feel tormented by panic attacks of claustrophobia. All three of us look haggard, our faces drawn and shiny with sweat, exhausted by constant travel and probably suffering side effects from strong malaria pills. That night, we sleep in hammocks on the boat. The dogs of Toki start barking and carry on for ten minutes, each bark echoing at the same volume a split second later on the opposite side of the river. Sleep is barely possible. A bat is flying about, either in the boat or in my imagination, and nearby I hear an animal snorting loudly like a train.

23 November. My face is swollen to the size of a football from mosquito bites. Emilio Fuentes has returned from Caracas with a message from anthropologist Jacques Lizot, a student of Claude Lévi-Strauss. The author of a beautiful book – *Tales of the Yanomami* – Lizot had also made a powerful filmed document of Yanomami shamanism – *Initiation of a Shaman* – in collaboration with Raoul Held. We can visit the Yanomami groups he works with, so long as no Maquiritari go with us, since the acculturated Maquiritari will exploit the vulnerable Yanomami if they can. We travel towards Mavaca, and nearby Tayari-teri, the Yanomami village where Lizot had lived for six years and where he had shot *Initiation of a Shaman*. The journey seems to take ages. We stop briefly when we pass a group of Yanomami Indians who jump into the boat, pointing at us and laughing. When the light fails, we crunch to a halt on a small beach where claustrophobia creeps up on me. I eat a meal of rice and cabbage then walk for ten yards, half the length of this sand spit, to sit and look at the sky. In this void I can see nothing except myself, the faint outline of the boat and a thousand stars. Frogs and toads puncture the stillness with qwok-qwok drones, bell-like chinking and bursts of machine-gun rattling. Close by but invisible, fish leap and fall back in the river with loud splashes. Even in this

perfect spectacle of light glimmers and sound fireworks, my head is spinning in a delirium of exhaustion and dislocation.

24 November. At the river's edge near Mavaca, we visit a shaman named Torokoiwa, recommended by Jacques Lizot. He lives in a small clearing of five shelters with a number of women and children. Pleased to hear that we are Lizot-teri, he agrees to chant and take *ebena*. This hallucinogen is made from powdered tree bark of the *Virola elongata* species, mixed with crushed seeds of *Anadenanthera peregrina* containing dimethyltryptamines which bear a structural resemblance to serotonin, a neurotransmitter naturally present in the brain. Torokoiwa is anxious to acquire a new hammock. We have none to spare, so a money deal is struck instead. He strips down to swimming trunks and squats. A small girl blows *ebena* powder into his nose through a long tube, enveloping his head in a green cloud, making him wince and dribble. He chants with a strong voice which jumps to falsetto. Growling and shouting, he paces up and down, gesticulating, sometimes stopping to ruffle my hair or Nestor's, finally squatting by one of the women to perform some healing on her.

After Torokoiwa has eaten some Quaker porridge oats, we travel with him to Tayari-teri. We have a tape from Lizot which we play to Machitowe, a young man who recorded sound on *Initiation of a Shaman*. Machitowe agrees to take us to Ocamo, where Emilio lives, but meanwhile, we have arrived at the beginning of a group shamanising session led by a charismatic older shaman, the most powerful of this place. After some prevarication, they decide we can record and photograph. Under the shade of the *shabono*, a vast circular shelter of sloping palm screens open to the sky in its centre, a group of six shamans take *ebena*. In the middle of them sits their patient, a sick-looking man wearing shorts. Blown forcibly through long cane tubes, the *ebena* powder causes retching, spitting, grimaces, growling and vomiting. Subdued, sporadic chants; the group sends imaginary missiles against their enemies with invisible blowpipes and bows, invoking and calling under control the *hekura* spirits which live within their chests; then the shaman picks up real weapons – a bow with its seven foot arrow, a large machete, finally an axe – and starts his dance, marching back and forth, chanting rhythmically, voicing the sounds of spirit animals and birds, transforming into a *hekura* spirit. The rhythm erupts into screams. He shapes his body into extreme angles, walking the path of the *shorori*, described by Jacques Lizot as "water demons and masters of subterranean fire". The hazards of this journey break through into our world. He rolls in the dust, rubbing his body as the demonic heat burns his skin. His chant to the *motoreri*, the leaf of the whirlwind spirit, breaks down in shrieks and an eerie, quavering falsetto.

As the *ebena* takes its full effect, the other shamans join in with the chanting – glassy-eyed, spitting, retching, vomiting loudly, strands of snot hanging from their noses and streaking their chests. Then some of them run to the other side of the *shabono*, tearing at the ground, striking at the high palm-screen walls, shouting and screaming in a state of near hysteria. Mutual massage follows, as they calm each other. All aspects of this *hekuramou* are symbolic. The mucus is not wiped away, for example, because this is believed to be the excrement of those spirits living in the shaman's chest. Demons are thieves who are sent by enemy shamans to steal the *noreshi*, or spirit parts of human souls, especially those of children. As sorcerers who can voyage through the four levels of the universe, plunging into actualisations of myth and history, floating in free space and time, the shamans undertake the burden of responsibility within their community to retrieve these souls. Healing is an intense psychodramatic theatre of cruelty, in which the sick become a battleground for the gruesome antagonism of tamed and malevolent spirits. Skin burns or oozes blood, the wind blows as the spirits move about, the shamans massage their patient, drawing out evil spirits through an extremity and then throwing it or vomiting it far from the unhealthy woman or man. This is the only form of medicine traditionally used by the Yanomami. As the American anthropologist Napoleon Chagnon has written: "They rely exclusively on the cures that the *shabori* [the shamans] effect, fighting supernatural ills with supernatural medicine."

Both the shaman and his own resident *hekura* spirits enjoy the effects of the *ebena*. Encounters with the spirit world need not depend on hallucinogens, yet the initiation of a shaman is a lengthy and traumatic process of death and rebirth, a reprogramming which introduces the human individual into secrets of an otherwise complex, invisible and volatile universe. The necessity for a shaman to maintain dangerous spirits within his own body, subdued yet ready to be unleashed, has an obvious psychological interpretation. The world is coherent but precarious, and for human society to remain in balance with the rest of the cosmos, the shamanic specialists must confront and absorb images of chaos, terror, disgust, wonder, fear, violence and fierce beauty. Plant hallucinogens, chanting, movement, poetic and occult language and the framework of origin myths are the transitional gateways, the technical means of access to a state of consciousness and an arena of action which the young shaman is taught as if it were a negotiable 3-D map, a synaesthetic virtual world, complete with colour, sound, smell, danger and pain.

25 November. We leave Tayari before 5 a.m. with Machitowe and another small boy from the village. As the light comes up, the river radiates the mystery of a Kurosawa film. Mist hangs in shreds from the treetops and rises off the surface of the grey river in short columns and high wisps. We pass by Ocamo mission at speed for fear that the Yanomami living there might see us and attack their Tayari enemies. No signs of human life, but many parrots, large herons and fluorescent blue butterflies. In the hot sun I fall asleep in the boat. Towards the end of a seven-hour journey we startle a group of naked Yanomami women by the river's edge. Arriving at Wabutawi-teri, we find Emilio waiting for us. The people here

are friendly and inquisitive. Where did Emilio find us? He tells them he found us in Ocamo, looking for music, but the music near the mission was so bad that he told us to come to Wabutawi-teri where the music was very good. That night I record a circular dance, performed by the women and young girls for a feast. During taping, all the men gather round me, peering at the machine. They all shoosh each other to keep quiet but somebody farts and they all break up laughing. Then Emilio persuades two men to perform an improvised duo exchange, usually done when another group visits. The function is to exchange greetings, news and views, but the speed of this rhythmic vocal counterpoint is breathtaking. The recording seems to be going well, but Emilio bursts in angrily and stops them. What they have been saying is that the foreigners are stupid to want to record their music and they are going to con lots of presents from us. Keeping a straight face is very difficult. Then some boys step up to sing a song which alternates soloist and a chorus of tones pitched so closely that they generate beat frequencies. That night I go to sleep listening to someone chanting a myth in the distance.

26 November. Emilio's trunk full of documentary notes has been stolen so we accompany him across the river in a search to find it. As soon as we go ashore, a group of about thirty Yanomami appear out of the trees. They have walked from Brazil to visit this village, they tell Emilio. All of them are very small, their faces so tiny that the tobacco wads crammed under their lower lips dominate every expression. One of them is carrying some kind of white worm or centipede – about a foot long – on a stick. They pull our hair with much amusement. As we get back in the boat, an older warrior begins to shout at Machitowe, waving his bow and arrows. Two other men jump in the water and pull our boat back to shore. "What's your family name?" the man is shouting. "Don't touch the engine. Come back here to talk." The look on Machitowe's face suggests that talk will lead to his death. Emilio shouts back in a mixture of determination and fear and we pull away

before the situation can escalate. That evening we are taken to see *ebena* and the ashes of the dead being consumed in a rite of ancestral communion. No question of recording this. We stand in awed silence at the edge of a shelter as the porridge of the spirits is eaten to the sound of quiet mass sobbing. Inside, the light is too low to see anything other than silhouettes. After so much drama, this dignified ceremony is very moving. When night falls, I record the same circular dance as last night, this time performed by the young men and boys. By now, nobody is interested in the technology. Tonight, the sky sparkles with stars. The *shabono* is dark save for a few flickering fires; a frog calls qwok-qwok-qwok and insects hiss. A brief disturbance as a big bird-eating spider runs past a fire. One of the women snatches up a burning piece of wood and bashes it down on the spider which will be eaten later. The men shuffle around their wide circle, each circumnavigation taking five minutes or so, punctuated by a swell then a fade of heterophonic singing and high-pitched whistle. I sit on the ground for more than one hour, wearing headphones, listening to the sounds move to my left and diminish as they reach the far point of the circle, then grow louder on my right until they return to the centre. The effect is magical. Later, I fall asleep to the sound of the chanting, the frog's qwok-qwok, the night-insect buzz; after dawn, I awake to birdsong, a woodpecker's drumming and a different chant.

28 November. Emilio is going to a petroglyph site today to collect plants so he arranges for us to record the old shaman of Wabutawi-teri taking *ebena*. The heat is intense and we lie in our hammocks, sweat pouring in streams. When we take the recording gear to the *shabono* we quickly realise that none of the shamans are happy with our presence at their *hekuramou* so we leave. A little later, one of the young men comes to tell us that we can record the *hekuramou* after all. We pick up everything and walk back to the *shabono*, only to be greeted by more hostility from the old shaman. We leave again. Then the young men come back once more to tell us,

really, this time will be fine. They can barely contain their mirth so we stay put, listening to shamanic roaring and growling in the distance. When Emilio returns, he investigates and finds that the old man had changed his mind and decided that he would agree to recording only if Emilio was present. Our acceptance of the situation seems prudent when we learn that the women hide all weapons when the old man shamanises and the men make a circle around him as a precaution against the violence which can erupt when he chooses to unleash demonic spirits.

29 November. Machitowe is bored. Our last day here. Rain. An old man squats by Emilio's desk, holding his bow and long arrows, sucking on a tobacco wad. I record him singing rain songs. Despite his fierce appearance he claims to be shy, so a guard has to be posted on the path. Rain songs are improvised, usually sung privately in a hammock, the tempo changing according to the rhythm of the rain. As we leave, flocks of birds burst from the trees above our heads, calling with a sound like sleigh bells, wheeling in all directions; parrots scream as they take off, their tails streaming out behind them; eagles hover above and turtles basking on logs collapse into the water as we approach. That night we stay at the medical station at Mavaca. Rigging up a mosquito net I disturb a huge spider, its white body the size of a hard-boiled egg spotted with black markings, its legs four inches in span. Four days later we are stuck in Tama-Tama mission, forced to endure mosquito bites and the smell of sewage, army and missionary interrogations, Maquiritari complaints that nobody studies their (vanishing) culture, tirades from the doctor against Lizot, who he claims has published "lies" about the genocide of the Yanomami. By now, I am deaf in one ear, my back is painful, I have ulcers on my tongue and mouth, my feet are blistered, my ankles are covered in bites, I want to kill all missionaries. I lie in my hammock, watching a picture postcard tropical sunset, the sky a bruise of black, blue and faded yellows. Thunder, lightning and torrential rain follow. Two Maquiritari

Indians walk in, carrying a tape machine which plays The Bee
Gees' "Staying Alive" and "Boogie Oogie Oogie" by A Taste of
Honey. The latter had been a UK hit in June, so I sink into a
disco reverie of homesickness mixed with the pleasure of total displacement.

4 December. Travelling back through rain, fog, high winds
and dense clouds of white winged flies. The boat is loaded
with a consignment of bananas. As we reach the confluence
of the Orinoco and the Atabapo, the waters flow side by side
without mixing, one blue-grey, the other greenish-brown.
When we stop at San Fernando de Atabapo, we find everybody is drunk. Herrera has won the election. We go to a shop
which sells fluffy dogs, clockwork divers, plastic mermaids,
plastic cowboy boots and other essentials, much of it veiled
by spiders' webs. Coming through here on the way into the
jungle we had seen soldiers water skiing on the river. Retro-
spective thoughts of Robert Duvall's surfing obsession in
Apocalypse Now (not released until the following year), or
Joseph Conrad's *Heart of Darkness*, are impossible to discount. Some days later, we arrive back at our original starting
point, where we load a truck which drives us to Puerto
Ayacucho. On dry land, my perceptions seem distorted. Some
ducks at the side of the road look as if they could be four feet
tall. Any zoological aberration has become eminently feasible.
In the town we help Simon to deliver his bananas and go with
him to the shacks where Maquiritari and Yanomami urbanites
live: dank sheds lined with newsprint, prison cells draught-
proofed in spurious information. That night *Soylent Green* is
showing at the cinema. We kill time by drinking beer, watching soldiers armed with automatic weapons arrest Indians.
Dogs sleep in the cinema aisles, salsa booms from the club
next door, loudspeaker hum obscures the dialogue of the film,
but the message is clear. After the breakdown of society, people subsist on a substance called soylent green. As Charlton
Heston discovers, this compound is manufactured from recycled corpses. Sixteen years later the prospect seems less

far-fetched, now that we know the Japanese have perfected hamburgers made from detoxified human shit. At the time, however, our minds drifted back to the emotional ceremony at Wabutawe-teri, and the eating of human ashes mixed with hallucinogenic plants. The next morning we leave for the airport. The taxi is driven by a grotesquely fat man wearing a plastic apron. The accelerator of his car is made from wood and attached by string to the dashboard. He believes we are missionaries. When we arrived in this town at the end of October, there were no television sets. We pass a shop. Outside, another fat man is sitting in a chair, watching television, presumably deciding whether to buy or not to buy. His family stand around him, waiting for his decision. When we reach the small airport, we discover that a French entrepreneur made a deal with the Venezuelan air force to transport TV sets into Amazonas.

listening below/the surface

Nightfall. A sound recordist sits in a small cabin, isolated in the frozen wastes of Antarctica. He drops a hydrophone through a small hole in the ice, then sits by his tape-recorder, headphones buried under layers of thermal clothing. He presses the record switch and suddenly, dramatically, he is projected into a dark, submarine, ice-vaulted cathedral of clicks, echoes, white noise and the tumbling melismatic whistles of high-frequency Weddell seal calls. Like time-lapse photography and microscopy, audio recording revealed inaccessible worlds, if not for the first time, then in graphic and retrievable detail.

frozen words

In *Gargantua and Pantagruel*, a serial satire written by François Rabelais between 1532 and 1534, the captain of a ship tells his crew not to be afraid when they reach the edge of the frozen sea. Sounds of a bloody battle between the Arimaspians and Cloud-Riders had been frozen and are now melting as spring approaches. Pantagruel finds some that have not yet thawed, frozen words and jokes which look like crystallised sweets, and throws them on the deck where they lie, colourful but inert. Warmed between the hands, they melt, sounding their words as they do so. One, a frozen cannon shot, explodes like an unpricked chestnut thrown on to a fire. Others are battle cries which melt together in a riot of sound poetry – hin, crack, brededin, bou, bou, trac, trrrr – that recalls Marinetti's Futurist free words, fruits of the inspiration of machine war.

Sounds of nature provoke strong emotional and mythic responses in humans, often generating strikingly similar images and stories which bridge time and geographical location. Sounds which originate underwater yet can be heard on land are particularly mysterious. During the mating season of the toadfish, the male of the species roars like a foghorn or kazoo every thirty seconds, loudly enough to be heard above water. Native Americans interpreted the humming as spirit voices and battle sounds which had been frozen in air and were thawing noisily. In Sausalito, California, sleepless and somewhat spooked houseboat owners launched a toadfish festival – complete with aquatic costumes and a kazoo-blowing parade – in June 1988 after being driven to distraction by this annual droning. Prior to discovering the true source of this nightly chorus, the residents of Sausalito came up with a number of fanciful theories to explain the drone: a sunken Japanese ship loaded with electric massagers, the CIA pumping nerve gas into the bay, the Sausalito City Council humming into storm drains.

echo return

"Nature is the supreme resource", composer Olivier Messiaen once said in a lecture. Few nature sounds have captured public imagination so thoroughly as the humpback whale songs recorded by Roger Payne. Originally available on disc by mail order from a Del-Mar, California, address, the recordings were issued by Capitol Records on *Songs of the Humpback Whale* (1970) and *Deep Voices* (1977). In those seven years, the first album sold more than 100,000 copies. Not particularly impressive, perhaps, when compared with the phenomenal sales of Gregorian chant from Silos Monastery, shifting more than 1,000,000 units in 1994 to a neo-spiritual market niche otherwise occupied by Enya, Le Mystère des Voix Bulgares, Jan Garbarek with the Hilliard Ensemble and the so-called holy minimalists – Arvo Pärt, John Tavener and Gorécki. But discounting the Singing Dogs, Pinky and Perky, Big Bird and other anthropomorphic oddities, these were the first non-human recording stars to dent the mass market. The whale songs were imitated by musicians or incorporated into electronic music, folk songs, contemporary classical pieces by Tavener and Alan Hovhaness, countless feature films and television documentaries; then the New Age movement appropriated them, almost as a central icon. The magisterial, weightless calm of these sounds became synonymous with technologically enhanced meditation, floatation, dolphin therapy, crystals and New Age videos. A new genre of functional music emerged: whale songs augmented by near-subliminal New Age noodling. Then the whales became fashionable again, as post-acid rave merged with the neo-hippie traveller aesthetic. By 1993, their cries could be heard echoing under the frantic beats of otherwise resolutely urban jungle tracks, such as L.T.J. Bukem's "Enchanted". Humpback whales had evolved from great leviathans into the cliché that could not be stopped.

Marine biologists and submarine crews had been recording underwater sounds for decades and sailors had been hearing them for centuries before this outbreak of whale-song fever. "Oh yes, we used to, you know, put the wooden paddle in the water", one arctic hunter has said, "and press it against our ears. That way we can hear the different types of animal that we want to go and hunt. My people have heard it for four thousand years." So why, in 1970, did these echoing flock calls capture the public imagination? After all, one eminent marine bioacoustician has suggested that some whale sounds may be non-mystical gastric rumbles. Roger Payne began his career as a biological acoustics researcher by studying another type of spatially sensitive animal call that could only be heard to its full extent through sophisticated recording technology: the ultrasonic sonar of bats. He moved on from bats to owls, birds which use acute hearing abilities to catch their prey in darkness, and then a pivotal incident shifted his work to what became a lifelong study of whales. Working at Tufts University in America, he heard on the radio that a dead whale had washed ashore. Never having seen a whale before, he drove out to Revere Beach, Massachusetts, at night in the rain. There he found an eight-foot porpoise lying on the sand, its rain-slick curves shining in the torch beam. "Someone had hacked off its flukes for a souvenir", Payne wrote, "and two other people had carved their initials deeply into its side. Someone else had stuck a cigar butt into its blow-hole. I removed the cigar and I stood there for a long time with feelings I can't describe."

Confronted with this macabre little tableau of eco-vandalism, Payne made a decision to turn his scientific knowledge to a didactic purpose and, as he wrote, "to use the first possible opportunity to learn enough about whales so I might have some effect on their fate". His decision was timely. In 1970, ecology, conservation and animal liberation were issues of growing public concern. During that year, the Institute of Contemporary Arts in London hosted a series of twenty-two lectures entitled *Ecology In Theory and Practice*, covering subjects ranging from sewage and ocean resources to Raymond Williams's overview of the concept of nature. Payne's experience on Revere Beach added a vital component to ecology's scientific bias. The whale songs he came to record were mysterious and strangely moving, the sheer beauty of their solitary, echoing moans encapsulating that same poignant sense of loss and alienation that would drive conservation into mysticism, political activism and sabotage.

"I am receiving mail from spiritualists who purport to channel dolphins in squeaky, sixteenth century, Biblical accents", writes Jim Nollman is his book *Spiritual Ecology*. Behind the faintly weary bemusement, he probably accepts his role as a focal point for such bizarre correspondence. Nollman is an American musician who has founded a company called Interspecies Communication, "the first organisation dedicated to promoting dialogue between humans and wild animals". Having developed techniques and technologies (such as an electronic underwater sound system) to cross this great divide, he has played music with wolves, whales and many other species, and as his book recounts, he is sometimes embroiled in situations which give him cause to think long and hard about the contradictions which well-meaning ecologists can precipitate. In 1988, for example, Greenpeace persuaded him to join an Alaskan adventure, an attempt to free three gray whales stuck in an ice hole. Not entirely convinced that the whales should be freed to satisfy the whims of conservationists and a resulting media circus, Nollman added his musical input to a variety of expensive and supposedly more rational mechanical interventions and succeeded where they had failed. Informed by shamanism, by Gregory Bateson's insistence that the exclusion of "things" from their context distorts our view of the interconnectedness of the world, and by the philosophy of deep ecology, Nollman still challenges some of the terminology and basic assumptions of ecology's outer fringes. "[T]hat adjective, *deep*", he writes, "has always confused me because it tries too hard to imply a secularized version of what the deep ecologists themselves comprehend as a *spiritual* relationship to nature."

deep listening

"Deep Listening™ is a trademark of The Pauline Oliveros Foundation, Inc." it says on the cover of a CD called *The Ready Made Boomerang*. That sounds serious. Luckily, there is a photograph of four members of The Deep Listening Band – Pauline Oliveros playing an accordion, trombonist Stuart Dempster, clarinettist William O. Smith and sound designer Panaiotis – placed just underneath this implicit threat. They look like a quartet of sea dogs, just home from hunting the great white whale, holed up in a shoreside bunker and improvising some underworld shanties.

Pauline Oliveros began making music as a group improviser in the early 1950s in San Francisco, playing French horn with Terry Riley, who played piano, and Loren Rush, who doubled on string bass and *koto*. In 1961 she began making electronic pieces, but was drawn more towards theatre, mixed-media and other expansive environments in preference to the laboratory conditions of the studio. "I was a young person in a field in which everybody was hiding in technical considerations", she says, talking from her home in upstate New York. "Hiding their feelings, hiding their motivations. It still goes on – the techno-jocks that are out there. Technocracy feels so safe. I had to prove myself, prove I could be a jock too." As a logical culmination of this outward-looking orientation, she now leads workshops in sound, health and deep listening, and collaborates on mixed-media presentations such as *Njinga the Queen King: Return of a Warrior*. In recent years, she has also released *The Ready Made Boomerang* and *Deep Listening*, both albums recorded in the huge underground resonating space of Fort Worden Cistern in Port Townsend, Washington.

The musical exploitation of cavernous resonance is ancient, perhaps as ancient as any other form of sonic experiment. At the beginning of this book I gave one example of an archaeologist who believes that the animistic cave paintings of pre-history were created in sites where there was a correspondence between the echoes and the animal depicted. There is some documentation of the awe induced by echoing geological and meteorological sounds among the rainforest Indians who lived close to the Ecuadorian and Peruvian

Andes. The signal drum of the Jivaro was said to be an imitation of a giant drum played by the Iguanchi, a shaman who had died, become spirit and caused otherwise inexplicable booming noises within the mountain whenever he was annoyed. But noise – the instrument of darkness – is used to scare away the unknown and unseen, also. Many musics have delighted in noise, seemingly to inflate the diminutive human body to a scale which can cope with the vastness of its surroundings (both physical and spiritual). This vastness, whether natural, architectural or digital, inevitably suggests mystery, sadness or loneliness. Many Chinese poems, for example, were devoted specifically to the eerie hoots of gibbons, echoing across river gorges. In his book *The Gibbon In China* Robert Hans van Gulik writes: "The graceful movements of the gibbon and his saddening calls are referred to by nearly every poet who wrote from the 3rd to the 7th century." He gives examples of some, such as Shên Yüeh's: "I do not know whether their calls are near or far, for I only see mountains rising after mountain. The gibbons love to sing on the eastern range, waiting for the answer from those on the western cliff."

Reverberation also invokes the sacred. Recordings of Buddhist and Gregorian chants are made in their intended settings of monasteries, cathedrals or mountains; some ethnographic field recordings of ritual have been pepped up by post-production reverb, in order to imbue them with added mystery. A fairly well-known Ocora recording of a Burundi praise singer named François Muduga, who accompanies his apparently sinister whispered vocal on the *inanga* zither, sounds as if it was recorded in the deepest, darkest cave of Central Africa. In fact, a photograph shows him playing in bright sunlight in the open air, the only reflective surface in sight a skinny tree trunk. Since the whisper – which makes Mr Muduga sound like a distillation of *gris-gris* period Dr John, Howlin' Wolf, Captain Beefheart and Can's Damo Suzuki – is a common technique for making parity between the volume levels of voice and zither, the extra echo can only be regarded as a sensationalist deception. But whether the echoes are synthetic or natural – Jamaican dub, a north African call to dawn prayer shattering the early morning silence as it blasts out of a tower-mounted loudspeaker, Elvis Presley's "Heartbreak Hotel" or a Javanese gamelan recorded under the high roof of a royal palace – there is no escaping their power to suggest actual, virtual and fantasy spaces.

"The instrumental items of the [Tibetan] Buddhist liturgy originally were outdoor features", writes Walter Kaufmann in his book, *Tibetan Buddhist Chant*. Discussing the sound symbolism of Tibetan instruments, he says: "The *rag-dung* drone is primarily of ritual nature, representing fearful, rumbling, and threatening sounds related to the terror deities while its purely musical function is of lesser importance." The photographs and sleevenotes to another Ocora album, *Musique Sacrée Tibetaine*, paint a vivid picture of loud, outdoor instruments used deliberately to vibrate cold air and fill every reverberant geological hollow with sonic dread. In a description of the ceremony of welcome, sound recordist Georges Luneau writes: "Four monks posted at the edge of the terrace of the monastery courtyard scan the far reaches of the valley. As soon as they glimpse the guest of honour they sound their enormous *dun-chen* horns, whose deep bass tones reverberate in the steep, white heights of the mountain. The silent snow captures and amplifies this extension of the human voice as it rings out to welcome the guest. Simultaneously a fire of sweet-smelling herbs is lit. Soon afterwards the *rgya-glin* oboes are heard. The lama climbs slowly upwards and the music does not cease until he has crossed the threshold of the monastery."

Other musicians and composers have explored the properties of acoustic echoes. In the late nineteenth century, Charles Ives's father, George, used to play musical instruments over the pond in Danbury, Connecticut. He was, Frank R. Rossiter wrote in *Charles Ives & His America*, "captivated by the tone quality of the echo that returned to him across the water – an experience that his son attempted to recapture, years later, in his chamber music piece *The Pond*." Charles Ives was inspired by Henry David Thoreau's belief in the "tonic of wildness", expressing a wish to "hear the silence of the night . . . the silence rings; it is musical and thrills me". In one of his compositions, *The Housatonic at Stockridge*, he depicted the singing from a church across the river, heard through leaves, mist, running water. As for indoor echoes, if the building is as impressive outside as in, then the exercise translates seamlessly from architectural acoustics into marketing concept. Jazz flautist Paul Horn's *Inside the Taj Mahal* and *Inside the Great Pyramid* are superior precursors of New Age music in their meditative, quasi-Eastern feel. Not only reverberations, but the buildings themselves invest the playing with apparent significance. In 1610, Monteverdi simulated echoes in his *Vespers*; Alvin Lucier's composition for pulses reflected by room echoes, written in 1968, was given the same title for reasons which, as Lucier has explained, are pertinent both to biomimetics and the awe inspired by resonance: "The title *Vespers* was chosen for the dual purpose of suggesting the dark ceremony and sanctifying atmosphere of the evening service of the Catholic religion and to pay homage to the common bat of North America of the family *Vespertilonidae*."

Ecology, anthropology, physics, semiotics, land art and conceptual art levered music into an area where sound and listening could take precedence over the intention of the composer. Alvin Curran, Evan Parker, David Dunn, Pauline Oliveros, Stuart Dempster, Albert Mayr, Paul Burwell, Hugh Davies, Michael Parsons and the late Stuart Marshall investigated other aspects of echoes and the articulation or mapping of space, ranging from the peculiarities of indoor acoustics to echoes across water and distance and natural amphitheatres. David Dunn has described one of his own pieces as follows: "*Nexus I* was realized four miles into the interior of the Grand Canyon in Arizona. Three trumpets responded to scored events in relationship to the environment resulting in stimulation of the extended resonance characteristics of the space and its life forms." In Xebec's *Sound Arts*, composer Mamoru Fujieda has written his impressions of an Alvin Curran piece, heard at the SoundCulture 1991 audio festival, held in Sydney: "The event that left the deepest impression on me was the performance called *Maritime Rites* by the American experimental composer Alvin Curran, which occurred on the final day of the festival. In this one-hour performance using all of Sydney Port and its harbour as a backdrop, boats and ferries which happened to traverse the bay became the instruments. In addition to this, two boats were specially prepared with a group of musicians playing two of Australia's native instruments: didgeridoo and the conch shell. From various directions, as the sounds of the fog horns rang out in union, a magnificent sound echoed all over the harbour."

Stuart Marshall and I shared a work table during our first year as art students at Hornsey in 1967–68. My conviction was that contemporary composition was arid; his equally fervent prejudice was that jazz equalled the commercial trad of Kenny Ball. So he told me about La Monte Young and I loaned him my copy of Ornette Coleman's *This Is Our Music*. Mutual listening blockages were cleansed and, with our hearing refreshed, we went out to hear music that dwelled at that crossroads, particularly the improvising of AMM. During the 1970s he spent some time in America studying with Alvin Lucier. "Western music has traditionally demanded the repression of space", Stuart wrote in a *Studio International* article called "Alvin Lucier's Music of Signs In Space". "Most music is performed for an audience who are all in the same seat. To a certain extent music performance must address itself to the performance space but only to subjugate its specificities." Written in 1976, his conclusion seems more relevant than ever: "Lucier's most recent work poses important questions about the relationship of the subject to music as a signifying practice. It focuses attention literally on the *position* of the subject. In no sense can an audience member be considered the mere passive recipient of musical meaning. In these pieces the stress on the articulation of perception makes the subject active as the place where musical meaning is created. Everything in is motion and no one can perceive the work as totality. This is a new notion of musical temporality which is intrinsically linked to musical space."

Alvin Lucier presaged many current concerns with his computer simulations of fantasy spaces (*The Bird of Bremen Flies Through the House of the Burghers*), drones and harmonics (*Music On a Long Thin Wire*) and explorations of biofeedback (*Clocker*, a piece in which the rhythm of a ticking clock is altered in real time through electrodes connected between the performer and a lie detector, and *Music For Solo Performer*, the first musical composition to use amplified brain waves as a sound source). There is an air of dry pseudo-science about some of these pieces, however, almost as if they were lifted out of the gilt-edged pages of a late-Victorian acoustics textbook. Pauline Oliveros was one of the biofeedback activators on the recorded version of *Music For Solo Performer*. For her, there are bigger issues at stake, some of which can be related to the sound ecology programme of Canada's World Soundscape Project, and some of which concern our psychic and corporeal health. I ask her to define the Deep Listening concept. "In 1988, that's when we went into that big cistern and recorded. Then we discovered we had enough material for a CD. When I was trying to write the liner notes, I was trying to come to some conclusion about what it was we were actually doing in there. The two words came together – deep listening – because it's a very challenging space to create music in, when you have forty-five seconds reverberation coming back at you. The sound is so well mirrored, so to speak, that it's hard to tell direct sound from the reflective sound. It puts you in the deep listening space. You're hearing the past, of sound that you made; you're continuing it, possibly, so you're right in the present, and you're anticipating the future, which is coming at you from the past."

She laughs. "So it puts you into the simultaneity of time, which is quite wonderful, but it's challenging to maintain it and stay concentrated. So that's what I thought we were doing, and listening to one another as well. The space itself becomes a very active partner in the creation but how you listen to it is how it gets shaped. Once I had made that discovery of putting those two words together – deep listening – it felt like a nice logo to make a connection to the work I had been doing all these years and continue to do."

She describes awesome resonant spaces as otherworldly. "Cathedrals were constructed for that purpose, to have sound which has a supernatural presence. We have enough of them. Grand Central Station is a tremendous reverberant space. Railroad stations were built like that – big pyramids. Both Stuart Dempster and I had been interested in reverberant spaces over a lifetime. Both of us being horn players: I play the French horn as well as the accordion, Stuart playing the trombone and digeridoo. As a young performer I was aware of the kinds of rooms I was playing my instrument in. I noticed, of course, that in a very dry space the tone didn't sound so good and in a more reverberant space, I began to get a more full, round, rich tone."

From the early 1970s, Pauline Oliveros has been writing "sonic meditations". She gives me an example. "The very first one was called *Teach Yourself To Fly*. The instruction goes something like this:

Observe your breath
and try to remain an observer of the breath
when you feel in tune with the breath cycle
gradually let the breath become audible
without trying to place your voice
just let the breath vibrate the vocal chords naturally
and gradually increase the intensity
until it comes to the point when it's time to decrease
then go back to the breath."

sonic healing/pharmaceutical method

In 1990, the manufacturer of Nurofen, a pain relief product, used two pieces of music for a television advert in a classic "before and after" formulation. The headache half of the commercial was illustrated by a piece of Japanese *gagaku*, the elegant court music which dates back almost unchanged to the beginning of the eighth century. Headache relief comes when the *gagaku* is replaced by Mike Oldfield's comically twee yet distressingly clumsy slice of exotica kitsch, "Etude", taken from his soundtrack to *The Killing Fields*.

listening below the surface

From Pauline's deep listening logo and the sonic meditations came another idea: the deep listening training sessions. "Every year I lead a retreat in New Mexico, in the Sangre de Cristo mountains in June", she explains. "People come to spend a week together to do different things which I call deep listening, or we try to find out what deep listening is, because it opens out, you know? It implies listening below the surface and also listening inwardly. So in these sessions with people I try and provide guidelines so that different forms of attention can be practised. So that you can come away with a fuller sense of the variety of experiences that you can have by listening and not tuning out. That's what it's about.

"In these sessions I try to get into the more subtle vibrations of the body, as close to the cellular level as possible and even the vibrations of the energy that goes through the body. And then also working on sounding. Sounding to increase sensitivity to the more subtle vibrations of the body. Sounding vocally – I always do these sessions without instruments because it gets real fundamental with vocalising." I ask her if she feels there is a relationship between these vibrational investigations and shamanic techniques of ecstasy. She laughs. "Well, it's the in thing right now. You can be a weekend shaman, take a course in being a shaman. We have a spiritual supermarket going where all these different tastes of different traditions are being presented in different ways. It's not necessarily bad. It depends on the motivation. There's a value to gaining some understanding of practical traditions. I think the shamanic journeying practice is very powerful, very rewarding and rich in terms of gaining access to the inner world and getting valuable messages from the inner teachers that are there. I'm very interested in that. We do journeying almost every night at the retreat - journeying in different ways, say journeying for oneself or journeying for a partner or journeying on a theme. I want to connect with listening in the broadest sense; not only listening to sound and vibrations but understanding that we *are* vibrations. We're made of it. It's working back to a spiritual development. Sound is the leading energy in that development."

12 theatre of sound

World Soundscape Project; Thomas Köner; Hans Jenny; Plunderphonics; progressive rock; Paul Schütze

digital archaeology

In a hitherto neglected museum basement a cupboard is opened. Untouched since Victorian times, it contains the preserved drone of a mosquito. The digital restorer gently shifts acoustic dust and grime from this frozen moment of sound with a virtual toothbrush. The drone grows stronger in the surrounding silence but the sound is old and impossibly fragile. It disintegrates suddenly and the digital restorer wakes with a start, sitting upright in bed in a cold sweat.

theatre of sound

"This blurring of the edges between music and environmental sounds may eventually prove to be the most striking feature of all twentieth-century music", wrote composer and World Soundscape Project founder R. Murray Schafer in his book *The Tuning of the World*. Based at Simon Fraser University, British Columbia, the World Soundscape Project was, and is, dedicated to the study and documentation of sounds in their environment. A double album and accompanying book released by the Project – *The Vancouver Soundscape* – includes recordings of air horns and steam whistles, mournfully blasting and hooting across cold landscapes. "One of the strangest things happened a few years back when we had a very cold spell", a Vancouver lighthouse keeper told WSP researchers. "There were patches of ice all over the Bay. When the echo came back from the ice it sounded like somebody ripping a large sheet of cloth."

Singular memories and vanishing sounds are the stock-in-trade of the project. "Perhaps the only animal sound in the Vancouver area that can compare in intensity with the mechanical operations of the sawmill is that of the Hoolack gibbons, recorded in the Stanley Park Zoo, where it was measured at a peak level of 110 dBA", say the album sleevenotes. Another WSP publication, *European Sound Diary*, notes sound impressions garnered during a trip from Sweden through to Scotland in 1975. The book can seem obsessional, though the fact that a written audio diary is unusual and a photographic record is commonplace says something about our attitude to sound. Everything from car horns to street conversations comes under the scrutiny of the WSP diarists. "I think I'm going to have a heart attack", one of the researchers says as they emerge into the noise and dirt surrounding Liverpool Street station in the mid 1970s.

Didactic and conservationist, equally focused on acoustic philosophy and practical sound design, the project under R. Murray Schafer leaned towards nostalgic yearnings for a pre-electronic, even pre-industrial soundscape. Throughout all WSP material, the strongest hatred is reserved for Muzak (or Moozak, as they term it). Schafer must have shuddered to see himself quoted in Joseph Lanza's pro-Muzak/easy listening polemic, *Elevator Music*, yet the concentration on sound events is highly subjective. Distant ambulance sirens may be one person's purgatory and another's poetry. "If we have a hope of improving the acoustic design of the world", Schafer wrote in *The Tuning of the World*, "it will be realizable only after the recovery of silence as a positive state in our lives. Still the noise in the mind: that is the first task – then everything else will follow in time." Under bombardment from increasing noise pollution levels, we can sympathise with Schafer and long for a world free of road drills and excessively loud barcode reader bleeps without sharing his desire to return to an Edenic state of pure, permanent quietude.

notation

Musicologist Samuel Akpabot notates a *kara* flute ensemble of the Birom people in northern Nigeria as follows: Player 1 stops to do a little dance; player 2 stops to blow his nose; player 3 stops to urinate and spit; player 4 stops to laugh at player 3 and chat with the crowd; players 3 and 4 stop to argue; player 5 stops to tune his drum. Notation is the critical word. Similar notations of musical events appear daily in newspapers and magazines, except they are called reviews.

thresholds

"Intrinsically non-visual, most of Max Neuhaus's works exist on the threshold of perception – sound sources are placed so that they cannot be seen and the sounds become a natural element of the space – ever-present yet almost imperceptible."

Sonorità Prospettiche: Suono Ambiente Immagine
(catalogue of sound art exhibited in Rimini, 1982, dedicated to Athanasius Kircher, the seventeenth-century science-magic explorer who devised speaking statues, mechanical organs and the megaphone, studied acoustics and notated birdsong)

Paradoxically, unusually quiet music highlights the supposedly polluting sounds of our environment. A recording studio is a quiet place until you attempt to record sounds on the threshold of hearing. "The more you try and achieve this mathematical impossibility, the more it recedes", says Max Eastley, creator of sound sculptures which can be audible but almost invisible or visible but almost inaudible. He cites Edgar Allan Poe's "The Tell-Tale Heart", a story of hypersensitive hearing, faint moans and creaking hinges in which the central protaganist silences an old man by murdering him, only to hear a beating sound, like a watch wrapped in cotton, the noise of the buried heart beating louder and louder in the acoustic space of his guilt. "You have to accept what's there. To hear nothing, you have to be dead."

Felix Hess assembled a sound installation of fifty robot "sound creatures" at Xebec Hall, Kobe. Called *Chirping and Silence,* the installation was inspired by the communication eco-system of frog choruses. Since the sound was interrupted by extraneous sounds, silence in the gallery was vital. The following description appeared in *A Document On Xebec* : "We had imagined that the foyer, on an afternoon when nothing was being held there, was extremely tranquil, but not even one of them began to call out in response to any of the others. So first we turned off the air conditioner in the room, and then we turned off the one on the second floor. Then we turned off the refrigerator and the electric cooking equipment in the adjoining café, the power of the multi-vision in the foyer, and the power of the vending machine in a space about ten metres away. One by one we took away these continual noises, which together created a kind of drone there . . . Hess was very interested in this and said things like, 'From now on maybe I should do a performance of turning off sounds'. By presenting us with small, delicate sounds, Hess's work rapidly opened up our ears."

"While composing and developing a piece, my passion for 'inaudible' sounds is a guiding principle", writes Thomas Köner, creator of threshold recordings produced with gong sound, contact microphones and studio processing. "I choose and build my music from elements which cannot be perceived by the normal ear. Perhaps these sounds that are so closely related to silence transport some of their origins into the music, like a memory." He talks about diffusion of light, sound sources that can't be localised, which shift in focus. Another composer, Paul Schütze, wrote in *The Wire* magazine about Köner's fugitive music: "Recently listening to Thomas Köner's *Permafrost*, I found that by the end of the disc my sense of aural perspective was so altered that the music seemed to continue in the sounds around me. Tube trains passing beneath the building, distant boilers, the air conditioning, and the elevator engines had been pulled into concert. This effect lasted for about forty minutes during which I could not get anything to return to its 'normal position' in the 'mix' of my flat."

soundhouses

The leaf-hole cricket chews a pear-shaped hole near the centre of a leaf, rests its forelegs on the surface of the leaf and scrapes its elytra, so increasing the amplitude of its song. The mole cricket digs a loudspeaker-like burrow and then sits inside, rear end airwards, and stridulates, so increasing the amplitude of its song. The howler monkey has greatly enlarged hyoid bones which form a resonating chamber in its throat, so increasing the amplitude of its song.

boundary and surface

"Context is half the work", artist John Latham once wrote, and as the terrifying noise of an amplified electric saw ripping through books demonstrated to me long before I had come across this epigram, to give 50 per cent or more over to context is to open music out into an immersive environment, a theatre of chaos and complexity. Counterbalancing moves to rationalise music into finite, controllable sequences of numbers (whether digital, Pythagorean, Qabalistic or the serialism of Milton Babbitt and Pierre Boulez), a large proportion of music made during the past hundred years has implicitly or violently rejected absolutes: the absolutes of political or religious dogma; the expedient absolutes of copyright; the beginning and end of a piece; the distinction between composer and performer, performer and audience, music and surroundings; the rejection of absolute boundaries and standards with which one piece of music can be judged against another.

theatre of illusions

"The magician is assisted by a boy, to whom (in the dark) he speaks at a distance through a tube formed of the windpipes of cranes, storks, or swans . . . A skull is made from the omentum of an ox, Etruscan wax, and gypsum and is connected with the windpipe of a crane through which an assistant speaks. Then burning coals and incense are put around it, and the skull vanishes (by the wax melting)." Various magical tricks from nearly one thousand years ago, documented by Hippolytos in the *Refutation of all Heresies*. Similar ventriloquial deceptions, primitive prophesies of the wired city, undid the Wizard of Oz.

wave forms

In *Dramas, Fields, and Metaphors*, anthropologist Victor Turner wrote that "man is both a structural and an antistructural entity, who *grows* through anti-structure and *conserves* through structure". Open structures which begin as revolutions often deteriorate into master plans designed to encompass the universe and autocratically eradicate all anomalous forms of music. So a return to listening, to hearing the world, is the most radical structure of all, since it is hard to envisage a master plan emerging out of such an amorphous, uncontrollable method. This is not to say that cosmological and social inferences cannot be drawn from observing the effects of sound.

A Swiss scientist named Hans Jenny studied experimental periodicity for many years, taking remarkable photographs of otherwise hidden effects of vibration, sound, speech, even Mozart and Bach, on liquid masses and powders. Collected in his book *Cymatics* (the study of wave forms), these enlarged images of mercury drops, gases, silver salt, lycopodium powder and solidifying pastes seem to show lunar deserts, Tantric diagrams, bubbling viscous swamps and creatures from the notebooks of H.R. Giger. Hans Jenny regarded his work as part of a greater study, described as "a triadic world model (the trinity of configuration, wave, power)". Jenny, who died in 1972, was a painter, musician, scientist and colour-light designer for the theatre. Inspired by researchers such as Chladni, who vibrated sand with a violin bow in 1787 and declared "the sound is painting", he saw affinities between the rhythms created by vibrating liquids with sound and the rhythms of history, human relations, biorhythms, the rhythms of poetry and music. "But it must be stressed", he concluded, "that these affinities are not merely metaphors or analogies but involve the recognition of homologous systems."

Cymatics was dedicated to the memory of Rudolf Steiner, the Austrian founder of the anthroposophic school of mystical thought, and Jenny's work turns up in a Steiner-published book by Theodor Schwenk, *Sensitive Chaos*. Introducing his study of flow motion in water, air and clouds, Schwenk makes suggestions for "a way on beyond pure phenomenology, towards an ability to 'read' . . . Through watching water and air with unprejudiced eyes, our way of thinking becomes changed and more suited to the understanding of what is alive." A 1960s precursor of the chaos maths fractals of the 1980s, *Sensitive Chaos* recalls the exhortations of John Cage, Pauline Oliveros or Roland Kirk to listen (without prejudice). Even the book jacket illustration is almost identical in its blue colour and swirling forms to Richard Pedreguera's cover art for Sun Ra's *Cosmic Tones for Mental Therapy* album, released on Ra's El Saturn label at around the same time. The only significant difference is that in Pedreguera's painting, a head – almost certainly Ra's – is forming in the centre of this vortical landscape.

Musicians can find material which matches their own discoveries in these searches for universal harmony among vibrations and wave forms. But an art based purely on observing nature should make us look back to ancient China, when Confucianists accused Taoists of immersing themselves in nature at the great cost of ignoring the social. There is a Rudolf Steiner school just around the corner from where I live. For a time, paintings from the school were pinned around the walls of the park café – delicate, amorphous, controlled abstractions based on the wave forms documented by Schwenk and Jenny. Attractive at first viewing, these paintings began to seem oppressive to me in their rigid, formulaic exclusion of representation, drama, contrast, variety or direct reference to anything more substantial than pastel-shaded aether.

theatre of the world

The year after Antonin Artaud wrote with delirious enthusiasm about the Balinese dance-drama he had seen performed at the 1931 Colonial Exhibition in Paris, he published the first manifesto of his Theatre of Cruelty. Artaud proposed an inner theatre of dreams, fantasies and obsessions, activated by masks, lighting like a "flight of fire arrows", ritual costumes, violent physical images of horrible crimes and famous personalities. "It must be aimed at the system by exact means", he wrote in another manifesto, *No More Masterpieces*, "the same means as the sympathetic music used by some tribes which we admire on records but are incapable of originating ourselves." He also envisaged new musical instruments, used as objects on stage and producing "an unbearably piercing sound." Just as Sir Francis Bacon's frequently quoted passage from his utopian *New Atlantis* of 1624 – "Wee have also Sound-Houses, where wee practice and demonstrate all Sounds and their Generation. Wee have Harmonies which you have not, of Quarter-Sounds . . . Wee represent and imitate all Articulate Sounds and Letters, and the Voices and Notes of Beasts and Birds . . . Strange and Artificial Echoes . . . meanes to convey Sounds in Trunks and Pipes, in strange Lines and Distances" – seems to us like a prediction of music and telecommunications in the twentieth century, so Artaud's manifesto of cruelty sounds cruelly reminiscent of half the rock videos on MTV.

theatre of illusions II

Tokwit, female war dancer of the northwest coast Kwakiutl Indians, entered a false-bottomed box during the winter ceremonials. She was apparently burned to death. Making an exit into a previously dug trench, she would communicate from the underworld through a series of kelp (seaweed) speaking tunes.

the electronic forest

Media has turned the world into a theatre. Music reflects this environment (what Jon Hassell has called the electronic forest) and, inevitably, many musicians create work which is lost and helpless in the forest, musics from which they disappear, leaving a vacuum at the centre of empty formlessness. If I listen to the New Age end of post-Fourth World/ ambient composing – albums such as Steve Roach's *Dreamtime Returns* or David Parsons's *Yatra* – I hear a false-frontage polyvinyl reproduction of nature and myth. The construction of this theatre is so transparently thin that I feel I can look behind the image to find the composer, inactive and supine, blissed out by his own airbrushed update of all those vulgar myths, carniverous plants, stinging bugs and natural disasters.

"Research into albums that have featured Pipes and similar sounds have shown that it is the sound and the music content that has sold the album, and it is NOT necessary to have a named artist playing the instrument."

PolyGram Press release for *Pan Pipe Moods*, January 1995

Others create work which throws a stream of theoretical and ethical questions (problems, some would say) into the mix. Sample and turntable specialists such as John Oswald, John Wall, Nicolas Collins, David Shea, Phillip Jeck and Christian Marclay avoid most of the draconian copyright enforcements enacted on hip-hop and house samplers, yet by using the work of other musicians as raw material, they focus attention on appropriation (or plunderphonics, as John Oswald has called it) as a, or *the*, central issue of the process. Representatives for Michael Jackson and Sony Records were incensed by Oswald's reassembly of Jackson's "Bad" and his use of Jackson's image (collaged on to a naked female body) for the cover of *Plunderphonic,* his not-for-sale CD of reconfigured Stravinsky, James Brown, Beatles, Dolly Parton, Glenn Gould, Metallica, 101 Strings, etc. Oswald lives in Toronto, so Jackson's people exerted pressure on the Canadian Recording Industry Association, which in turn compelled Oswald to give up all remaining copies of his album to be physically crushed.

Sampling is the most extreme contemporary example of a music which absorbs into itself the music which surrounds it. I first met Oswald in New York City in 1979, having travelled there with improvisers Steve Beresford and Nigel Coombes. Without theorising it beforehand, Beresford, Coombes and I were playing music that jumped across stylistic boundaries with little regard for synchronicity or "good taste" – the kind of instant jump-cut improvising that some critics would call post-modern. In New York we met and played with other musicians who felt exactly the same way: Oswald, John Zorn, Eugene Chadbourne, Polly Bradfield, Charles K. Noyes, Bob Ostertag and Toshinori Kondo among them. Eugene Chadbourne, for example, had formed a band which combined country music (which he loved) with manic free improvisation. Zorn has explained it as a generational thing of growing up with a diverse record collection. As a teenager he began taking the effects he liked from Elliot Carter or Charles Ives pieces and slotting them into his own compositions. "It was almost like a William Burroughs cut-up technique", he said to me in 1988. "I'm basically a thief. There's no hierarchy, where if you listen to classical music you do it drinking champagne and if you listen to blues it's with a shot of whisky in a dirty little bar. That kind of attitude – that one is dirty and the other is clean – is ridiculous."

In New York, Oswald drank beer with bourbon chasers. Although he played slippery alto saxophone and danced, his mind was on fantasy reconstructions of gender and identity through technological manipulation. As early as 1975, he had snipped, restitched and collaged Led Zeppelin with a crazed radio preacher into a prophetic piece called "Power". During a visit to London to promote his plunderphonic reconstruction of the Grateful Dead's "Dark Star" on *Grayfolded*, we got together to talk about the issues raised by sampling. Sampling is neither a technically nor an ideologically homogenous process. Some composers – John Wall, for example – manipulate CD-sourced raw material in a digital sampler to create an integral aesthetic that is both referential and utterly unfamiliar; others – Christian Marclay and Phillip Jeck – overlay records by other artists, exploiting the iconic cultural significance and technical idiosyncracies of vinyl.

For Oswald, there are many conceptual parameters beneath the obvious issue of copyright theft. "I was really interested in that idea of legitimate quotation, which isn't built into the system", he says. "You don't have quote marks in musical notation or in recordings, for that matter. But you can annotate your sources. I tend to call the portions of things that I use Electro-quotations. The thing that's perhaps perverse in the analogy with literature is that I'm very rarely just quoting. Although I tend not to filter or distort the sound, I transform it so much in time that it's not just free quotation. It's some sort of elaboration. It's like the commentary is built in. What you usually get in journalism or literature is that the quotation doesn't usually represent the whole essay. It's something that's used as a trigger point for a commentary or elaboration. In music, I think you can do those kind of things simultaneously. You can have all sorts of things happening where the quotation is recognisable as itself, even though it's been transformed in some way. So that's when you get into this Electro-quotation thing, when the source is still familiar. It's Electro-quotation if you're making an electronic quote of something and it's Plunderphonics if you're screwing around with that quote."

Sampling outrages those who believe in the sanctity of authorship and ownership. But, at the opposite extreme, musics which attempt to make a nostalgic, exaggerated return to the nineteenth century before Debussy, the huge symphonic expressions of the composer as a single god, at the centre of creation and in control of all his works, can only seem ludicrous at a time when computers think faster, clone replications at will and spread information over vast distances in intricate, often unidentifiable webs. In 1975, a colleague of mine – Jeffery Shaw, now a virtual artist (or artist of virtuality, perhaps) – was commissioned to provide Rick Wakeman with inflatable castle turrets for his extravaganza, *Myths and Legends of King Arthur*, staged on ice at Wembley. He passed me a free ticket and I can still recall my fascinated horror, watching blade-footed damsels and unsteady knights carrying cardboard swords circle the transported, caped Wakeman as he executed scalar flights from top to bottom of the banked keyboards at which he – Liberace and Superman – was the epicentre. Wakeman played the fool in this milieu, of course, but many of his colleagues in progressive rock and jazz rock believed in the regressive philosophies of command-centre grandiosity, replete with lengthy solos, meaningless time-signature changes, conspicuous dexterity, narrative development and the mystico-sexual inevitability of symphonic climax.

The progressive ethos of the genius conducting from the mountaintop also lies at the heart of much New Age music. Kitaro, for example, was originally influenced by English progressive rock and the German synthesiser music of 1970s bands such as Tangerine Dream. Like most New Age musicians, he objects to the term, though not as strongly as some European exponents and functionaries of the genre, such as Hugo Faas, the German manager of Swiss New Age harpist Andreas Vollenweider. "New Age sounds not good translated into German", Fass told me. "It sounds like the fascists." Kitaro once believed that the atmosphere of music should be created through the exclusive use of beautiful sounds. Born into a small farming community in central Japan, he played in Tokyo-based bands until sick of *Spinal Tap*-style internal strife. After going solo, he transformed so-called "classic rock" into a kind of cosmic muzak, full of pomp, melodrama and titles such as "In the Beginning" and "The New Dawn". In 1990, he told me that he was building a recording studio in America's Rocky Mountains to escape from the noise and crowds of Japan. "I don't want to be a business", he claimed. "I can spend time in a deeper place. I want to meditate for a whole year and then after that I can compose music."

Progressive rock drew from programme music, a type of composing which portrays specific scenes or events. In a sense, Debussy could be described as a programme composer, yet like the paintings of Turner, his descriptiveness tends to dissolve the subject, implying the non-fixity that is more characteristic of the twentieth century. Programme music was the precursor of synthetic electronic ambience – the *Environments* series of albums, for example, which were designed to insinuate tranquil rural moods into the stress zones of indoor urban life. Among the most famous, distinguished and enduringly popular, not to say overworked, examples of programme music are Mendelssohn's *Fingal's Cave*, Beethoven's *Pastoral Symphony*, Vaughan Williams's *The Lark Ascending*, Sibelius's *Finlandia* and Richard Strauss's *Also sprach Zarathustra*. Strauss's "astonishing orchestral virtuosity tempted him to a parade of realism that in its extreme form led to bathos" chides Leslie Orrey, author of *Programme Music*. Bathos was mistaken for profundity by the likes of Emerson, Lake and Palmer and even now, the most unlikely pop, rock or swingbeat star will signal the big entry with dry ice, retina-blistering white light and the blasting fanfares of *Also sprach Zarathustra* (in all probability believing it to have been written by a film composer such as John Williams for *2001: A Space Odyssey*).

sound design

Despite all these caveats, the process of composing by imagining, then depicting, inner landscapes and scenarios which remain private to the composer can create striking results. "It's something I do", admits Paul Schütze, once an Australian-based soundtrack composer for cinema, now the London-based creator of albums such as *Apart*, *The Surgery of Touch*, *The Rapture of Metals* and *New Maps of Hell*. "But it's hard to know whether I do that because I spent so long doing film or whether I gravitated to film because I do that first. Interestingly, I think the reason I stopped doing film is because, even though film potentially facilitates the total design of a pan-aural event by including musical and non-musical sound, it doesn't really take advantage of that. With the few exceptions that we all are acutely aware of, like Alan Splet's work with David Lynch, Walter Mirch's work with Coppola and Scorsese, and a very few other individual isolated examples such as the Coen brothers' films like *Blood Simple* and *Hudsucker Proxy*, film doesn't allow this. It's logical, because film is a massively expensive medium."

But cinema is a theatre of exaggeration in which every minute sound we hear is foregrounded with hallucinogenic clarity: the harsh scrape of a beard as Henry Fonda is shaved or the interplay between tiny sound events and Ennio Morricone's music scores in Sergio Leone's spaghetti westerns; the hugely amplified noise of kicks, punches, even the passage of arms through the air in Chinese martial arts film; the tense creak of boat timbers, the squish of a knife into flesh, the ricochet of bullets off rocks in countless westerns. "There's a wonderful story about *Taxi Driver*", says Schütze. "I think it was the first and only film where, when the censors saw the film, the only requirement they had in order to pass it for a screening certificate was a sound cut. What completely freaked them out was the fact that Walter Mirch had taken the idea of the gun, which is a tremendously symbolic and disturbing thing, and he put cannon fire underneath the gunshots. So these gunshots are not a pop; these gunshots are like your lungs are blown out through the back of the theatre, which is probably what it would feel like if you were holding the gun. I think the censors realised that this was subjective sound from the character's perspective. You were feeling the recoil because you were holding the gun, therefore you were empathising with Travis Bickle which is a deeply disturbing thing to realise you're doing. I think this is a controversial thing to say, because the music score [by Bernard Herrmann] is so highly regarded, but I think it's almost expendable. The sound that was there is so powerful that if you took the music score away you would actually make the film more disturbing, not less.

"With a lot of scores, music scores interpose themselves between the visceral quality of the film and the audience. *Eraserhead* is a brilliant example of running a film on abstract sound design. What Alan Splet did for films, he took abstract 'space' music – the whole idea that anything abstract was airborne – and he grounded it, rubbed its face in the wet cement and said, 'Look, this is where you are, this is what you know about, this is really what scares you. This is your reality. It's terrifying and it's incredibly beautiful at the same time.' So suddenly, that film gave a voice to the whole industrial, land-grounded, earth-ambient genre – everyone from Zoviet France, to Coil, to Lustmord. There are hundreds of them and it also provided the backdrop from a lot of industrial bands like Front 242 and Hoodlum Priest. I think you'd be hard-pressed to find a fully developed example of this that predated that film. I could be completely wrong on this and have my theory blown out of the water."

Having grown up in a cinematic environment, in which film's hyperreal theatre of sound animates everyday noise outside the cinema, some musicians are influenced into a prophetic form of composing which is not so much soundtrack for an imaginary film as sound design for an imaginary life. "I think there's a very strong sense in a lot of contemporary music that the formal musical elements are the legitimate bones of the composition and the rest of it is decoration or icing or bridge passages", Schütze concludes. "It's fairly rare to hear it amalgamated in such a way as one isn't given precedence over the other, aside from the fact that a listener's ear will give precedence to something that is more structurally coherent, whatever that means. So I actually think the real arena for this is outside film."

13 ocean of sound

David Lynch; John Lilly; Kate Bush; David Sylvian; shamanism; ambient; information ocean

"I feel a little bit strange," says David Lynch. Well, what else? We are sitting in a large, L-shaped room in his home. One wall, vast as a drive-in movie screen, is glass; behind it lies the vegetal mystery and darkness of the Hollywood Hills at night. Lynch lost his dog in this darkness, eaten by coyotes, he maintains. The room echoes with our voices and explosive snaps from a log fire, spearing the cold air, ricocheting off the walls and ceiling. Three items of 1950s' furniture occupy the broad expanse of floor, megalithic in their hapless, solitary arrangement. Lynch may well have deliberately placed these few chairs at shouting distance from each other in order to make relaxation and intimacy as difficult as possible.

Although *Twin Peaks*, designed by Lynch and writer Mark Frost for ABC-TV, degenerated into aimlessness, the original pilot contained moments of genuine strangeness, particularly the music and the red-curtain ending. The otherworldly quality of this latter scene came partly from the fact that it was shot in reverse. "The whole thing was shot backwards", says Lynch. "You start at the end and work to the beginning. All the camera moves, therefore, are backwards. All their walking is backwards and all their talking is backwards but the whole idea of it, of course, is that it will not and it should not look exactly realistic but it should look somewhat realistic. We had to rehearse all that. There were just two actors and they had to learn their lines backwards. They had their lines printed on a tape backwards and they'd just listen over and over to it. Some sounds backwards are just impossible to duplicate. I wanted to do more of this thing – it's really a nifty look and feel. The timing is funny."

This nifty mood, reminiscent of ectoplasmic spiritualist seances, carried over into the music, which was sung by Julee Cruise and created by Angelo Badalamenti with Lynch writing lyrics. Lynch sent Badalamenti a column of forty words, written on an envelope. Badalamenti recalls this envelope when I talk to him on the telephone. "He sent me a lyric called 'Mysteries of Love' ", says Badalamenti. "It was like six lines of poetry. I called him and asked him, 'What do you want me to do with this? What kind of music?' He said, 'Make it like the waves of the ocean. Make the music like a beautiful wind and like the song chanting through time. And cosmic.' So I said, 'Oh, I'm glad you told me'." This fruitful partnership went on to produce performance pieces, television commercials and an album – *Floating Into the Night*. If Chet Baker had sung lyrics over Nino Rota orchestrations of Santo and Johnny's "Sleepwalk" and The Chantays' "Pipeline" then the results might have sounded similar to Julee Cruise's oceanic crooning.

the mediumship of the tape recorder

Dr Konstantin Raudive, once a student of Carl Jung and a former professor of psychology at the Universities of Uppsala and Riga, believed that a tape recorder left running in record mode in a quiet room can capture the voices of the dead. This phenomenon, if it exists, was prophesied by Thomas Edison, inventor of the phonograph, but discovered by a musician and film producer named Friedrich Jürgenson at the end of the 1950s. Taking a tape recorder out to the Swedish countryside to record birdsong, he also picked up faint conversations which, coincidentally or not, were discussions of nocturnal bird vocalisations. Jürgenson published a book, *Voices From the Universe*, which alerted parapsychologists. In 1971, Pye Records (the same company that released many important pop and R&B records in the 1960s) participated in experiments aimed at testing the theory. During an eighteen-minute recording, the engineer heard nothing over his headphones, although the VU meter indicated constant signals. At the playback, those present heard over two hundred "voices". These "psychophonic" voices sound like swarms of aural garbage, the aether talk of subliminal toadfish captured in the global babble of dead city radio transmissions that fills our so-called silence. Perhaps they are spirits trying to tell us something. But what?

immersion

"Postmodern humans swim in a third transparent medium now materialising. Every fact that can be digitized, is."
Kevin Kelly, *Out of Control: the new biology of machines*

Oceans and islands. Two of the most common metaphorical images at the end of the millennium. Islamic activists in Iran seek to ban satellite dishes, alarmed by floods of Western decadence flowing in on a sea of electronic cultural imperialism. John Perry Barlow, cyberspace guru and Grateful Dead lyricist, describes the emergent electronic connectedness as an ocean of information.

On our watery planet, we return to the sea for a diagnosis of our current condition. Submersion into deep and mysterious pools represents an intensely romantic desire for dispersion into nature, the unconscious, the womb, the chaotic stuff of which life is made. As a genteel, chlorine-scented expression of this primordial longing, the popularity of swimming as recreation is a relatively modern obsession. "Ever since George III had set the mood by swimming off Weymouth to the accompaniment of a chamber orchestra", writes Charles Sprawson in *Haunts of the Black Masseur*, "a string of resorts had grown up along the coasts of England." Now a replica of his bathing machine sits in Weymouth's Sealife Centre, and in the buildings which surround it, rays and sharks glide and wheel in their tanks to soundtrack loops of New Age music, divorced from the rhythms of the sea, out of time.

Kings and queens have always had their ambient music: the symbol of ultimate power and wealth, a soundtrack orchestra to smooth transitional moments, ease sleep and digestion, mollify the gods of disorder, dramatise rites and pomp. This was their own personal Muzak system and sleeping pill prescription. But with the advent of the Walkman, the Discman, the DATman, the car radio, tape and CD player, we have all become monarchs, at least in the sense that we can cut ourselves off from our surroundings, or, as Akio Morita envisaged when he co-designed the Sony Walkman, our families. The image of bathing in sound is a recurrent theme of the past hundred years: Debussy's *Images* and Ravel's *Jeux d'eau* ripple around the listener; Arnold Schoenberg's *The Changing Chord-Summer Morning By a Lake-Colours* wraps us in flickering submarine light; Gyorgy Ligeti's *Atmosphères* envelops us in steam; Morton Feldman's *Durations* drips down in a slowly configuring tatoo of sonic colours; Toru Takemitsu's film scores bathe us in the shadow world of Jun'Ichiro Tanizaki; Gavin Bryars's *The Sinking of the Titanic* sinks us into the abyss of fading echoes, rusting treasures and bloated corpses.

In a more commercial sphere, liquid musics that fall somewhere between experiment and easy listening teeter on the edge of formless ambience: Les Baxter's "Sunken City"; My Bloody Valentine's "Loomer"; Reload's whale sounds and samples from *The Deep* on *A Collection of Short Stories*; The Cocteau Twins' *Echoes In a Shallow Bay* EP; Holger Czukay's "Cool In the Pool"; The Beach Boys' "Cool, Cool Water", which moves from cool finger-snapping surf, pool and suntan culture into a swirling, glossolalic drowning section, created for *Smile* at a time when Brian Wilson was descending into a deep dark trench of psychedelic incapacity and Mike Love was fasting and meditating with such fervour that he began to believe that he might be able to talk to the birds. In fact, of all the Beach Boys, the one who came closest to the oceanic was Dennis Wilson, whose solo album – *Pacific Ocean Blue* – hovered compellingly between surfer's ecstasy, nature worship and alcoholic sentimentality. Six years after that album, Dennis Wilson drowned in Marina Del Ray, his diving capabilities blunted by alcohol, Valium and cocaine. After special dispensation from President Ronald Reagan, he was buried in the Pacific.

In 1993, I found myself flat on my back in the total darkness of a floatation tank, listening to ambient techno tracks by Black Dog, B12, Derrick May, Aphex Twin and The Orb. This promotional gimmick, dreamed up by the record company as a way of making a compilation album into a news story, underlined other connections between ambient music and floatation. Some years earlier, I had written a story about a floatation centre in South London called Lux Aeterna, named after the Ligeti piece that features in the soundtrack of Stanley Kubrick's *2001: A Space Odyssey*. Aimed at the informed yuppie, perhaps a person not unlike the Mickey Rourke character in *9½ Weeks* with his Nakamichi tape deck and ambient musical backdrops, this now defunct establishment played Brian Eno albums in the background as you waited for your float sitting on Tom Dixon chairs. And in Tokyo in 1993, a poster advertised an event organised by Eden In the Sky Code: 05/Space Lab Yellow, called *Respect To John Lilly*. "Ambient Underground Movement – party for next generation", it promised, with a scheduled seminar and workshop with John Lilly from 20:00 to 21:00 and then ambient dance with DJ Mooky, interactive VJ Sato and space direction by LF-Research.

More than anybody, John Lilly forged links between dolphin intelligence, sensory deprivation, immersion and psychedelics that have resurfaced in the culture which surrounds ambient music. He has been caricatured in two films,

The Day of the Dolphin and *Altered States*. With his schemes for reprogramming the human biocomputer, Lilly has moved from being the scientific equivalent of Dr Doolittle to being the unscientific equivalent of Dr Spock – learning to communicate with dolphins, then immersing himself for extended periods in sensory deprivation tanks under the influence of powerful hallucinogenics and finally becoming a guru for the rave New Age. A monologue by Lilly, excerpted from his book *The Centre of the Cyclone*, is accompanied by the ambient electronic music of Ryoji Ikeda and Yoshio Ojima on a Japanese CD entitled *Silence*. And on a Danish CD compilation of ambient, entitled *Boredom Is Deep and Mysterious*, Opiate have a track called "John Lilly In Loop".

Immersion is one of the key words of the late twentieth century. Bass is immersive, echoes are immersive, noise is immersive. With massive volume and density, categories barely matter: Neil Young or The Cocteau Twins heard live, Philip Glass in his early days, Slayer, Suicide, Phill Niblock, Brian Jones's post-production ultra-phasing of Joujouka's trance musicians, the Velvet Underground's "I Heard Her Call My Name", Saw Throat's *Inde$troy*, "And The Gods Made Love" by Jimi Hendrix, the Burundi drummers, Peter Brötzmann's *Machine Gun*, a Jah Shaka dub session, Eric B & Rakim heard live. Music is felt at its vibrational level, permeating every cell, shaking every bone, derailing the conscious, analytical mind.

Opiates, floating free (as The Byrds sang in "Dolphins Smile"), vibrational bliss. Evident here is a nostalgia, or a yearning, to float free in a liquid world of non-linear time, heightened sense perceptions and infinitely subtle communications, as opposed to the everyday world of divided time, building blocks, sequential language and objectification which we must negotiate with our awkward, upright, two-legged stance. Psychology returns us inevitably to our foetal condition, sleeping gently in the womb, or to a pre-mobile infant state when the world is colour, sound, smell and touch.

But does it end there? After ten years of studying dolphin communication in the Virgin Islands and Hawaii, Gregory Bateson,
anthropologist, psychologist and cyberneticist, wrote the following passage in a 1966 essay published in *Steps To An
Ecology of Mind* : "I personally do not believe that the dolphins have anything that a human linguist would call a
'Language'. I do not think that any animals without hands
would be stupid enough to arrive at so outlandish a mode of
communication. To use a syntax and category system appropriate for a discussion of things that can be handled, while
really discussing the patterns and contingencies of relations,
is fantastic."

For anybody who uses a computer, things that can be handled begin to vanish from the world, increasingly represented
by 2-D icons on a screen. The panic is on. Hard copy is disappearing. All sound – acoustic or electronic – can be
manipulated in the digital domain. Books are disappearing.
Packaging and paper are said to be disappearing (though no
sign of that yet). If you live in the Western world, then indus-
trial-era hard labour appears to be disappearing (except for a
vague awareness of distant deadening toil taking place in factories dedicated to new technology manufacture). At Xebec
Hall in Kobe, I discover a paper entitled "The Future Form of
Visual Art" written by Toshiharu Ito. "In contrast to human
beings who have invented tools to make things and in doing
so invented a culture", he writes, "whales and dolphins may
have established a culture without objects, consisting only of
communication. Moreover, their cultural structure may have
a property which is sympathetic to the new media society
which has begun to surround us. This could be indicating the
opening of a new civilisation that is totally different to the
conventional form. Naturally, such a form would change the
significance of art itself. An information network is permeat-
ing into our daily life environment and new direct linkage
media like holophonics and phosphotron are advancing to the
next stage of development. In one sense, mankind which is

placed in such an informational environment can be compared with the dolphins or whales in a new kind of sea."

a wicked voice

"Singer, thing of evil, stupid and wicked slave of the voice, of that instrument which was not invented by the human intellect, but begotten of the body, and which, instead of moving the soul, merely stirs up the dregs of our nature! For what is the voice but the Beast calling, awakening that other Beast which all great art has sought to chain up, as the archangel chains up, in old pictures, the demon with his woman's face."

Vernon Lee, "A Wicked Voice", in *Supernatural Tales*

And how does the wicked body, the human voice, survive in the information sea? Kate Bush serves me tea and toast in a private room of a London pub. I had always felt that her music was five years behind public taste, definitely a long way from my taste, but, in retrospect, *The Dreaming* album of 1982 anticipated all that would blossom into credibility in the 1990s: didgeridoos, bullroarers, imitations of animal vocalisations, simulations of native Australian clapstick rhythms, Indian vocalised drum rhythms, jazz bass lines, passages of free improvisation accompanied by insect sounds, Irish and Greek folk instruments merged with digital technology and sampled into new alchemical compounds.

dream-text

"From scattered parts of the world are also found instances of ceremonies, dances and songs which appear to originate in the sought or unsought dreams and visions of primitive peoples."

J. Steward Lincoln, *The Dream in Primitive Cultures*

As I have suggested before, recording is a dream-text, a vision of possible worlds, with the studio (despite the mundane knobs and faders, the racks of technology, the bland carpets and utility chairs, the teak and vinyl) as the otherworld. I put this idea to Kate Bush. "I think that all art deals with dream-worlds", she responds, "because I think most of it is creating illusion. It's creating an illusion to affect someone in a specific way, which is to reach out to people. Technology should be there to make things easier to translate things on to tape, but it's not the soul of the music. The human element – that's the soul. I think that computers, particularly, could lead us into a completely new age of spiritualism. This hi-tech world can encourage and embrace very old music. Maybe computers are going to teach us a tremendous amount about ourselves and the planet, because in some ways it's the first objective viewpoint we'll be taking that has a very high intelligence. I think it could be fantastically exciting if we put the combination of soul and computers together."

In Celtic mythology, the ninth wave was a boundary, a divide between homeland and alien worlds. Beyond the ninth wave was exile. *Hounds of Love*, Kate Bush's 1985 album, was two releases in one. The first side had its hit singles – "Cloudbursting", "Running Up That Hill", "Hounds of Love"; the second side was "The Ninth Wave", with its seven reflections on drowning, floating on the sea or drifting in space, witch trials, exile, emergence and rebirth. The cover photographs emphasised this schizophrenia. On the front, Kate is the confident, sensual, "public" performer – pouting red mouth, pink skin against violet fabric, framed by dark red hair, bedded by two sleek, soft, honeycoated gundogs. On the back, she appears in monochrome, either drowning face-up or emerging from water, her arms draped with seaweed, her eyes averted from the public's (voyeur) gaze. Also on the back cover was an extract from one of Alfred Tennyson's romantic eulogies for the Celtic hero of British legend, King Arthur:

> "Wave after wave, each mightier than the last,
> 'Til last, a ninth one, gathering half the deep
> And full of voices, slowly rose and plunged
> Roaring, and all the wave was in a flame"

Oceanic, incandescent, ecstatic. Sex and pagan spirit. Birth and death. "Although there's a lot of ethnic music that I find really moving", she says, " there's something about Celtic music that really does touch me. The sound of Irish pipes – it's the sound of elation. It's like a big wave. I do get this very oceanic vision. Big waves rolling in."

A correlation between ocean, islands, birds, music and the unconscious can be found in Celtic myths dating back to before the ninth century. In *The Voyage of Maildun*, the travellers hear a murmuring confusion of voices at a distance. Following the sound, they eventually come to an island – the Isle of Speaking Birds – where huge numbers of brown, black and speckled birds are shouting and speaking in human tongues. In other stories there are islands of dazzlingly colourful birds, said to be the souls of holy men, singing fairy music, and demonic swans which chase and torment flocks of screaming birds, the souls of people who have committed crimes. In *Pagan Celtic Britain*, Anne Ross makes reference to birds whose magical music sends people to sleep so that lovers can enjoy better sex; shrieking ravens that emerge from the sea; death coming as a screaming black nocturnal bird or a bird without wings or feathers; raven goddesses which could prophesy; children who transmute into swans, blessed with the gift of singing so beautifully that those who hear their bird music fall into deep sleep.

Ever since post-acid-house techno-paganism took hold as a lifestyle option, shamanism has been invoked in a routine way, as if swallowing Ecstasy and dancing all night to techno records, let alone taking a weekend course in shamanic journeying, can transform the beleaguered, profane urban body into a shamanic state overnight. At a *Wire* magazine seminar on techno, held at London's ICA in 1993, a memorable exchange took place between Fraser Clark, self-proclaimed pro-psychedelic guru of the zippie (Zen-inspired professional pagan) movement and Derrick May, guru (self-proclaimed and otherwise) to all disciples of Detroit techno. According to Clark, rave culture (which he claims to have invented)

brought the youth of Britain closer to the earth. All-night dancing in the open air was shamanic, he insisted. More than that,
it was *African*. "If that's African dancing", May responded,
"then my ancestors needed their asses kicked." Without wish-
ing to join the bootcamp of fundamentalist animal-skin
shamanic academics, I have serious doubts about automatic
assumptions that the kind of free-floating ecstatic states induced by drugs, dancing and probable dehydration are
identical to shamanism's cosmologically centred spirit
journeys.

In 1994, I was commissioned to write database material on
shamanism and associated subjects for The Shamen's CD-i/CD-
ROM. I spoke with psychedelic plant guru Terence McKenna
and The Shamen's Colin Angus at the time that The Shamen
released "Re-evolution", an ambient single featuring
McKenna's monologue on shamanism, the archaic revival and
plant hallucinogens. After decades of boiling up infusions of
psychotropic leaves and fungi, McKenna had become a born-
again techno freak. "You require electronic instruments to
invoke and duplicate the kinds of acoustical phenomena you
encounter on psychedelics", he maintained (a false distinction, I think, unless he includes software and digital sampling
in his definition of "instruments"). "The instruments are being used to invoke a nature that has almost slipped from our
cognition. We don't live in that kind of nature. To us, nature
is a park. Real nature is very much like the ambience of dense
electronic music."

But a rock-shaman convergence goes back further. In 1988
I was asked to write an essay for David Sylvian's *In Praise of
Shamans* world tour. In conversations, Sylvian made a
number of statements which suggested the method at the root
of his music's openness. Fishing in the dark was one of them.
"I think one of the strongest qualities I have is my ability to
create atmospheres", he said in one of these discussions. "I
think that music has to enable the listeners to reflect upon
themselves. I want my imagination to be given free rein and

not be dictated to by the music. I try not to dictate with music." So the audience is half the work, perhaps part of the reason why Sylvian has such an obsessively devoted fan base. Mystery tantalises the listener into believing that there are answers somewhere at the end of the mysterious tunnel. With records such as "Ghosts", *Brilliant Trees*, *Flux + Mutability* and *In Praise of Shamans*, Sylvian found ways to deconstruct the pop song into relatively open works, semi-collectively created by musicians drawn from some of the key areas of music making of the past twenty-five years – from ECM-style jazz improvising, from Can and Azimuth, from ambient, electronic and Fourth World. Listed, the names are revealing: Holger Czukay, Markus Stockhausen, Jaki Liebezeit, Danny Thompson, B.J. Cole, Ryuichi Sakamoto, Kenny Wheeler, Bill Nelson, John Taylor, Frank Perry, Mark Isham, Jon Hassell, Robert Fripp, Percy Jones and members of Japan. It was as if Sylvian wanted to draw into himself all the potentials suggested by these musicians and reforge them in his own image.

Shamanistic cosmologies are strikingly uniform. There is the sky, or heaven; the earth, on which ordinary mortals live; and the underworld, the place of the dead. Shamans can travel through all these zones, though the journeying is not necessarily pleasant or easy. Studies of shamanism document physical illness, psychosis, visions of dismemberment, being eaten and regurgitated by spirits, trial by fire, drowning, mutilation, mystical death and rebirth. Shamans, as portrayed by Oliver Stone, may gaze serenely into the middle distance as rock stars commune with the Dionysian mysteries of beer, but archive photographs and films of shamans from Siberia, Mongolia and Amazonas show grizzled, haunted characters, lined with knowledge after travelling to hell and back. Ambient music is regarded, sometimes with comic militancy, as an escape from the unpleasant realities of raw emotion, psychological crisis, body mess and political discontent, but if ambient means only white-light bliss, then the musicians are mere functionaries, slaves to cool the brows of overheated

urban info-warriors, rather than shamans who travel to gruesome corpselands in order to mug demons for wisdom.

This demand that sound should bow to escapist needs is a
rejection of the potential implicit in music's unfolding perme-
ability over the past hundred years. Music – fluid, quick,
ethereal, outreaching, time-based, erotic and mathematical,
immersive and intangible, rational and unconscious, ambient
and solid – has anticipated the aether talk of the information
ocean.

memory

Sitting quietly in never-never land, I am listening to
summer fleas hibernating on my small female cat . . .

London, 1995

bibliography

Archer, Mildred, *Tippoo's Tiger*, Victoria & Albert Museum, London, 1959.

Artaud, Antonin, *Collected Works Volume 4*, Calder & Boyars, London, 1974.

Attali, Jacques, *Noise: The Political Economy of Music*, Manchester University Press, Manchester, 1985.

Bailey, Derek, *Improvisation: Its Nature and Practice In Music*, The British Library, London, 1992.

Ballard, J. G., *Vermilion Sands*, Carroll & Graf, New York, 1988.

Barthes, Roland, *Mythologies*, Jonathan Cape, London, 1972.

Bateson, Gregory, *Steps To An Ecology of Mind*, Chandler, San Francisco, 1973; Paladin, London, 1973.

Bharati, Agehananda (ed.), *The Realm of the Extra-Human: Agents and Audiences*, Mouton, The Hague, 1976.

Budge, E. A. Wallis, *The Book of the Dead*, Routledge & Kegan Paul, London, 1974.

Cage, John, *Silence*, Marion Boyars, London, 1978.

Canto, Christophe and Faliu, Odile, *The History of the Future: Images of the 21st Century*, Flammarion, Paris, 1993.

Carr, Ian, *Miles Davis*, Paladin, London, 1984.

Chagnon, Napoleon A., *Yanomamö: The Fierce People*, Holt, Rinehart and Winston, USA, 1968.

Charbonnier, Georges, *Entretiens avec Edgard Varèse*, Éditions Pierre Belfond, Paris, 1970.

Clifford, James, *The Predicament of Culture*, Harvard University Press, 1988.

Cohn, Norman, *The Pursuit of the Millennium*, Paladin, London, 1970.

Conrad, Joseph, *Almayer's Folly*, Oxford University Press, Oxford, 1992.

—, *Heart of Darkness*, Penguin, London, 1972.

Davis, Miles, with Troupe, Quincy, *Miles: The Autobiography*, Simon & Schuster, New York, 1989.

DeLillo, Don, *White Noise*, Picador, London, 1985.

Dick, Philip K., *We Can Build You*, Daw Books, USA, 1972.

Donà, Claudia, "Invisible Design", in *Design After Modernism:*

Beyond the Object, Ed. John Thackera, Thames and Hudson, London, 1988.

Drosnin, Michael, *Citizen Hughes*, Arrow, London, 1986.

Eco, Umberto, *A Theory of Semiotics*, Indiana University Press, Bloomington, 1976.

——, *Faith In Fakes*, Secker & Warburg, London, 1986.

——, *The Open Work*, Hutchinson Radius, London, 1989.

Eliade, Mircea, *Shamanism: Archaic Techniques of Ecstasy*, Routledge & Kegan Paul, London, 1964.

Fagg, William, *The Raffles Gamelan: A Historical Note*, The British Museum, London, 1970.

Flaubert, Gustave, *The Temptation of Saint Anthony*, Secker & Warburg, London, 1980.

Fletcher, Ian (ed.), *Decadence and the 1890s*, Edward Arnold, London, 1979.

Flint, R. W. (ed.), *Marinetti: Selected Writings*, Secker & Warburg, London, 1972.

Fowler, Gene and Crawford, Bill, *Border Radio*, Texas Monthly Press, 1987.

Geary, Christraud M., "Slit Gongs In the Cameroon: Sights and Sounds of Beauty and Power", in Brincard, Marie-Thérèse, *Sounding Forms: African Musical Instruments*, The American Federation of Arts, New York, 1989.

Gérardin, Lucien, *Bionics*, Weidenfeld and Nicolson, London, 1968.

Gheerbrant, Alain, *The Impossible Adventure*, Victor Gollancz, London, 1955.

Gibson, William, *Neuromancer*, Victor Gollancz, London, 1984.

Godwin, Jocelyn, *Arktos: The Polar Myth in Science, Symbolism and Nazi Survival*, Thames and Hudson, London, 1993.

——, *Athanasius Kircher*, Thames and Hudson, London, 1979.

——, *Harmonies of Heaven and Earth*, Thames and Hudson, London, 1987.

Goldberg, RoseLee, *Performance: Live Art 1909 to the Present*, Thames and Hudson, London, 1979.

Goldrosen, John J., *Buddy Holly*, Charisma Books, London, 1993.

Green, Celia and McCreery, Charles, *Lucid Dreaming: The Paradox of Consciousness During Sleep*, Routledge, London, 1994.

Greenfield, Karl Taro, *Speed Tribes*, Box Tree, London, 1994.

Gregory, Lady, *A Book of Saints and Wonders*, Colin Smythe, Gerrards Cross, 1971.

Griffin, Donald R., *Listening In the Dark*, Dover, New York, 1974.

Harding, James, *Erik Satie*, Secker & Warburg, London, 1975.

Harich-Schneider, Eta, *A History of Japanese Music*, Oxford University Press, Oxford, 1973.

Hardy, Thomas, *The Mayor of Casterbridge*, Oxford University Press, Oxford, 1987.

Heath, Chris, *Pet Shop Boys versus America*, Viking, London, 1993.

Helmholtz, Hermann, *On the Sensations of Tone*, Dover, New York, 1954.

Hillman, James and Ventura, Michael, *We've Had a Hundred Years of Psychotherapy and the World's Getting Worse*, Harper San Francisco, San Francisco, 1992.

Hilton, James, *Lost Horizon*, Macmillan, London, 1933.

Hoover, Thomas, *Zen Culture*, Arkana, London, 1989.

Huysmans, Joris-Karl, *Against Nature*, Penguin, London, 1959.

Jellis, Rosemary, *Bird Sounds and their Meaning*, BBC Publications, London, 1977.

Jenny, Hans, *Cymatics*, Basilius Press, Basel, 1967.

Jung, C. G., *Alchemical Studies*, Routledge & Kegan Paul, London, 1968.

Kaufmann, Walter, *Tibetan Buddhist Chant*, Indiana University Press, Bloomington, 1975.

Kelly, Kevin, *Out of Control: The New Biology of Machines*, Fourth Estate, London, 1994.

Kuhn, Annette (ed.), *Alien Zone*, Verso, London, 1990.

Kunst, Jaap, *Hindu-Javanese Musical Instruments*, Martinus Nijhoff, The Hague, 1968.

——, *Music In Java*, Martinus Nijhoff, The Hague, 1973.

Lanza, Joseph, *Elevator Music*, St Martin's Press, New York, 1994.

Lee, Vernon, *Supernatural Tales*, Peter Owen Ltd., London, 1987.

Lévi-Strauss, Claude, *The Raw and the Cooked*, Jonathan Cape, London, 1970.

——, *Introduction to a Science of Mythology: From Honey to Ashes*, Jonathan Cape, London, 1973.

Lilly, John C., *The Centre of the Cyclone*, Marion Boyars, London, 1990.

——, *The Scientist*, Ronin, California, 1988.

Lizot, Jacques, *Tales of the Yanomami*, Cambridge Studies in Social Anthropology, Cambridge University Press, Cambridge, 1985.

Lockspeiser, Edward, *Debussy*, J. M. Dent, London, 1936.

Louys, Pierre, *Aphrodite*, Panther, London, 1972.

Lovecraft, H. P., "From Beyond", in *Crawling Chaos*, Creation Press, London, 1992.

McDermott, John with Kramer, Eddie, *Hendrix: Setting the Record*

Straight, Warner Books, USA, 1994.

McLuhan, Marshall and Fiore, Quentin, *The Medium is the Message*, Penguin, London, 1967.

McPhee, Colin, *A House in Bali*, Oxford University Press, Oxford, 1979.

Maconie, Robin, *The Works of Stockhausen*.

Masotti, Franco, Masotti, Roberto, Rizzardi, Veniero and Taroni, Roberto (curators), *Sonorità Prospettiche: Suono Ambiente Immagine*, Commune di Rimini, Italy, 1982.

Mitchell, Mitch and Platt, John, *The Jimi Hendrix Experience*, Pyramid Books, London, 1990.

Moyle, Alice M., *Aboriginal Sound Instruments*, Australian Institute of Aboriginal Studies, Canberra, 1978.

Needham, Joseph, *Science and Civilisation In China*, vol. II, Cambridge University Press, Cambridge, 1956.

Nichols, Roger, *Debussy Remembered*, Faber and Faber, London, 1992.

Nollman, Jim, *Spiritual Ecology*, Bantam New Age Books, USA, 1990.

Nyman, Michael, *Experimental Music: Cage and Beyond*, Studio Vista, London, 1974.

Oldknow, Tina, "Muslim Soup", in *Brought to Book*, ed. Breakwell, Ian and Hammond, Paul, Penguin, London, 1994.

Orrey, Leslie, *Programme Music*, Davis-Poynter, London, 1975.

Ouellette, Fernand, *Edgard Varèse*, Calder & Boyars, London, 1973.

Partch, Harry, *Genesis of a Music*, Da Capo Press, New York, 1974.

Partington, J. R., *A History of Chemistry*, vol. I, Part I, Macmillan, London, 1970.

Poe, Edgar Allan, *Poe's Tales of Mystery and Imagination*, J. M. Dent, London, 1908.

Polin, Claire, "Why Minimalism Now?", in *Music and the Politics of Culture*, ed. Christopher Norris, Lawrence and Wishart, London, 1989.

Pynchon, Thomas, *The Crying of Lot 49*, Bantam Books, USA, 1967.

Rabelais, François, *Gargantua and Pantagruel*, Penguin, London, 1955.

Reisner, Robert George, *Bird: The Legend of Charlie Parker*, Citadel Press, New York, 1962.

Revill, David, *The Roaring Silence*, Bloomsbury, London, 1992.

Rheingold, Howard, *The Virtual Community: Finding Connections in a Computerised World*, Secker & Warburg, London, 1994.

Rossiter, Frank R., *Charles Ives and His America*, Victor Gollancz, London, 1976.

Roussel, Raymond, *Impressions of Africa*, Calder & Boyars, London, 1966.

Rudorff, Raymond, *Belle Epoque*, Hamish Hamilton, London, 1972.

Rushkoff, Douglas, *Cyberia: Life In the Trenches of Hyperspace*, HarperCollins, New York, 1994.

Russolo, Luigi, *The Art of Noises*, Pendragon Press, New York, 1986.

Said, Edward W., *Orientalism*, Penguin, London, 1985.

Sales, G. and Pye, D., *Ultrasonic Communication by Animals*, Chapman and Hall, London, 1974.

Sarno, Louis, *Song from the Forest*, Bantam Press, London, 1993.

Schafer, R. Murray (ed.), *European Sound Diary*, A.R.C. Publications, Vancouver, 1977.

——, *The Tuning of the World*, Alfred A. Knopf, New York, 1977.

——, (ed.) *The Vancouver Soundscape*, Simon Fraser University, Vancouver, Canada, 1978.

Schwenk, Theodor, *Sensitive Chaos*, Rudolf Steiner Press, London, 1965.

Sebeok, Thomas A. (ed.), *Animal Communication*, Indiana University Press, Bloomington, 1968.

——, *Zoosemiotics: At the Intersection of Nature and Culture*, Peter De Ridder Press, Netherlands, 1975.

Shimoda, Nobuhisa, *2010: The Centrifugal Force of Space, Sound & People: A Document on Xebec*, TOA Corporation, Japan, 1993.

Sprawson, Charles, *Haunts of the Black Masseur: The Swimmer as Hero*, Jonathan Cape, London, 1992.

Steward Lincoln, J., *The Dream in Primitive Cultures*, The Cresset Press, London, 1935.

Stockhausen, Karlheinz, *Towards a Cosmic Music*, Element Books, Dorset, 1989.

Storr, Anthony, *Music & the Mind*, HarperCollins, London, 1992.

Surjodiningrat, R. M. Wasisto, *Gamelan Dance and Wayang in Jogjakarta*, Gadjah Mada University Press, Jogjakarta, 1971.

Tanizaki, Jun'Ichiro, *In Praise of Shadows*, Jonathan Cape, London, 1991.

Tate, Greg, *Flyboy In the Buttermilk*, Fireside, New York, 1992.

Thakara, John (ed.), *Design After Modernism*, Thames and Hudson, London, 1988.

Thompson, Robert Farris, *Flash of the Spirit*, Vintage Books, New York, 1984.

Tisdall, Caroline and Angelo Bozzolla, *Futurism*, Thames and Hudson, London, 1977.

Thomson, David, *Suspects*, Secker & Warburg, London, 1985.

Torgovnick, Marianna, *Gone Primitive: Savage Intellects, Modern Lives*, University of Chicago, USA, 1990.

Tosches, Nick, *Dino*, Minerva, London, 1993.

Turner, Victor, *Dramas, Fields, and Metaphors*, Cornell University Press, Ithaca and London, 1974.

van Gulik, Robert Hans, *Hsi K'ang and his Poetical Essay on the Lute*, Sophia/Tuttle, Japan, 1968.

——, *The Gibbon in China*, Brill, Leiden, 1967.

——, *The Lore of the Chinese Lute*, Sophia/Tuttle, Japan, 1968.

Wachsmann, Klaus, *Spencer to Hood: A Changing View of Non-European Music*, Proceedings of the Royal Anthropological Institute of Great Britain and Ireland, London, 1973.

Wichmann, Siegfried (exhibition director), *World Cultures and Modern Art* (catalogue), Bruckmann Publishers, Munich, 1972.

Wilmer, Valerie, *As Serious As Your Life*, Quartet, London, 1977.

Wilson, Peter Lamborn, *Sacred Drift*, City Lights, San Francisco, 1993.

Worner, Karl H., *Stockhausen: Life and Work*, Faber and Faber, London, 1973.

Yokoi, Hiroshi, *St GIGA*, Japan, 1991.

Young, La Monte and Zazeela, Marian, *Selected Writings*, Heiner Friedrich, Munich, 1969.

discography

The following alphabetical list relates simply to this book. Intended as a selective, personal guide for readers who wish to hear some of the music I have written about, rather than a definitive discography of supposedly essential recordings, it could prove frustrating. Better to include deletions, vinyl limited editions, CD obscurities and interesting but awful records, however, than restrict myself to currently available, quality controlled releases. On the other hand, this is not a discography aimed at trainspotters, completists, original pressing fetishists, vinylmaniacs, CD purists or record collectors interested solely in market values. My apologies in advance, then, to anybody who sets out to buy certain items below: the catalogue numbers are taken from a mixture of deletions, new issues, reissues and barely issued and should be regarded as a starting point only. Where no artist name is appropriate but the nature of the recording is obvious, I have listed the title. Needless to say, no correspondence can be entered into regarding the author's record collection. For further advice, These Records mail order service – 387 Wandsworth Road, London SW8 2JL – may be helpful.

African Headcharge, *Great Vintage Volume 1*, On-U CD2.
Akira (soundtrack by Yamashiro Shoji), Demon DSCD 6.
AMM, *AMM Music*, Elektra EUK-256.
Aphex Twin, *Selected Ambient Works Volume II*, Warp CD 21.
Ash Ra, *New Age of Earth*, Virgin OVED 45.
Ayler, Albert, *Swing Low Sweet Spiritual*, Osmosis 4001.
Baker, Chet, *Chet Baker Sings*, Pacific Jazz PJ-1222.
Bali: Gamelan Music from Sebatu, Archiv Produktion 2723 014.
Baxter, Les, *Jewels of the Sea*, Capitol ST 1537.
Beach Boys, *Landlocked*, HNG-10 (bootleg).
—, *Smile*, ST 2580 (bootleg).
—, *Pet Sounds*, Capitol CDP 7 48421 2.
—, *Smiley Smile*, Capitol CDP 7 93696 2.
The Beatles, *White Album*, EMI PCS 7068.

Biosphere, *Microgravity*, Apollo AMBCD 3921.

The Black Dog, *Temple of Transparent Balls*, GPR LP 1.

Bow Gamelan Ensemble, Audio Arts cassette.

Bowie, David, *Heroes*, EMI EMD 1025.

—, *Low*, EMI EMD 1027.

Brian Jones Presents the Pipes of Pan at Joujouka, Coc 49100.

Brown, James, *Startime*, Polydor 849 108-2.

Brötzmann, Peter, *Machine Gun*, FMP.

Bryars, Gavin, *The Sinking of the Titanic*, Obscure 1.

Budd, Harold, *Abandoned Cities/The Serpent* (In Quicksilver), LAND 08.

—, *Lovely Thunder*, EG EGED 46.

—, *The Pavilion of Dreams*, Obscure OBS 10.

Burroughs, William, *Break Through In Grey Room*, Sub Rosa CD 006-8.

Bush, Kate, *The Dreaming*, EMI EMC 3419.

—, *Hounds of Love*, EMI EJ 24 0384 1.

—, *The Sensual World*, EMI CDP 7930 7 82.

Bukem, L. T. J., *Music/Enchanted*, Good Looking Records 12" single GLR 004.

Cage, John, *John Cage*, Cramps CRSLP 6101.

—, *Mr John Cage's Prepared Piano*, Decca Headline HEAD 9.

—, *Music For Keyboard 1935–1948*, CBS CM2S 819.

—, *Variations IV*, Everest 3230.

—, and Tudor, David, *Indeterminacy*, Folkways FT 3704.

Cherry, Don, *Organic Music*, Caprice RIKS DLP 1.

—, *Relativity Suite*, JCOA/Virgin J2001.

Cocteau Twins, *Echoes of a Shallow Bay*, 4AD BAD 511.

Cohen, Ira, *The Poetry of Ira Cohen*, Sub Rosa Aural Documents SR62.

Coleman, Ornette, *Beauty Is a Rare Thing: The Complete Atlantic Recordings*, Rhino R2 71410.

—, *Virgin Beauty*, CBS Portrait PRT 461193 1.

Coltrane, Alice and Santana, Devadip Carlos, *Illuminations*, CBS 69063.

Coltrane, John, *Infinity*, Impulse AS-9225.

—, *Transition*, Impulse AS-9195.

Cruise, Julee, *Floating Into the Night*, Warner Brothers 9 25859-2.

Curran, Alvin, *Canti e Vedute del Giardino Magnetico*, Ananda no. 1.

Czukay, Holger and Dammers, Rolf, *Canaxis*, Spoon CD 15.

The Dagar Brothers, *A Musical Anthology of the Orient: India III*,

Baren Reiter Musicaphon BM 30 L 2018.

David, Miles, *Agharta*, Columbia COL 467897 2.

——, *The Birth of the Cool*, Capitol CAPS 1024.

——, *Bitches Brew*, CBS 460602 2.

——, *In Concert*, Columbia COL 476910 2.

——, *On the Corner*, CBS 65246.

——, *Pangaea*, CBS 467087 2.

——, *Sketches of Spain*, CBS 32023.

Debussy, Claude, *Chansons de Bilitis*, Candide CE 31024.

——, *Images/Estampes/Deux Arabesques*, Supraphon 0 11 0699.

——, *La mer*, CBS 72533.

——, *Prélude a l'après-midi d'un faune/Jeux/Nocturnes*, CBS/
Odyssey 32 16 0226.

——/ Ravel, Maurice, *String Quartets*, Deutsche Grammophon 445
509-2.

Deep Listening Band, *The Ready Made Boomerang*, New Albion
NA 044CD.

Deep Voices: The Second Whale Record, Capitol ST-11598.

Dolphy, Eric, *Other Aspects*, Blue Note BT 85131.

——, *Out to Lunch*, Blue Note BST 84163.

Dr John the night tripper, *Gris-Gris*, Atco SD 33-234.

808 State, *Ninety*, ZTT 246 461-2.

Ellington, Duke, *The Blanton–Webster Band*, Bluebird 5659-1-RB

Ellis, Don, *Shock Treatment*, Columbia CS 9668.

Eno, Brian, *Ambient 4: On Land*, EG EEGCD 20.

——, *Another Green World*, Island ILPS 9351.

——, *Apollo: Atmospheres & Soundtracks*, EG EGLP 53.

——, *Music For Films*, Editions EG EEGCD 5.

——, *Neroli*, All Saints ASCD 15.

——, *Thursday Afternoon*, EG EGCD 64.

——, and Byrne, David, *My Life In the Bush of Ghosts*, EG EGCD 48.

Environments: The Magic of Psychoactive Sound, Syntonic Research
Inc., SD 66010.

Evans, Bill, *Spring Leaves*, Milestone CA 271.

Feldman, Morton, *Triadic Memories*, Sub Rosa SUBCD012-35.

4-Hero, *Parallel Universe*, Reinforced LP0004.

Fripp, Robert/Eno, Brian, *The Essential Fripp and Eno*, Virgin EG
CDVE920.

Future Sound of London, *ISDN*, Virgin CDV 2755.

Le Gamelan Balinais de Lotring, CBS 88059.

Gazzelloni, Severino, *Flute Works by Debussy, Varèse, etc.*, Heliodor
Wergo 2549 002.

Göttsching, Manuel, *E2-E4*, Racket Records RRK 15037.

Hancock, Herbie, *The Complete Warner Bros. Recordings*, Warner Archives 9362-45732-2.

Hassell, Jon, *Aka/Darbari/Java (Magic Realism)*, EG EEGCD 31.

—, *City: Works of Fiction*, Opal/Warner Bros. 9 26153-2.

—, *Dream Theory in Malaya*, EG EEGCD 13.

—, and Bluescreen, *Dressing For Pleasure*, Warner Bros. 9 45523-2.

—/ Eno, Brian, *Possible Musics*, EGEEGCD 7.

Hassell, Jon vs. 808 State, *Voiceprint*, All Saints ASCD17.

Hekura: Yanomamö Shamanism from Southern Venezuela, !Quartz 004.

Hendrix, Jimi, *Electric Ladyland*, Track 613 010.

—, *Live & Unreleased: The Radio Show*, Castle Communications HBCD 100.

—, *Nine To the Universe*, Polydor Super Pols 1023.

Higher Intelligence Agency, *Colourform*, Beyond RBADCD5.

Hillage, Steve, *Rainbow Dome Musick*, Virgin CDVR 1.

Horn, Paul, *Inside*, Epic BXN 26466.

Human Arts Ensemble, *Under The Sun*, Universal Justice Records TS 73-776.

Indian Ocean (Arthur Russell), *School Bell/Treehouse*, Sleeping Bag 12" single SLX-0023X.

Irresistible Force (Mixmaster Morris), *Space Is the Place*, Rising High RSN 5.

Java: Bedoyo Ketawang, Galloway Records, Musique Du Monde 7.

The Jesus and Mary Chain, *Psycho Candy*, Blanco Y Negro 240 790-1.

King Tubby, *Dub Gone Crazy*, Blood & Fire BAFCD 002.

—, *King Tubby's Special 1973–1976*, Trojan TRLD 409.

Kirchin, Basil, *Worlds Within Worlds*, EMI Columbia SCX 6463.

—, *Worlds Within Worlds*, Island Help 18.

Kirk, Roland, *Left & Right*, Atlantic 588 178.

The KLF, *Chill Out*, JAMS LP 5.

Köner, Thomas, *Permafrost*, Barooni BAR 009.

Kraftwerk, *Autobahn*, EMI Auto 1.

—, *Computer World*, EMI EMC 3370.

—, *Electric Cafe*, EMI EMD 1001.

—, *The Man-Machine*, Capitol E-ST 11728.

—, *Trans-Europe Express*, EMI E-ST 11603.

Kurnia, Detty, *Coyor Panon*, Flame Tree FLTRCD 519.

LFO, *Frequencies*, Warp CD 3.

Loop Guru, *The Third Chamber*, Loop CD 001.

Lucier, Alvin, *Music for Solo Performer*, Lovely Music VR 1014.

Lull, *Cold Summer*, Sentrax SNTX 490.

Marclay, Christian, *Record Without a Cover*, Recycled Records.

Maxfield, Richard, *Electronic Recordings*, Advance Recordings FGR-8S.

——, Reich, Steve, Oliveros, Pauline, *New Sounds In Electronic Music*, Odyssey 32 16 0160.

May, Derrick, Craig, Carl, Atkins, Juan, Pennington, James, *Relics*, Transmat/Buzz bzzlp 106106.

McLaughlin, John, *Devotion*, Douglas 4.

Meek, Joe, *The Joe Meek Story*, Decca DPA 3035/6.

Merry Christmas Mr Lawrence (soundtrack composed by Ryuichi Sakamoto), Virgin V2276.

Messiaen, Olivier, *Oiseaux exotiques*, Supraphon SUA ST 50749.

MEV/AMM, *Live Electronic Music Improvised*, Mainstream MS/5002.

Mr Fingers (Larry Heard), *Amnesia*, Jack Trax FING 2.

Mitchell, Roscoe, *Sound*, Delmark DL 408.

Model 500, *Night Drive (Thru Babylon)*, Metroplex/Macola 12" single MRC-0994.

The Gerry Mulligan Quartet, *Gerry Mulligan Quartet*, Vogue LAE 12050.

The Music Improvisation Company, *1968–1971*, Incus 17.

Music of the Venezuelan Yekuana Indians, Folkways FE 4104.

A Musical Anthology of the Orient: Japan V, Baren Reiter Musicaphon BM 30 L 2016.

Musik für Ch'in, Museum Collection Berlin MC7.

Musique du Burundi, Ocora OCR 40.

Musique sacrée Tibétaine, Ocora OCR 71.

μ-ziq, *Tango n'Vectif*, Rephlex 013.

My Bloody Valentine, *Loveless*, Creation CRE CD 060.

Namlook, Pete, *Silence*, FAX PK 08/25.

Niblock, Phill, *Four Full Flutes*, Experimental Intermedia Foundation XI 101.

Oiseaux du Venezuela, L'Oiseau Musicien G11.

Oliveros/Dempster/Panaiotis, *Deep Listening*, New Albion NA 022 CD.

Ono, Yoko, *Onobox*, Ryko RCD 10224.

The Orb, *A Huge Ever Growing Pulsating Brain That Rules From the Centre of the Ultraworld*, W.A.U. Mr Modo 12" single MWS 017T.

——, *The Kiss EP*, W.A.U. Mr Modo MWS 010T.

Oswald, John, *Plunderphonic*, (not-for-sale CD).

Pablo, Augustus, *East of the River Nile*, Rockers Production.

Parker, Charlie, *Bird With Strings: Live at The Apollo, Carnegie Hall & Birdland*, CBS 82292.

—, *The Verve Years (1948–50)*, Verve 2610 026.

Partch, Harry, *The World of Harry Partch*, CBS MS7207.

Perry, Lee, *The Upsetter Box Set*, Trojan Perry 1.

Phuture, *Acid Tracks*, Trax 12" single TX142A.

Pink Floyd, *The Piper At the Gates of Dawn*, EMI SCX 6157.

Pran Nath, Pandit, *Earth Groove*, Transatlantic TRA 193.

—, *India's Master Vocalist*, Shandar, SR 10007.

—, *Ragas of Morning & Night*, Gramavision 18-7018.

Prime, Michael, *Aquifers*, RRR-CD-09.

Prince Far-I, *Cry Tuff Dub Encounters Chapter III*, Daddy Kool DKLP 15.

Psyche (Carl Craig), *Crackdown*, Kool Kat/Transmat 12" EP KOOLT 603.

Public Enemy, *It Takes a Nation of Millions To Hold Us Back*, Def Jam 462415 1.

Reese and Santonio, *The Sound*, KMS/Kool Kat Kool T15.

Reload, *A Collection of Short Stories*, Infonet inf 4 cd.

Riley, Terry, *A Rainbow In Curved Air*, Columbia MS 7315.

—, *Happy Ending*, Warner Brothers 46 125.

—, *In C*, CBS 64565.

—, *Persian Surgery Dervishes*, Shanti 83.501.

—, *Shri Camel*, CBS M 35164.

The Ronettes, *Sing Their Greatest Hits*, Phil Spector International Super 2307 003.

Russell, Arthur, *Instrumentals*, Another Side of Les Disques Crépuscule, Side 8401.

—, *Let's Go Swimming*, Rough Trade 12" single RTT 184.

—, *World of Echo*, Rough Trade 114.

Sakamoto, Ryuichi, *B-2 Unit*, Island/Alfa ILPS 9656.

Satie, Erik, *Piano Music Volume 1*, Decca Vox STGBY 633.

—, *Vexations*, Harlekijn Holland Produkties SAT 001.

Saw Throat, *Inde$troy*, Manic Ears ACHE 019.

Scanner, *Scanner*, Ash 1.1.

Schoenberg, Arnold, *5 Pieces for Orchestra, Op. 16*, Sony SMK 48 463.

Schütze, Paul, *Apart*, Virgin AMBT6.

—, *New Maps of Hell*, Extreme XCD 015.

—, *The Surgery of Touch*, Sentrax SNTX 175.

Sequential, *Prophet/The Mission*, Pod 025 12" single.

The Sheltering Sky (soundtrack by Ryuichi Sakamoto, Richard Horowitz, etc.), Virgin CDV 2652.

Shomyo – Buddhist Ritual from Japan, Dai Hannya Ceremony – Shingon Sect, Philips 6586 021.

Shore, Howard and Coleman, Ornette, *Naked Lunch*, Milan 262 732.

Sinatra, Frank, *In the Wee Small Hours of the Morning*, Capitol CAPS 1008.

Skinny Puppy, *VIVIsectVI*, CAPITOL C1-91040.

Songs of the Humpback Whale, Capitol ST-620.

Sounds and the Ultra-Sounds of the Bottle-Nose Dolphin (recorded by John Lilly), Folkways FX 6132.

Spacetime Continuum with Terence McKenna, *Alien Dreamtime*, Astralwerks ASW6107-2.

Spontaneous Music Ensemble, *Karyobin*, Chronoscope CPE 2001-2.

St GIGA/Sound of the Earth series, *Ambient Soundscape II: Prayers for the Spirit of Nature*, Disques Kinza (Japan) TOCT-6920.

Stalling, Carl, *The Carl Stalling Project*, Warner Bros. 9 26027-2.

Stockhausen, Karlheinz, *Telemusik*, DGG 137012.

Sueño Latino, *Sueño Latino*, BCM Records 12" single BCM 323.

Sumac, Yma, *Voice of The Xtabay*, Capitol SM-684.

Summer, Donna, *Love To Love You Baby*, GTO GTLP 008.

Sun Ra, *Angels and Demons at Play*, Saturn 407.

——, *Art Forms of Dimensions Tomorrow*, Saturn 9956.

——, *Cosmic Tones for Mental Therapy*, El Saturn KH-2772.

——, *Cosmic Visions*, Blast First BF FP 101V.

——, *Heliocentric Worlds Volume 1*, ESP 1014.

——, *Heliocentric Worlds Volume 2*, ESP 1017.

——, *The Magic City*, Saturn 403.

——, *The Nubians of Plutonia*, El Saturn 406.

——, *Strange Strings*, Saturn 502.

——, *Sun Ra Volume 1*, Shandar SR 10.001.

Sylvian, David, *Weatherbox*, DSCD1.

——, and Czukay, Holger, *Plight and Premonition*, Virgin CDVE 11.

Symbols and Instruments, *Mood/Science of Numbers/Tear Drops of Yesterday*, Network/KMS 12" single NWKT 5.

Takemitsu, Toru, *Film Music by Toru Takemitsu*, JVC VICG-5127.

Throbbing Gristle, *20 Jazz Funk Greats*, Industrial TGCD 4.

Tristano, Lennie/Dameron, Tadd, *Crosscurrents*, Affinity AFF 149.

Twin Peaks (soundtrack by Angelo Badalamenti), Warner Bros 9 26316-2.

The United States of America, *The United States of America*, CBS 63340.

The Upsetters (Lee Perry), *Super Ape*, Mango 260858.

U2, *Achtung Baby*, Island CIDU 28.

—, *Zooropa*, Island CIDU 29.

The Vancouver Soundscape, World Soundscape Project EPN 186.

Varèse, Edgard, *Nocturnal/Ecuatorial*, Vanguard VSL 11073.

—, *Intégrales, etc.*, Vox Candide STGBY 643.

—, *Arcana, etc.*, Decca SXL 6550.

Various, *Ambient 4: Isolationism*, Virgin AMBT 4.

—, *(Artificial Intelligence II)*, Warp CD 23.

—, *Circadian Rhythm*, Incus 33.

—, (Fluxus sound artists), *Flux Tellus*, Tellus cassette #24.

—, *Futurism & Dada Reviewed*, Sub Rosa SUBCD012-19.

—, *Silence*, Spiral Editions (Japan) 36CD-NO20.

The Velvet Underground, *White Light/White Heat*, MGM SVLP 9201.

Wilson, Dennis, *Pacific Ocean Blue*, Caribou CRB 81672.

Wolff, Henry and Hennings, Nancy, *Tibetan Bells*, Island HELP 3.

Young, La Monte, *The Second Dream of The High Tension Line Stepdown Transformer from The Four Dreams of China*, Gramavision R2 79467.

—, *12 I 64 AM NYC the first twelve Sunday Morning Blues*, (unreleased tape).

—, and Zazeela, Marian, *The Theatre of Eternal Music*, Shandar 83.510.

—, and Zazeela, Marian, *31 VII 69 10:26–10:49 PM*, Edition X (limited edition) München.

Young, Neil and Crazy Horse, *Arc-Weld*, Reprise 7599-26746-2.

Zappa, Frank, *Uncle Meat*, Bizarre/Transatlantic TRA 197.

Zawinul, Joe, *Zawinul*, Atlantic SD 1579.

Zorn, John, *Film Works*, Eva WWCX 2024.

index